PRIESTLY MINISTRY AND THE PEOPLE OF GOD

Priestly Ministry and the People of God

Hopes and Horizons

Richard R. Gaillardetz

Thomas H. Groome

Richard Lennan

Editors

ORBIS BOOKS

Maryknoll, New York 10545

ORBIS BOOKS
Maryknoll, New York 10545

Founded in 1970, Orbis Books endeavors to publish works that enlighten the mind, nourish the spirit, and challenge the conscience. The publishing arm of the Maryknoll Fathers and Brothers, Orbis seeks to explore the global dimensions of the Christian faith and mission, to invite dialogue with diverse cultures and religious traditions, and to serve the cause of reconciliation and peace. The books published reflect the views of their authors and do not represent the official position of the Maryknoll Society. To learn more about Orbis Books, please visit our website at www.orbisbooks.com.

Library of Congress Cataloging-in-Publication Data

Names: Gaillardetz, Richard R., 1958– editor. | Groome, Thomas H., editor. |
    Lennan, Richard, editor.
Title: Priestly ministry and the people of God : hopes and horizons /
    Richard R. Gaillardetz, Thomas H. Groome, Richard Lennan, editors.
Description: Maryknoll, New York : Orbis Books, [2022] | Includes
    bibliographical references.
Identifiers: LCCN 2021035166 (print) | LCCN 2021035167 (ebook) |
    ISBN 9781626984615 (print) | ISBN 9781608339242 (ebook)
Subjects: LCSH : Priesthood—Catholic Church.
Classification: LCC BX1912 .P7527 2022 (print) | LCC BX1912 (ebook) |
    DDC 262/.142—dc23
LC record available at https://lccn.loc.gov/2021035166
LC ebook record available at https://lccn.loc.gov/2021035167

Contents

LIST OF ABBREVIATIONS

CARA	Center for Applied Research in the Apostolate
CCC	*Catechism of the Catholic Church*
DV	*Dei Verbum*
EG	*Evangelii Gaudium*
GS	*Gaudium et Spes*
JSTB	Jesuit School of Theology at Berkeley
LG	*Lumen Gentium*
LS	*Laudato Si'*
OS	*Ordinatio Sacerdotalis*
PDV	*Pastores Dabo Vobis*
PO	*Presbyterorum Ordinis*
PPF6	Program of Priestly Formation, 6th edition
QA	*Querida Amazonia*
RF	*Ratio Fundamentalis*
SC	*Sacrosanctum Concilium*
STM	Boston College School of Theology and Ministry
TSPG	"To Serve the People of God: Renewing the Conversation on Priesthood and Ministry"
UT	*Ultimis Temporibus*

Introduction

Thomas H. Groome

With this collection, we bring to completion—though not conclusion—conversation about the future of Catholic priesthood that began at Boston College (BC) some years ago. In September 2016, the Church in the 21st Century (C21) Center at Boston College established a faculty seminar to study and imagine "the future of priesthood." The sentiment was that, while the state of priesthood shows ample signs of crisis, this might also be a moment of grace to forge a new horizon so urgently needed.

The seminar group was made up of twelve working members and a student scribe. Of those, six were distinguished theologians with particular competence on the theme, three were priests, two were university personnel who work in spiritual formation, two were Boston College PhD students in theology, and two were priest leaders from the Archdiocese of Boston; there were eight men and five women in all. Richard Lennan, Richard Gaillardetz, and I served as cochairs.

The ninety-minute breakfast seminar met four times each semester for two years, adding a final gathering, making a total of seventeen meetings. The first three semesters were spent in intense study and conversation, with the fourth dedicated to writing a consensus statement that went through many drafts. While concerned for the state of Catholic ministry, in general, we realized early on that it would be wise to limit our focus to diocesan priesthood, in particular. Further, while we hoped our research might bear fruit for the whole church, we limited our focus to our context here in the United States.

The seminar members were far from uniform in their views regarding priesthood. This diversity became a blessing in that it prompted us to step back from the controversial issues and to ask the deeper questions: What does it mean to be ordained? What are the nature, purposes, and needed charisms for priesthood? How should the church craft the selection, preparation, and ongoing education of its priests?

We discerned that a *practical* theological approach to our theme was advisable. This meant beginning with contemporary research on the present practice of diocesan priesthood in the United States by looking at statistics, trends, and projections—the Center for Applied Research in the Apostolate (CARA) research was invaluable. We studied what is happening with collaborative parishes and with the recruiting of international priests to fill a perceived shortage. We considered the faculties and formation practices of our seminaries, the integrating of diocesan priesthood with the explosion of full-time lay ecclesial ministers, now numbering more than forty thousand in the United States.

Then, faithful to such a practical theological approach, we added theoretical research by reviewing the grounding in scripture and tradition of ordained ministry in the early church and across the centuries, at Vatican II, and into the present day. We read all of the relevant church documents, including *Pastores Dabo Vobis* of Pope John Paul II (1992), *The Gift of the Priestly Vocation* of the Congregation for Clergy (2016), and others. We brought in scholars from other universities to share their research on ministry.

After such practical and then theoretical research, we moved in our fourth semester to writing a foundational and consensus statement— about eight thousand words—suitable for any interested person to read. The result was the document, "To Serve the People of God: Renewing the Conversation on Priesthood and Ministry" (TSPG) issued jointly by the Boston College Department of Theology and its School of Theology and Ministry. It was first published in *Origins*[1] and is reproduced in its entirety in the opening of the first part of this volume.

We shared our document with all the bishops of the English-speaking world, as well as the presidents of all the Episcopal Conferences worldwide, in both English and Spanish. It was communicated to Pope Francis through Cardinal Parolin, Vatican Secretary of State. Cardinal Parolin wrote appre-

---

[1] "To Serve the People of God: Renewing the Conversation on Priesthood and Ministry," *Origins* 48, no. 31 (2018). The document was well received, with very appreciative reviews in a number of publications. For example, in *America* magazine, Professors Steve Bevans and Robin Ryan of the Catholic Theological Union in Chicago commented that it is "one of the best reflections on priesthood we have ever read."

ciatively, "I am grateful for your efforts aimed at renewing the theology of priesthood and ministry and I express my hope that your work will bear fruit in the life of the Church." The document was also shared with and appreciated by scholars preparing the Pan Amazon Synod (October 2019). All of this encouraged us to continue the conversation.

On January 2 and 3, 2020, we gathered a group of forty people at the Boston College retreat center in Dover, Massachusetts, for an intense conversation on the document. We were particularly honored by the presence and participation of Cardinal Blasé J. Cupich of Chicago, Cardinal Joseph W. Tobin of Newark, and Cardinal Reinhard Marx, archbishop of Munich and Freising and then-president of the German Bishops' Conference. Cardinal Sean O'Malley of Boston presided and preached at the opening liturgy. In addition, present were six bishops; seven priests, who were either rectors of a seminary or deans of a theologate; seven theologians from other universities; some lay leaders; and the members of the original seminar.

The agenda was a thorough conversation of TSPG. This was aided by three presentations by Professors Lennan, Gaillardetz, and Bergin, who elucidated the text. Throughout the conference, Cardinals Marx, Tobin, and Cupich also made brief presentations. Most of the time, however, we engaged in small- and whole-group conversations. To say that the discourse was "lively" would be an understatement. At the end, the conference issued a "communiqué" that summarized some of its insights and recommendations.[2]

Soon thereafter, the COVID-19 epidemic struck and delayed any further in-person conversation. Perhaps the hiatus will prove in time to be a mixed blessing. On the one hand, this difficult period has been particularly challenging for the worship life of the church, reducing us to virtual liturgies and sorely missing reception of the Eucharist. On the other hand, many families, with parish programs and Catholic schools being closed, began to read and reflect together on the Sunday scriptures and be more intentional in the catechesis of their children. Then, in the larger church, there has been heightened emphasis on synodality to guide the life and practices of regional churches, and the reappointment of a committee by Pope Francis to study

---

[2] See Conference Co-Chairs, "Communiqué of Conference on 'To Serve the People of God: Renewing the Conversation on Priesthood and Ministry'"; Richard Lennan, "Ministry in the Life of the Church"; Richard Gaillardetz, "A Profile of a Well-Formed Priest"; Liam Bergin, "Shaping the Future"—all in *Origins* 49, no. 33 (2016).

the possibility of women in the diaconate. All of this and more encourages fresh conversations.

This present volume renews the good work. The first part includes the full text of TSPG and the three elaborating essays by Professors Lennan, Gaillardetz, and Bergin, followed by a reflection from Cardinal Marx that he delivered at the conference. The second part has sixteen essays from participants at that conference, including an archbishop, a bishop, seminary rectors, pastoral ministers, and academic theologians. Our invitation to all was to write a readable essay of some three thousand words, expressing their best hopes for the future of priesthood. We encouraged the authors to write from their own context and experience, and particularly from their hearts and deepest desires.

Our best hope is that this volume is a catalyst of fresh conversations across the ideological spectrum regarding priesthood. We hope it is read by bishops and vocation directors, by theological faculties and seminaries, and by the whole people of God. Thinking especially of adult faith education programs in parishes, we asked the authors to add reflective questions to their essays.

What sounded loudly at the January 2020 gathering is that the priesthood is cherished and lies at the heart of our Catholic faith and people. Also palpable was that effective *preaching*, *pastoring*, and *presiding* are essential to the nurturing of our faith, as was the deep desire to have such priestly ministry flourish going forward. While this volume brings some completion to the work of the original Boston College faculty seminar on priesthood, we hope the conversation and the fruits of our good work will long endure.

Part I

The Document

To Serve the People of God

Renewing the Conversation on Priesthood and Ministry

[December 18, 2018]

Introduction

The Church and the world need mature and well-balanced priests, fearless and generous pastors, capable of closeness, listening and mercy.[1]

1. Pope Francis has stated repeatedly his desire to breathe fresh air into the theology and practice of the ordained priesthood. That desire aligns Pope Francis with the Second Vatican Council (1962–65), which recognized that "the often vastly changed circumstances of the pastoral and human scene" required a renewed theology of the priesthood.[2] In addressing that need, the council retrieved neglected riches of the Church's tradition, interpreting them in light of the contemporary context.

2. "To Serve the People of God," which is the fruit of Boston College's "Seminar on Priesthood and Ministry for the Contemporary Church," sponsored by the School of Theology and Ministry and the Department of Theology at Boston College, also aspires to present the priesthood in ways attentive to both the faith of the Church and current circumstances. The seminar that produced the text was a two-year project exploring the history, theology, and practice of the ordained priesthood within the wider ministerial life of the Catholic community.

---

[1] Pope Francis, "To Participants in the International Conference on Pastoral Work for Vocations Sponsored by the Congregation for the Clergy" (2016), http://w2.vatican.va/content/francesco/en/speeches/2016/october/documents/papa-francesco_20161021_pastorale-vocazionale.html.

[2] Second Vatican Council, *Presbyterorum Ordinis*, "Decree on the Life and Ministry of Priests" (1965), article 1. The texts of Vatican II are taken from Austin Flannery ed., *Vatican Council II*, rev. ed. (Collegeville, MN: Liturgical Press, 2014).

3. Gathered together for research and discussion in the seminar were women and men who are lay and ordained theologians and ministers working in pastoral and academic settings. In its composition and way of proceeding, the seminar embodied what this text itself promotes: the collaboration of all ministers for the sake of the Church's mission in the world.

4. This paper seeks to encourage conversation about the priesthood and contribute to the Church's discernment of appropriate theology and practices of formation for future priests. The text focuses particularly on diocesan priests and their formation. If priests are to be "shepherds with the 'smell of the sheep,'" as Pope Francis urges, suitable formation is of primary importance.[3] Pope Francis seeks priests willing "to serve the people of God, to serve the poor, men and women who are outcasts, living on the fringes of society, to serve children and the elderly."[4] Programs of formation should nurture and channel that willingness.

5. Formation for the priesthood is an essential enterprise of the Church. It flows from an understanding of the ways in which the ordained priesthood participates in the life of the Church and its mission in the world. The arguments and conclusions in this text echo Vatican II's retrieval of the ecclesial identity of priests. This perspective interprets the specificity of priests within their relationship to the community of faith and the mission shared by all the baptized.

6. When such a perspective is lacking, as has happened in Catholic history, ordination can appear to create a gulf between priests and the other members of the Church, with whom priests form the one body of the baptized. Similarly, a concentration on functions unique to priests also runs the risk of isolating priests from the community of faith, or even of defining priests in terms of power over the community. If priesthood becomes a path to power, priests can understand themselves as gatekeepers of "discipline, rules and organization," rather than as disciples among disciples.[5] Programs of formation can shape priests attuned to shared service

---

[3] Pope Francis, "Homily for the Chrism Mass" (2013), http://w2.vatican.va/content/francesco/en/homilies/2013/documents/papa-francesco_20130328_messa-crismale.html.

[4] Pope Francis, "Meeting with Clergy, Men and Women Religious and Seminarians" (2015), http://w2.vatican.va/content/francesco/en/speeches/2015/november/documents/papa-francesco_20151126_kenya-religiosi.html.

[5] Pope Francis, "Message of Pope Francis to Participants in the Pilgrimage-

within the community of faith, rather than control over it. To do so, these programs must be underpinned by the wisdom of the theological tradition and committed to the Church's "responsibility of reading the signs of the times and interpreting them in the light of the Gospel."[6]

7. "Signs of the times," of course, are many and varied. They are also often unique to countries and cultures. For that reason, Vatican II acknowledged that "the wide diversity of peoples and countries" requires local churches to develop programs of formation fashioned for their own context.[7] This text has its grounding in the Catholic Church in the United States of America, a grounding whose distinctive contours likewise require a particular approach to the ministry and formation of diocesan priests. The authors of this paper recognize that its analysis will not be fully applicable beyond the United States, but hope that its approach may be beneficial for other local churches as they reflect on ecclesial ministry.

8. As part of the wider civic community, Catholics in the United States experience a range of influences whose impact is manifold and momentous. Those influences encompass ever-widening disparities in social, educational, and economic opportunity, and also debates on race, gender, marriage, and climate change. The effects of technology, including the ramifications of social media on perceptions of truth, also affect members of the Church as much as any other group in civil society. In addition, some contemporary social developments in the United States, notably the exponential increase in Hispanic immigrants and the shedding of religious affiliations by the "nones," have immediate implications for all ministers within the Catholic community.[8]

9. The present moment of Catholic history adds its own list of issues with specific consequences for the Church's ordained ministry. Prominent among topics that call for urgent attention by programs of formation is the

---

Meeting at the Shrine of Our Lady of Guadalupe" (2013), http://w2.vatican.va/content/francesco/en/messages/pont-messages/2013/documents/papa-francesco_20131116_videomessaggio-guadalupe.html.

[6] Second Vatican Council, *Gaudium et Spes*, "Pastoral Constitution on the Church in the Modern World" (1965), article 4.

[7] Second Vatican Council, *Optatam Totius*, "Decree on the Training of Priests" (1965), article 1.

[8] For an analysis of the "nones," including the perspective of those baptized as Catholics, see Kaya Oakes, *The Nones Are Alright: A New Generation of Believers, Seekers, and Those in Between* (Maryknoll, NY: Orbis, 2015).

sustained and growing demand that all baptized men and women be able to share responsibility and participate together in the Church's life and ministries. The continuing damage done by clerical sexual abuse, including the radically flawed ways in which bishops responded to survivors of abuse, is also highly significant for the future of the priesthood.

10. The increasing gap between the number of Catholics in parishes and the number of priests ministering in those parishes is another area of the Church's life that must engage anyone concerned about the future of the diocesan priesthood.[9] The fact that the declining number of priests coincides with the burgeoning of lay ecclesial ministry, whose roots are in Vatican II's recovery of the centrality of baptism, makes plain that the future of the Church's ministry will not simply duplicate its past, or even its present.[10] Lay ministry is not a substitute or competitor for the ministry of ordained priests, but rather a gift of the Holy Spirit and an integral part of the Church's mission today. Imagining and implementing policies and practices conducive to more effective collaboration between various forms of ministry, as well as the thriving of each particular form, is essential for the life and mission of the Catholic community.

11. "To Serve the People of God" adds its analysis of priestly ministry, and its suggestions for the future, to the body of official works that have accompanied the Church's reflection on priestly life since the 1960s. What began at Vatican II with *Presbyterorum Ordinis* and *Optatam Totius* has continued with *Pastores Dabo Vobis* (1992), *The Directory on the Ministry and Life of Priests* (1994), and numerous other sources that include, most recently, *The Gift of the Priestly Vocation* (2016). For Catholics in the United States, the local application of those texts has come through the Program of Priestly Formation (1st edition: 1991; 5th edition: 2005; 6th edition: 2019).

12. This paper situates its discussion within the Church's current discipline and teaching. While this stance may disappoint those who believe

---

[9] For information on demographic trends in the priesthood see, for example, Katarina Schuth, *Seminary Formation: Recent History–Current Circumstances–New Directions* (Collegeville, MN: Liturgical Press, 2016), and Mary L. Gautier, Paul M. Perl, and Stephen J. Fichter, *Same Call, Different Men: The Evolution of the Priesthood since Vatican II* (Collegeville, MN: Liturgical Press, 2012).

[10] For an overview of the number of Catholics involved in preparing for various forms of ministry, see Mary L. Gautier and Jonathan Holland, *Catholic Ministry Formation Enrollment: Statistical Overview for 2016–2017* (Washington, DC: Center for Applied Research in the Apostolate, 2018).

that there can be no future for the priesthood without the ordination of women and married men, the *consensus fidelium*, the "breathing-together" of the whole Church, does not yet exist in relation to those possibilities.[11] Irrespective of who is to be ordained, however, the community of faith must be clear in its understanding and expectations of priestly ministry. It is this imperative that the paper prioritizes, leaving other questions to the ongoing discernment of the Church.

13. Affirming that continuity in faith differs from immutability, "To Serve the People of God" looks towards a creatively faithful future for the Church's ordained ministry.[12] The members of the seminar are confident that the Christian community and its leaders, guided by the Holy Spirit and united in faith, hope, and love, will exercise the wisdom and courage essential to the construction of a future rich in possibilities, a future embodying all that the grace of God enables.

Part One
Ministry in the Life of the Church

14. The Second Vatican Council showcased God's self-revelation in love—grace—as the foundation of Christian life, faith, and worship. This section of "To Serve the People of God" frames the Church's mission and ministry, including the ordained priesthood, in light of that revelation. The text connects all ecclesial ministries to the Church's mission to embody and mediate grace in the world. As it pursues that mission, the Church must ensure that the practice of ministry, and programs of formation for ministry, respond to the movement of the Holy Spirit in different cultural and historical contexts.

The Mission of the Triune God

15. To the eyes of faith, creation reveals God as life-giver (Rom 1:19–20). God gives life as an act of love, establishing a relationship with all that

---

[11] The "breathing-together" of the Church derives from John Henry Newman, *On Consulting the Faithful in Matters of Doctrine* (1859), ed. John Coulson (London: Collins, 1986); the notion of *consensus fidelium* receives a detailed treatment in Ormond Rush, *The Eyes of Faith: The Sense of the Faithful and the Church's Reception of Revelation* (Washington, DC: Catholic University of America Press, 2009).

[12] On the distinction between "continuity" and "immutability," see Avery Dulles, *The Catholicity of the Church* (Oxford: Clarendon Press, 1985), 99.

exists. In the covenants with Israel, covenants that God initiates, the breadth and depth of God's love take shape in a singular promise: "I will walk among you and be your God, and you shall be my people" (Lev 26:12).[13] In Jesus Christ, "the mediator and the fullness of Revelation," Christians recognize the climax of God's self-communication in love and the fulfillment of God's covenant promise.[14]

16. In Jesus, through the Holy Spirit, God the Father "in his great love speaks to humankind as friends and enters into their life, so as to invite and receive them into relationship with himself."[15] In Jesus, God reveals the justice, mercy, and compassion emblematic of God's reign. As crucified and risen, Jesus guarantees that the life-giving Word of God will speak the final word in the story of creation, leading to its fulfillment in God's realized kingdom.

17. The unique mission of the Holy Spirit is to be the "Advocate" (John 14:16), the Spirit of truth, who "reminds" (John 14:26) humanity of the teaching of Jesus and of all that God has accomplished in Christ. In doing so, the Spirit "offers everyone the possibility of sharing in this paschal mystery in a manner known to God."[16] The Spirit extends God's creative and saving love by empowering the followers of Jesus Christ to live in the world as his disciples: "Christ is now at work in human hearts by the power of his Spirit; not only does he arouse in them a desire for the world to come but he quickens, purifies, and strengthens the generous aspirations of humankind to make life more humane and to conquer the earth for this purpose."[17]

18. "Grace" encapsulates God's life-giving love that draws all creation into communion with God the Father, through Christ and the Spirit. As the self-offering of the God who has reconciled all things in Christ (2 Cor 5:18), grace can overcome all alienation and division. Without inhibiting human freedom, grace draws humanity into an ever-deepening communion with God and with God's creation through love, peace, generosity, and the other gifts that express the presence of the Spirit (Gal 5:22). These gifts, accessible even amidst the present-day ambiguities of human life, offer a foretaste of God's fulfilled reign.

---

[13] See also Exod 6:7; Jer 30:22; Ezek 36:28; Rev 21:3.
[14] Second Vatican Council, *Dei Verbum*, "Dogmatic Constitution on Divine Revelation" (1964), article 2.
[15] *Dei Verbum*, article 2.
[16] *Gaudium et Spes*, article 22.
[17] *Gaudium et Spes*, article 38.

The Church as a Community for Mission

19. The Christian tradition, while acknowledging the universality of grace, professes the Church to be a unique expression of God's effective love in the world. Since Christ and the Spirit are its "co-instituting" principles, the Church is more than a human organization.[18] At the same time, the Church, even as it embodies grace in history, is never less than a human organization. To illuminate the Church's paradoxical identity, Vatican II refers to the Church as being "in the nature of a sacrament," a term that links grace with the Church's historical and social existence.[19]

20. As sacrament, the Christian community is "a sign and instrument, that is, of communion with God and of unity among all people."[20] As sacrament, the Church "receives the mission of proclaiming and establishing among all peoples the kingdom of Christ and of God, and she is, on earth, the seed and beginning of that kingdom."[21] There is, then, an irreducible bond between the Church's sacramentality and its mission: "All those who in faith look towards Jesus, the author of salvation and the principle of unity and peace, God has gathered together and established as the Church, that it may be for each and everyone the visible sacrament of this saving unity [with God]."[22] To accomplish their mission, members of the Church "are to share with all people the spiritual goods of this life and the life to come."[23]

21. The Church's sacramental identity shapes its existence as a visible community, a structured body of faithful disciples.[24] Reflecting God's Trinitarian life, grace forms the Church as a people who, through sharing the Holy Spirit received in baptism, are to be one, holy, catholic, and apostolic. The Church's unity is that of a communion, a unity of difference that witnesses to the catholic dimension of God's grace, which "is neither divisive nor oppressive

---

[18] Yves Congar, *I Believe in the Holy Spirit*, trans. D. Smith, vol. 2 (New York: Seabury, 1983), 9.

[19] Second Vatican Council, *Lumen Gentium*, "Dogmatic Constitution on the Church" (1964), article 1.

[20] *Lumen Gentium*, article 1.

[21] *Lumen Gentium*, article 5.

[22] *Lumen Gentium*, article 9.

[23] Second Vatican Council, *Ad Gentes*, "Decree on the Church's Missionary Activity" (1965), article 7.

[24] *Lumen Gentium*, article 8.

but gathers up genuine difference in an inclusive wholeness."[25] Effective unity and catholicity in the Church require ongoing conversion to deeper holiness, as well as creative fidelity to the apostolic tradition; these are all sure signs of the Spirit.

22. The community of the Church is a "pilgrim" people, simultaneously inseparable from history and oriented towards the fullness of God's kingdom.[26] As such, the Christian community experiences not only the ways in which God's reign is already evident in the world, but the human and ecclesial realities still requiring the transformation that God's Spirit can accomplish. Discerning how they might embody this life-giving Spirit more faithfully and creatively in each time and place is integral to the pilgrimage that the Church's members undertake.

23. To sustain its pilgrimage and guide its discernment, the community of the Church turns constantly to the liturgy, especially the eucharistic liturgy, in which "grace is poured forth upon us as from a fountain."[27] Through the word and sacrament of the liturgy, the Spirit strengthens communities, and their individual members, to live the Gospel with greater freedom and deeper dedication to mercy, compassion, and generosity.

24. The integrity of the Church in history, no less than the robustness of its mission, requires that all the baptized appropriate their call to be disciples of Jesus Christ through the Holy Spirit. The relationship with Jesus Christ, "the way, and the truth, and the life" (John 14:6), is the heart of discipleship. Through grace, that relationship gradually transforms disciples: "it is no longer I who live, but Christ who lives in me" (Gal 2:20). Since the Spirit operates in manifold ways, discipleship is a multifaceted activity: it ranges from serving "the least of these" (Matt 25:45) to making "a defense to anyone who calls you to account for the hope that is in you" (1 Pet 3:15). In all of its forms, discipleship engages history and culture: "we go out towards God only by entering into the world."[28]

25. Discipleship is nurtured within the communion of the Church. As the first generation of Christians "were together and had all things in common"

[25] Richard Gaillardetz, *Ecclesiology for a Global Church: A People Called and Sent* (Maryknoll, NY: Orbis, 2008), 35.

[26] *Lumen Gentium*, articles 48–51.

[27] Second Vatican Council, *Sacrosanctum Concilium*, "Dogmatic Constitution on the Sacred Liturgy" (1963), article 10.

[28] Karl Rahner, *Hearer of the Word: Laying the Foundation for a Philosophy of Religion*, trans. J. Donceel (New York: Continuum, 1994), 120.

(Acts 2:44), so the members of today's Church are to "witness also by their believing life together."[29] The nurturing of disciples in order that the whole Church might be a sacrament "for the life of the world" (John 6:51) provides the context for understanding the role of ministry in the ecclesial community.

Ministry within the Mission of the Church

26. Ministry is fundamentally ecclesial, emerging from the life of the Church and its mission.[30] The Pauline letters emphasize that, through the Spirit, all forms of ministry are for the sake of the community of faith: for the "one body" (Rom 12:4); "the common good" (1 Cor 12:7); and "God's Church" (1 Tim 3:5). These texts make clear that ministry is not inward-looking, but at the service of the Church's engagement with the world. Thus understood, ministry is "the vocation of leading disciples in the life of discipleship for the sake of God's mission in the world."[31]

27. Ministers are disciples before they are ministers; they remain disciples even as they engage in ministry. Ministry does not substitute for the mission of all disciples, but strengthens the members of the Christian community to enact in their specific circumstances the faith, hope, and love that the Spirit empowers. As an ecclesial act, ministry requires the conversion of ministers to the grace of Jesus Christ at the heart of the Church and a continual deepening of their bonds to the ecclesial community. Consequently, participation in ministry, for both lay and ordained ministers, is neither a promotion beyond the ranks of the baptized nor an indicator of superior holiness.

28. What is unique to ministers is their particular relationship to other members of the body of the Church: "Ordered Church ministry is a reality broader than the ministry of the ordained (though inclusive of it) and narrower than Christian discipleship. Ordered ministry refers to any and all ministries that, once formally undertaken, draw one into a new ecclesial relationship within the life of the Church; in undertaking

---

[29] Gerhard Lohfink, *Jesus of Nazareth: What He Wanted, Who He Was*, trans. L. Maloney (Collegeville, MN: Michael Glazier, 2012), 109.

[30] See Richard Lennan, "The Church as Mission," in *The Disciples' Call: Theologies of Vocation from Scripture to the Present Day*, ed. Christopher Jamison (London: Bloomsbury, 2013), 43–63.

[31] Kathleen Cahalan, *Introducing the Practice of Ministry* (Collegeville, MN: Liturgical Press, 2010), 50.

an ordered ministry, one is ecclesially repositioned."[32] Ministers, priests included, are to serve the community of baptized disciples in its responsibility for the one mission of the Church in the world.

29. For the sake of the Church's mission, ministers guide and support the members of the body of Christ, encouraging them to respond to the Spirit of their baptism. The heart of ministry, therefore, lies in forms of service that aid the realization of the Church's mission, a mission that takes on new requirements in an ever-changing world. Building on that description, the following section of the paper explores the principal features of the ministry that the Church's ordained priests exercise.

Part Two
A Profile of the Well-Formed Priest

30. The ministerial effectiveness of ordained priests is interwoven with their growth in personal maturity and Christian discipleship. In identifying why this is so, Part Two offers a profile of priests who embody those characteristics. The relational dimension of the priesthood is integral to this profile: relationships shape priests, as they do all people. For priests, the relationships with the Trinitarian God and with the people of God are pivotal.

Priests within the Community of Disciples

31. Ordination, when situated within a relational approach to the priesthood, can never be understood simply as a ritual event that is independent of the humanity, faith, and the capacity for service that formation seeks to nurture and enhance in seminarians.[33] As an act of the ecclesial community, ordination builds on the sacraments of Christian initiation that launch all disciples on their journey of faith and service. For all the baptized, the journey of discipleship has a priestly dimension: "persevering in prayer and praising God, [disciples of Christ] should present themselves as a sacrifice, living, holy and pleasing to God."[34]

---

[32] Richard Gaillardetz, "The Ecclesiological Foundations of Ministry within an Ordered Community," in *Ordering the Baptismal Priesthood: Theologies of Lay and Ordained Ministry*, ed. Susan Wood (Collegeville, MN: Liturgical Press, 2003), 36.

[33] Nathan Mitchell, *Mission and Ministry: History and Theology in the Sacrament of Order* (Wilmington, DE: Michael Glazier, 1986), 236–37.

[34] *Lumen Gentium*, article 10.

32. Holy orders, however, adds a new dimension to the discipleship of priests: "priests by the anointing of the Holy Spirit, are signed with a special character and conformed to Christ the priest in such a way that they can act in the person of Christ, the head."[35] In the context of the ordination, "character" indicates a particular relationship between Christ and the priest within the ecclesial community. The grace of this relationship enables and empowers priestly ministry. Just as baptism and confirmation, the other sacraments to which "character" applies, establish the identity of believers as disciples, orienting them to share in the Church's mission, the character of holy orders is also for mission. Through the grace of ordination, priests "exist and act in order to proclaim the Gospel to the world and to build up the Church in the name and person of Christ the head and shepherd."[36] This expanded identity of priests, which repositions them within the community of faith, is for the sake of the community's mission. Priests, in short, are to "promote the baptismal priesthood of the entire people of God, leading it to its full ecclesial realization."[37]

33. As ministers of word, sacrament, and service, priests are "sent to give what one cannot give on the basis of natural resources or powers."[38] Since the relationship with Christ and the Spirit initiates and sustains priestly ministry, that ministry summons priests to grow in holiness: "the very holiness of priests is of the greatest benefit for the fruitful fulfillment of their ministry."[39] An ever-deepening conversion to Christ and the Spirit nurtures priests as ministers of God's merciful presence in the world: "Mercy is our way of making the entire life of God's people a sacrament. Being merciful is not only 'a way of life,' but '*the* way of life.'"[40] For priests themselves, an appreciation of God's mercy for others and for themselves can cultivate freedom from the dangers of "workaholism," acquisitiveness,

---

[35] *Presbyterorum Ordinis,* article 2.

[36] Pope John Paul II, *Pastores Dabo Vobis,* "On the Formation of Priests in the Circumstances of the Present Day" (1992), article 15.

[37] *Pastores Dabo Vobis*, article 17.

[38] Joseph Ratzinger, "Biblical Foundations of Priesthood," *Communio* 17 (1990): 620.

[39] *Presbyterorum Ordinis,* article 12.

[40] Pope Francis, "Extraordinary Jubilee of Mercy: Spiritual Retreat Given by Pope Francis on the Occasion of the Jubilee for Priests Third Meditation" (2016) (emphasis in original), http://w2.vatican.va/content/francesco/en/speeches/2016/june/documents/papa-francesco_20160602_giubileo-sacerdoti-terza-meditazione.html.

and clericalism. The latter "forgets that the visibility and sacramentality of the Church belong to all the People of God not only to the few chosen and enlightened."[41]

34. To support and deepen the ongoing conversion to grace, fruitful priestly ministry requires sustenance from relationships within the Christian community and the wider world. For priests, as for all disciples, it is "the faith, hope and love of their friends and companions in discipleship who will sustain and renew their deeper needs in faith, hope and love."[42] The capacity for relationships marked by mutual support, challenge, and forgiveness is important not merely for the psychological health of priests, but for the effectiveness of their ministry: "true ministry must be mutual. When the members of a community of faith cannot truly know and love their shepherd, shepherding quickly becomes a subtle way of exercising power over others and begins to show authoritarian and dictatorial traits."[43] This feature of well-formed priests makes plain why human formation must be "the basis of all priestly formation."[44]

Priestly Ministry and the Goals of Formation

35. It is possible to distill from Vatican II, and the teaching of the Church since the council, five central aspects of priestly ministry. The next section of this text focuses on those five aspects, identifying not only their foundation in the relationship that priests have to God and the community of faith, but also their implications for programs of formation.

36. *(1) The priest as preacher.* Since evangelization is a pressing challenge for the Church today, particularly in the age of digital communications and social media, preaching is at the heart of priestly ministry. Indeed, Vatican II designated the authentic proclamation of the word of God in Scripture as the "primary duty" of priests.[45] This proclamation

---

[41] Pope Francis, "Letter to Cardinal Ouellet," 2016, https://w2.vatican.va/content/francesco/en/letters/2016/documents/papa-francesco_20160319_pont-comm-america-latina.html. For a detailed study of the causes and effects of "clericalism," see George Wilson, *Clericalism: The Death of Priesthood* (Collegeville, MN: Liturgical Press, 2008).

[42] Enda McDonagh, "The Risk of Priesthood," *The Furrow* 51 (2000): 596.

[43] Henri Nouwen, *In the Name of Jesus: Reflections on Christian Leadership* (New York: Crossroad, 1989), 43–44.

[44] *Pastores Dabo Vobis*, article 43.

[45] *Presbyterorum Ordinis,* article 4.

requires priests to be committed to growth as "a living contemplation of the Word and not simply a cultic technician or manager."[46] The word of God that priests are to proclaim to others, must first touch their own lives and stimulate continuing conversion to Jesus Christ. The priest as preacher must be "a person of faith speaking."[47] For effective preaching, this person of faith must recognize "the complex social, political and economic forces that are shaping the contemporary world." This context touches the lives of priests as much as those to whom they preach.[48]

37. It is essential that anyone ordained to presbyteral ministry have the capacity to preach the Gospel with the creativity that engages people's lives, while also being faithful to the Good News proclaimed in the liturgical readings. Since a homily seeks to be "a kind of music which inspires encouragement, strength and enthusiasm," it necessitates education both in a theology that can speak to contemporary men and women and in an appropriate set of communication and pedagogical skills.[49] Pope Francis stresses that "the homily is the touchstone for judging a pastor's closeness and ability to communicate to his people."[50] Preaching that does not express such qualities greatly inhibits the effectiveness of priestly ministry. Indeed, a priest unable to preach well would be a contradiction in terms.

38. *(2) The priest as leader of worship and prayer.* A key element in the ministry of any priest is liturgical presiding and being a "pray-er" in various ecclesial and civic settings. The role of priests in the liturgy "is not simply to engage 'in a ceremony.'"[51] In presiding at the liturgy, priests "gather the community through gospel and blessing into the common ritual action . . . so that the communion of the Church as the body of Christ and Christ's presence in this communion of Spirit may truly be expressed."[52]

---

[46] Joseph Ratzinger, "Priestly Ministry: A Search for its Meaning," *Emmanuel* 76 (1970): 493.

[47] National Conference of Catholic Bishops, *Fulfilled in Your Hearing: The Homily in the Sunday Assembly* (1982), article 39; http://www.usccb.org/_cs_upload/8090_1.pdf.

[48] *Fulfilled in Your Hearing*, article 34.

[49] Pope Francis, *Evangelii Gaudium*, "On the Proclamation of the Gospel in Today's World," 2013, article 139.

[50] *Evangelii Gaudium*, article 135.

[51] Kevin Irwin, "A Spirituality for the Priest: Apostolic, Relational, Liturgical," in *Ministerial Priesthood in the Third Millennium*, ed. Ronald Witherup and Lawrence Terrien (Collegeville, MN: Liturgical Press, 2009), 100.

[52] David Power, "Representing Christ in Community and Sacrament," in

39. While priests fulfill a unique role in presiding at the liturgy, fruitful participation in the Church's worship for priests, as for all members of the Christian community, is inseparable from their life of faith, their relationship with the Church, and their manner of engagement with the wider world. Even the enrichment that priests are offered through the Eucharist comes to them more as recipients of that Eucharist, alongside their sisters and brothers in the Christian community, rather than only as a consequence of presiding at the eucharistic liturgy.[53]

40. *(3) The priest as collaborative leader.* Collaboration brings into relief the fact that "Christian initiation gives us a shared but differentiated responsibility for the life and mission of the Church, and calls us to work together on equal terms."[54] Respect for this "differentiated responsibility" challenges ministers in their work with each other and with the wider community to accept not only that "our different vocations and gifts are complementary and mutually enriching" but that "we are accountable to each other for how we work and what we do."[55]

41. The forms of ecclesial ministry that have emerged since the Second Vatican Council have increased markedly the opportunities for collaboration between priests and other ministers. The many lay men and women who have discerned vocations to these ministries, and engaged enthusiastically in theological, spiritual, pastoral, and personal formation, are the "co-workers" of the ordained.[56] As such, lay ministers bring gifts that can enhance the ministry of the church. It is certainly true that the pastoral experience and insights of priests often enable them to mentor their lay colleagues, but effective leadership in this new context also requires from priests an openness to learn from, work with, and support other ecclesial ministers, seeing in this collaboration, even in its challenges, a gift to their own ministry.

Being a Priest Today, ed. Donald Goergen (Collegeville, MN: Michael Glazier, 1992), 117.

[53] Karl Rahner, "The Consecration of the Layman to the Care of Souls," *Theological Investigations,* vol. 3, trans. K.-H. and B. Kruger (New York: Crossroad, 1982), 70.

[54] Catholic Bishops' Conference of England and Wales, *The Sign We Give,* 1995, 12, http://www.cbcew.org.uk/CBCEW-Home/Publications/The-Sign-We-Give-1995/(language)/eng-GB.

[55] Catholic Bishops' Conference of England and Wales, *The Sign We Give*, 12.

[56] For an overview of this development see United States Conference of Catholic Bishops, *Co-Workers in the Vineyard of the Lord: A Resource for Guiding the Development of Lay Ecclesial Ministry* (Washington, DC: USCCB, 2005).

42. All candidates for ordination must be prepared to work positively and equitably with women, who make up the majority of lay ecclesial ministers. The likelihood that priests will appreciate the leadership of women in ministry increases when women—single, married, and religious—have played a significant and positive role in diocesan seminaries. The experiences and insights of women can be a rich resource for formation programs, offering a broader vision than the one that prevails when the ordained alone are the architects and agents of formation.

43. *(4) The priest as a public representative of the Church.* The sacrament of orders is an action of Jesus Christ and the Holy Spirit through the Church. The ministry of ordained priests, then, is always an ecclesial ministry: "As an activity of the Church, pastoral office can only represent and act in the name of the Lord when it represents the life of faith of the Church."[57] As ecclesial ministers, priests represent the teaching, values, and wisdom of the Church to the wider world. This ecclesial dimension also has a particular expression in the relationship between the priest and the bishop.[58]

44. A consequence of the representative role of priests is that the wider civic and non-Catholic public often judges the Church by the words and actions of priests. This fact requires priests to be worthy representatives of the faith community by exercising responsibility in matters extending from sexuality, to the use of time, and to honest stewardship of personal and communal finances.[59]

45. *(5) The priest as practitioner of pastoral charity.* Recognizing that priests, as part of the complex modern world, could be "perplexed and distracted by the multiplicity of tasks facing them," Vatican II identified the exercise of "pastoral charity" as the means by which priests could integrate their lives.[60] The council stressed that pastoral charity could become the hallmark of priests only if priests committed themselves to "penetrating ever more intimately through prayer into the mystery of Christ."[61]

---

[57] Edward Kilmartin, "Apostolic Office: Sacrament of Christ," *Theological Studies* 36 (1975): 260.

[58] See *Presbyterorum Ordinis,* article 5, and *Christus Dominus,* "Decree on the Pastoral Office of Bishops in the Church" (1965), articles 28–33.

[59] See David Ranson, "Priest: Public, Personal and Private," *The Furrow* 53 (2002): 219–27.

[60] *Presbyterorum Ordinis,* article 14.

[61] *Presbyterorum Ordinis,* article 14.

46. If priests are to manifest the "joy of the Gospel," they must embody the love and mercy of God in consistent and recognizable ways. That responsibility, Pope Francis contends, is a consequence of the relationship between priests and Jesus: "when we let ourselves be chosen by Jesus, it is to serve: to serve the people of God, to serve the poor, men and women who are outcasts, living on the fringes of society, to serve children and the elderly."[62]

47. Pope Francis is clear that such service requires priests willing and able to encourage and nurture the people to whom they minister. He is likewise clear that encouragement and nurture differ from control over people and from any claim to be the sole sources of all wisdom among God's people: "Do we support them and accompany them, overcoming the temptation to manipulate them or infantilize them? Are we constantly open to letting ourselves be challenged in our efforts to advance the good of the Church and her mission in the world?"[63]

48. Priests must discern, individually and collectively, how they are to maintain the priority of pastoral ministry in the midst of other demands. Such discernment becomes particularly necessary when "the routine of inner Church business" threatens to extinguish "the flame of the primordial responsibility to proclaim the Gospel, the joyful news."[64] When "busyness" becomes a defining mark of priests, priestly ministry suffers: "Everybody knows that we are busy, but I don't think this is what we want them to know about us, not really, not first of all. We want them to know that we love them, that we are there for them in the ups and downs of their daily life."[65]

49. The need for priests able to give priority to pastoral charity in a world of competing demands is no less critical now than at the end of the council. The endeavor to satisfy that requirement underscores the importance of formation for ministry, the theme on which the next section of "To Serve the People of God" concentrates.

---

[62] Pope Francis, "Meeting with Clergy, Men and Women Religious and Seminarians," 2015, http://w2.vatican.va/content/francesco/en/speeches/2015/november/documents/papa-francesco_20151126_kenya-religiosi.html.

[63] Pope Francis, "Meeting with the Coordinating Committee of CELAM," 2013, http://w2.vatican.va/content/francesco/en/speeches/2013/july/documents/papa-francesco_20130728_gmg-celam-rio.html.

[64] Ratzinger, "Priestly Ministry," 499.

[65] Michael Heher, *The Lost Art of Walking on Water: Reimagining the Priesthood* (Mahwah, NJ: Paulist, 2004), 5.

Part Three
Shaping the Future

50. The primary claim of the previous section is that creative and collaborative priestly ministry in service of the Church requires priests committed to ongoing growth in faith and human maturity. The following pages identify ways in which programs of formation might aid the emergence of such priests, priests likely to provide effective ministry for the Church's present and future.

Formation for Effective Priestly Ministry

51. "Formation" summarizes the multi-faceted—human, spiritual, intellectual, and pastoral—and multi-stage—initial, seminary, and ongoing—process that nurtures the Church's ordained ministers prior to and after ordination.[66] While the elements of formation draw on myriad sources of human wisdom, Jesus himself, God's love incarnate in human history through the Holy Spirit, is the model for the integration of those elements. Thus, formation prompts priests to "deepen their love for Christ, the good shepherd, pattern their lives on his, [and] be ready to go out into the highways of the world to proclaim to all Christ the way, the truth and the life."[67]

52. Ever since the Council of Trent mandated in 1563 that local bishops should establish "a perpetual seminary of ministers of God," the formation of diocesan priests has largely taken place in seminaries. Although diocesan seminaries have nurtured many skilled and compassionate pastors, the enclosed settings of the seminary, often insulated from the everyday world of families, budgeting, commuting, and even grocery-shopping and laundry, can isolate seminarians.[68] This section of the text explores how seminaries might achieve richer outcomes for the church's mission by harvesting the spectrum of gifts available in the wider ecclesial community.

---

[66] For an overview of the four areas of formation, see *Pastores Dabo Vobis*, articles 42–59.

[67] *Pastores Dabo Vobis*, article 82.

[68] The Council of Trent, canon 18 of the "Decree on Reform," in "The True and Catholic Doctrine of the Sacrament of Order, to Condemn the Errors of Our Time" (July 15, 1563); the text can be found in *Decrees of the Ecumenical Councils*, vol. 2, ed. Norman Tanner (Washington, DC: Georgetown University Press, 1990), 742.

53. In its review of key areas of formation, the material in this section broadens the scope, personnel, and duration of the process of formation beyond what prevails currently in diocesan seminaries. The section makes the case that the formation of effective priests must be a priority for the whole Church, not merely for bishops and priests themselves. Aligned with this focus, the material that follows also emphasizes the necessity of ongoing formation, an emphasis that underscores formation as a lifelong activity, rather than one that concludes with ordination. A further concentration of the following pages is the need for formation programs to be alert to the social context and other factors that shape the Church of today and will influence the Church of tomorrow.

54. *(1) Vocations and recruitment.* The choice of candidates for formation has an impact on every aspect of seminary life and priestly ministry. This fact reinforces the urgency of discernment about the vocation of candidates for ordination. As Pope Francis notes, bishops in particular must accept responsibility for this discernment, resisting the pressure to increase numbers by accepting candidates indiscriminately: "Today we have so many problems, and in many dioceses, because some bishops made the mistake of taking those who at times have been expelled from other seminaries or religious houses because they need priests. Please! We must consider the good of the People of God."[69]

55. This text has connected "the good of the People of God" to all that serves the Church's mission. Pope Francis highlights missionary service as the test of authenticity for all Christians: "the ultimate criterion on which our lives will be judged is what we have done for others. Prayer is most precious, for it nourishes a daily commitment to love."[70] Consistent with that focus, candidates for ordination must embrace the mutuality between priestly ministry and the Church's missionary mandate to love and serve others. Accordingly, the community of faith must seek out and encourage candidates who are able to connect their faith with a life of self-giving: "Let the students most clearly realize that they are not destined for a life of power and honors, but to be dedicated wholly to the service of God and pastoral ministry."[71]

---

[69] Pope Francis, "Address to the Plenary of the Congregation for Clergy," 2014, http://w2.vatican.va/content/francesco/en/speeches/2014/october/documents/papa-francesco_20141003_plenaria-congregazione-clero.html.

[70] *Gaudete et Exsultate*, article 104.

[71] *Optatam Totius*, article 9.

56. The holiness integral to priestly ministry does not require a choice between personal spirituality and a life of service, between commitment to God and commitment to God's people. Holiness develops by holding together these two commitments. Consequently, all those engaged in guiding the discernment and formation of diocesan seminarians must challenge forms of piety that tend towards a disembodied "perfection" or neglect engagement with the world in which the Holy Spirit is at work: "It is not healthy to love silence while fleeing interaction with others, to want peace and quiet while avoiding activity, to seek prayer while disdaining service."[72]

57. Since diocesan priests must value communion, and be people who seek to unite differences for the sake of a shared discipleship, the capacity for relationship with a variety of women and men should be evident in those entering diocesan seminaries.[73] A principal task in assessing applicants for the seminary, therefore, must be discerning the presence of the human qualities conducive to the building of positive relationships. Psychological screening can make a major contribution to this process of discernment. Affirming the value of such screening recognizes that the capacity for healthy human relationships can reveal the presence of the Spirit, underscoring that grace is always an incarnate reality: "far from being timid, morose, acerbic or melancholy, or putting on a dreary face, the saints are joyful and full of good humor. Though completely realistic, they radiate a positive and hopeful spirit."[74]

58. *(2) Initial and Seminary Formation.* Although the seminary is the primary venue for academic and pastoral formation leading to ordination, spiritual and human formation can begin prior to philosophical and theological studies. Whatever the venue of formation, the likelihood that a program of formation will produce positive outcomes depends in large measure on the willingness of candidates to engage in "a journey of faith and of gradual and harmonious maturity."[75] Openness to formation manifests itself in qualities of trust, generosity, patience, and the desire to be with people and to serve them.

---

[72] *Gaudete et Exsultate*, article 26.

[73] See, for example, Denis Edwards, "Personal Symbol of Communion," in *The Spirituality of the Diocesan Priest*, ed. Donald Cozzens (Collegeville, MN: Liturgical Press, 1997), 73–84.

[74] *Gaudete et Exsultate*, article 122.

[75] Congregation for the Clergy, "The Gift of the Priestly Vocation" (2016), article 28.

59. Given the demands of contemporary culture, it is imperative that human formation be a priority in the earliest stages of preparation for priestly ministry. Human formation aims at the "affective maturity" that arises from "convinced and heartfelt obedience to the 'truth of one's own being,' to the 'meaning' of one's own existence."[76] Affective maturity is as essential to ministerial effectiveness as theological knowledge and the other goals of formation: "In order that [their] ministry may be humanly as credible and acceptable as possible, it is important that [priests] should mold [their] human personality in such a way that it becomes a bridge and not an obstacle for others in their meeting with Jesus Christ the Redeemer of humanity."[77]

60. Psycho-sexual development is a key component of affective maturity, a component whose importance the sexual abuse crisis has brought into sharp relief. Accordingly, initial and seminary formation must directly promote alternatives to "the celibate cloak of silence," that discourages attention to issues of sexuality.[78] An atmosphere in which particular theologies of the priesthood lead to a lack of transparency or damaging repression in sexual matters leaves priests, and the wider Church, vulnerable to a repetition of the behaviors that have damaged many lives, and the good standing of the Church, in recent decades.[79] History shows unequivocally that the failure to address such issues has only deleterious outcomes.

61. Since priests must be able to relate appropriately and comfortably with both men and women, it is essential that formation programs not limit themselves only to contributions from the ordained. The talents and insights of as wide a cross section of the Church's members as possible are required to prepare priests for the world and Church they will serve.

62. One aspect of current programs of formation for diocesan seminarians that warrants serious reconsideration is the relationship between the living situation of seminarians and the place where they study. Present practice in the United States generally privileges the seminary as the venue for all aspects of formation, thereby separating diocesan seminarians from lay and religious candidates for ministry, even though they are all under-

---

[76] *Pastores Dabo Vobis*, article 44.

[77] *Pastores Dabo Vobis*, article 43.

[78] Ranson, "Priest: Public, Personal and Private," 223.

[79] Eamonn Conway, "Operative Theologies of Priesthood: Have They Contributed to Child Sexual Abuse?," in *The Structural Betrayal of Trust*, ed. Regina Anmicht-Quinn, Hille Haker, and Maureen Junker-Kenny (London: SCM, 2004) [*Concilium* 2004/3], 72–86.

taking similar philosophical and theological studies. If, however, candidates for ordination study in universities and theological centers with others who are preparing for ministry, the shared learning is likely to contribute to a healthy future for ministry in the Church, a future in which collaboration and co-responsibility are typical. This development could come about while also respecting that the residence of seminarians may be specific to their formation. The benefits that accrue when diocesan seminarians and those in formation for lay ecclesial ministry are able to study together argue for the importance of adopting this approach whenever possible.

63. This change would introduce diocesan seminarians to the gifts and talents of those with whom they will work as ministers. It would also open them to a greater diversity in theologies and convictions than is likely to be common in diocesan seminaries. This diversity can be enriching; it certainly reflects the reality of the Church in which the ordained will serve. As such, the experience of diversity offers a means by which those activities of the seminary that focus on personal and spiritual formation could find both verification and challenge. With this in mind, diocesan authorities must ensure that "efforts to maintain old structures, houses and programs that are no longer viable in their present forms," do not preclude the possibility of creative and future-oriented approaches to formation.[80]

64. *(3) Ongoing Formation.* As professionals—a term that acknowl-edges the training and responsibility of priests, and is fully reconcilable with "vocation"—priests require formation that is life-long. In order to preach effectively and express the merciful compassion of God in their ministry, priests need consistent spiritual direction and attention to their spiri-tual lives. They require also updated theological reflection and continued development in key areas of ministry, including presiding, counseling, and pastoral planning.

65. Too often, programs for ongoing formation lack both the support of bishops and the commitment of priests themselves. Indeed, among the latter there can be an "intergenerational unwillingness" to participate in ongoing formation.[81] The heavy demands that conscientious priests face can also

---

[80] Luisa Saffiotti, "Forming Ministers for the Twenty-First Century," *Human Development* 26 (2005): 7.

[81] John Beal, "Performance Management of Catholic Clergy: 'Best Practice' or New Iconoclasm?," in *Best Practices in Catholic Church Ministry Performance Manage-ment*, ed. Charles Zech (Lanham, MD: Lexington, 2010), 61.

subvert ongoing formation. It is vital, therefore, that diocesan authorities work with priests to create a culture in which priests value post-ordination development and bishops encourage it. Since opportunities for ongoing formation can involve the absence of priests from their communities, it is crucial that bishops and priests help the members of those communities to recognize the importance of formation activities. That recognition can aid acceptance of the short-term disruption of normal schedules that the absence of priests may require. Since ongoing formation can enable priests to preach and preside more creatively, and be more enthusiastic in animating local communities, its benefits flow ultimately to the whole Church.

66. *(4) Environment of Ministry.* Priests today—and certainly tomorrow—cannot be "lone rangers." The willingness to work collaboratively with others, men and women who are volunteers and also those who are formally engaged as lay ecclesial ministers, is necessary for effective ministry. Since the whole Christian community shares through baptism in Christ's threefold ministry as priest, prophet, and shepherd, ordained priests must also be ready and able to collaborate with those they serve. Collaboration is more than simply a useful means to accomplish tasks: it is a way in which priests can be "sincere in their appreciation and promotion of lay people's dignity and of the special role the laity have to play in the Church's mission."[82] Collaboration, then, is an act of faith in the Spirit at work in the whole Church.

67. Collaboration can be challenging. It necessitates receptivity to possibilities that come from beyond oneself and requires the readiness to "cross borders that protect one's safe space, dispel illusions of being invulnerable and in total control, and surrender the inviolability of one's good idea."[83] As such, the imperative of collaboration and partnership in ministry reinforces the importance of a spiritual life that embraces an identity formed by being part of a shared mission, an identity that reflects God's own existence as a loving communion.

68. The contemporary reality of cultural diversity is another aspect of the Church's life in the United States that requires creativity from diocesan priests and those seminarians preparing for the diocesan priesthood. A will-

---

[82] *Presbyterorum Ordinis,* article 9.

[83] Daniel Gast and William Clark, "Collaboration in a Pastoral Key," in *Collaborative Pastoral Leadership*, ed. William Clark and Daniel Gast (Lanham, MD: Lexington, 2017), 197.

ingness to learn from other cultures is a necessary prerequisite for priests to evoke the gifts for ministry present throughout all groups in the Church.[84]

69. *(5) Openness to the future.* The Church's ordained ministry has a history precisely because it has changed over time. This fact suggests that further change can be expected as the future unfolds. In particular, it is clear that the presence and gifts of large numbers of women in ministry today, a phenomenon that, as this paper has noted, has moved the practice of ministry into new territory, ensures that "there can be no future for the church which women have not had a pivotal hand in shaping."[85] Among other prospects for change in the immediate future is the possibility of priestly ordination of mature married men (*viri probati*), an issue currently canvassed in various parts of the Church.

70. It is imperative that priests and those in formation for ordination embrace the reality of change and look towards the unknowable future with hope, rather than with anticipatory despair. Pope Benedict XVI stresses for all members of the Church the irreducible importance of hope: "Only the great certitude of hope that my own life and history in general, despite all failures, are held firm by the indestructible power of Love, and that this gives them their meaning and importance, only this kind of hope can then give the courage to act and persevere."[86] To meet the opportunities and challenges of the present and the future, priests and the Church as a whole require such hope, which is inseparable from courage, discernment, and an engaged and deep faith in the Holy Spirit's guidance of the pilgrim community.

Conclusion

71. Pope Francis cautions that ministry can lead to priests being "exhausted, broken into a thousand pieces, moved and even 'consumed' by the people."[87] He notes too that priests who "go out and give [the] people

---

[84] Allan Figueroa Deck, "Intercultural Competence: The Opportunities and the Present Reality," in *To Be One in Christ: Intercultural Formation and Ministry*, ed. Fernando Ortiz and Gerard McGlone (Collegeville, MN: Liturgical Press, 2015), 9–23.

[85] Elizabeth Johnson, "Imaging God, Embodying Christ: Women as a Sign of the Times," in *The Church Women Want: Catholic Women in Dialogue*, ed. Elizabeth Johnson (New York: Crossroad, 2002), 58.

[86] Pope Benedict XVI, *Spe Salvi*, "On Christian Hope," 2007, article 35.

[87] Pope Francis, "Homily for the Chrism Mass," 2015, http://w2.vatican.va/

what was entrusted to [priests]," can experience that the people to whom they minister "will make [priests] rejoice in that hundredfold which the Lord has promised to those who serve him."[88] Those two, seemingly contradictory statements from Pope Francis point to the way that priestly ministry reflects the central paradox of Christian faith: that life and death are inseparably connected.

72.   There have been many expressions of "death" for the priesthood in recent decades, the sexual abuse crisis and the reduction in vocations being the most obvious ones. While acknowledging those deficits, this text, echoing what the Second Vatican Council initiated, has featured the seeds of life in the current theology and practice of the priesthood, seeds present especially in the renewed appreciation of the ministry of the word and the opportunities for collaboration with lay ecclesial ministers. Above all, the approach in this work has emphasized that the ecclesial nature of the priesthood, its share in the mission proper to the whole Church, is integral to its thriving.

73.   "To Serve the People of God" is hopeful about the future of the priesthood. This hope reflects the conviction, mentioned in the Introduction, that consensus regarding the profile of a well-formed priest can provide a foundation for discussion of all issues that affect the ordained priesthood. To support the Church's discernment that particular people have received a call from God to minister as ordained priests, this text has outlined five characteristics essential for effective priestly ministry:

a.   the capacity to preach the word of God in ways that nurture the faith, hope, and love of the disciples of Christ;

b.   the ability to lead the Christian community in life-enhancing prayer and worship;

c.   the willingness and aptitude to be a collaborative leader among lay ecclesial ministers and the whole people of God;

d.   the disposition to lead an exemplary life of discipleship within the ecclesial community;

e.   the commitment to practice pastoral charity in service of the gospel.

---

content/francesco/en/homilies/2015/documents/papa-francesco_20150402_
omelia-crisma.html.

[88] Pope Francis, "Homily for the Chrism Mass," 2014, http://w2.vatican.va/
content/francesco/en/homilies/2014/documents/papa-francesco_20140417_
omelia-crisma.html.

74. The specifics of the priesthood's future, like all aspects of the Church's life, are unknown (and unknowable). Nonetheless, the God who desires to make all things "new" (Rev 21:5), the God who is "eternal newness," empowers the Church, through the Spirit, to construct a path to the future.[89] The analysis of the priesthood in this text offers a contemporary theological analysis for the Church to consider as it takes up its task. In so doing, the text encourages the embrace of Pope Francis's oft-repeated promotion of "boldness":

> Complacency is seductive; it tells us that there is no point in trying to change things, that there is nothing we can do, because this is the way things have always been and yet we always manage to survive. . . . Yet let us allow the Lord to rouse us from our torpor, to free us from our inertia. Let us rethink our usual way of doing things; let us open our eyes and ears, and above all our hearts, so as not to be complacent about things as they are, but unsettled by the living and effective word of the risen Lord.[90]

---

[89] *Gaudete et Exsultate*, article 135.
[90] *Gaudete et Exsultate*, article 137.

1

Ministry in the Life of the Church

Richard Lennan

"Climate emergency" was the Oxford "Word of the Year" in 2019. Since the warming of the planet does not respect national boundaries, constructive responses to this emergency require all nations to move from a stance of competition to one of interdependence. Pope Francis's appreciation of this imperative resounds through *Laudato Si'*, in which he emphasizes that the need to care for the earth, "our common home," makes a demand on all people. As he links the global perspective of climate science with insights from the creation stories in Genesis, Francis stresses that God, the author of life, unites all creatures "by unseen bonds" that produce "a kind of universal family, a sublime communion" (*LS* 89). Pope Francis's reasoning supports the conclusion that God sees all life as an ecosystem, one in which every part is in relationship to all others.

Ecosystems depend on relationships, on the interweaving of their various constituents. Each of these constituents, in turn, depend on the whole system, such that no single member can truly thrive unless all members thrive. Ecosystems are wonderfully catholic: the differences within them enhance the well-being of the whole, without threatening its unity. The document "To Serve the People of God" develops a similarly catholic portrait of the ordained priesthood, one that locates the specificity of its subject within various forms of relationship.

To provide the scaffolding for the approach that the document develops, the first part of the text sketches three ecosystems: the Trinity, the church, and ecclesial ministry. This chapter elaborates on those three facets, highlighting the particularity of each one, the relationships between them, and their implications for a contemporary theology of the priesthood.

The Trinity

One of the Second Vatican Council's great legacies is its portrayal of God's revelation. For Vatican II, revelation is not primarily the communication of information, even "truths," about God. Revelation is God's self-communication, by which God encounters human beings within their world. The self-giving of God in history bridges the divide between God and humanity; it provides avenues by which "people can draw near to the Father, through Christ, the Word made flesh, in the Holy Spirit, and thus become sharers in the divine nature" (*Dei Verbum*, 2). Remarkably, then, the creator God, the source of all life, "addresses men and women as [God's] friends, and lives among them, in order to invite and receive them into [God's] own company" (*DV* 2).

God's self-revelation, therefore, is for the sake of building communion. Revelation shows that the divine ecosystem that is the Trinity, far from being a "gated community" that glories in its separation, extends beyond itself to be the source and sustenance of all life. Just as the life-giving mission of the Trinity binds all creatures to God, so it binds all creatures to each other through their participation in God's own life.

Consequently, when Vatican II speaks in *Gaudium et Spes* of the followers of Christ sharing in the "joys and hopes . . . grief and anguish" (*GS* 1) of all people, it is doing more than expressing a worthy humanitarian vision. It is, in fact, articulating a statement of faith, one that recognizes that, because God does not separate human beings into different groups, people of faith must likewise eschew such divisions. The disciples of Christ, then, do not have an exclusive claim on God's love and attention, but are moving together with all people—and, indeed, all created life—to deeper communion within the ecosystem of the one God, who alone is their fulfillment. The specificity of Christians lies not in their detachment from others but in the nature of their engagement with all people and all creation, in their witness to the universality of God's life-giving presence.

The Trinitarian dynamics of creation, the Incarnation, and the working of grace in the world, all signal that authentic responses to God will involve life-giving relationships. So, too, they indicate that definitions of holiness must extend beyond interiority to encompass social action reflective of God's creative love. Such relationships and embodied holiness are to be hallmarks of the church, whose existence derives from God's action in history. The church, then, is the second ecosystem that provides context for the priesthood.

The Church

The church does not exist independently of its reality as a community of faith. Far from being a speculative claim, this assessment of the church has an unimpeachable grounding in the facts of history, as well as in both a theological and sociological analysis of the church. The Christian community has always understood itself as the product of God's initiative. Membership in the church is voluntary, but members are all responsive to God's call, to the invitation to become part of a people that has its source in God's revelation in Jesus Christ and the Holy Spirit, and its fulfillment in God's Trinitarian communion.

From the beginning of God's covenantal relationships with Israel, God has formed a "people," rather than relate to atomized individuals. Jesus, too, gathered a community around him. Jesus's friends, his disciples, learned through sharing their life with him, listening to him, and witnessing how he engaged with those in need of God's life-giving mercy and healing. The disciples also learned that their relationship with Jesus had implications for how they were to treat one another. Most importantly, they learned that "whoever wishes to be first among you must be slave of all" (Mark 10:44). Living this way was not an arbitrary imposition that Jesus inflicted on his followers, but a reflection of Jesus's own practice since he "came not to be served but to serve, and to give his life a ransom for many" (Mark 10:45).

The mission that the followers of Jesus received from him at the Last Supper was that they should do as he did. More particularly, the disciples were to "love one another as I have loved you" (John 15:12). The Last Supper also provides the primary expression of what loving others requires: the willingness to wash feet, to put oneself at the service of others. This service reinforces that connection to Jesus necessarily involves connection to others. In this vein, *Lumen Gentium*, Vatican II's document on the church, begins by describing the church as "a sacrament—a sign and instrument, that is of communion with God and of the unity of the entire human race" (*LG*, 1). The authenticity of the church, then, has its measure in the church's engagement with the world. This engagement gives expression to all that derives from the relationship that the community of faith has with the God of Jesus Christ.

It is surely not a chance event that the appearance of the Holy Spirit at Pentecost (see Acts 2) was to the disciples gathered together. It is certainly true that they were gathered in fear, unable to release the potential of their common faith in Jesus Christ. The gift of the Spirit transformed that fear into courage, into the boldness that led the first Christian community to become a body of evangelizers, sharing with all people the hope born of the life, death, and Resurrection of Jesus Christ through the Holy Spirit. A defining feature of the whole narrative of the Acts of the Apostles is the pivotal role of the community that prays together, commissions those going out to preach, discerns together how best to respond to the questions that emerged to challenge the fledgling community, and supports each other in the face of opposition and discouragement. In short, Acts is a portrait of the many features intrinsic to the church as ecosystem.

Perhaps the most compelling portrayal of the ecclesial ecosystem is St. Paul's description of the church as a "body" (1 Cor 12:12–31). For Paul, the whole body is the work of the Holy Spirit, so that the various parts attain their fullest identity only in relation to each other: "As it is, there are many members, yet one body" (1 Cor 12:20). Significantly, no member of the body can claim precedence over another since "in the one Spirit we were all baptized into one body" (1 Cor 12:13). Distinctions within the body, then, can never validly supplant the unity and interrelationships of the one community of the baptized.

In the last few years, Pope Francis's stress on the synodal reality of the church has brought into sharper relief some key consequences of the church's existence as a body of faithful disciples. One of these consequences is that the church is more likely to fulfill its mission creatively and constructively when the whole community of faith plays a role in discerning what it is that the Spirit is saying to the church in the present moment of the world's history. Synodality enables the gifts of all the baptized to have a voice; it reinforces that all members of the community of faith share the gifts of the Holy Spirit.

A synodal church is one in which dialogue matters. The core prerequisite for authentic dialogue is the willingness to be attentive to the Spirit, who does not operate simply from the top down but also from the bottom up. The Spirit nurtures the church's catholicity, its unity in diversity, rather than imposing uniformity. In a truly catholic church, there is a possibility that the full range of local churches—and groups within each local church—might contribute to the life and mission of the whole ecclesial community.

Vatican II's ecclesiology highlights the identity of the church as a "pilgrim." As pilgrim, the church is a community whose fulfillment lies in

God alone. As it moves through history, the community of faith is primarily to proclaim and witness to the reign of God, which offers hope and reconciliation to all people. Life within the pilgrim community requires the ongoing conversion of all members, and of all the structures that mediate the life of the community. This openness to conversion is a principal manifestation of the community's response to the grace of the Holy Spirit. The embrace of conversion ensures that members of the church do not mistake themselves for the creator God, and do not separate themselves from the rest of God's creation.

The baptism that marks the beginning of the Christian pilgrimage for all members of the church also initiates each Christian into the universal mode of the priesthood: the priesthood of the faithful. This priestly people is called to worship that leads inexorably to service of God in the world. This priestly people is one, yet diverse: it is catholic. An element of this catholicity is the ordained ministry, which does not supplant the wider community of the priestly faithful but has a particular relationship to it, for the sake of the church's one mission. This mission furnishes the rationale for all ministry in the church.

Ecclesial Ministry

Ministry is the third ecosystem that "To Serve the People of God" profiles. Ministry nests in the church's mission, just as the church nests in the mission of the Trinitarian God. Through word, sacrament, and pastoral presence, all ministry in the church that serves the Spirit's reconciling and empowering grace simultaneously serves the mission of the church in the world. By embodying mercy and compassion, ministers are to support and encourage the priestly people—as individuals and communities—as they strive to live as people of faith, hope, and love. Thus understood, ministry is at the service of the ecclesial community and its mission.

Much of the emphasis in discussions of ministry focus on the identity of the minister. The disadvantages of this approach are significant: it separates the minister from the rest of the community, as if ministers were "lone rangers"; it focuses on the person of the minister, rather than the work of ministry. Reclaiming ministry according to the model of Jesus himself—teaching and preaching, healing and reconciling, supporting and admonishing, consoling and encouraging, and eating with and welcoming—

reinforces that Christian life is an ecosystem in which all participants receive from others. Christian life, far from being the endeavor of individuals who pride themselves on their independence and self-sufficiency, is a joint enterprise, one that nobody can accomplish on their own. The work of ministry testifies to this communal reality.

By beginning with "mission" as being applicable to all members of the church, it is possible to develop a perspective on ministry that highlights its irreducibly communal or ecclesial dimension. Ministers have their "home" and grounding in the whole people of God. Their work as ministers is to nourish, encourage, and support the community of the baptized, to accompany the efforts of fellow pilgrims to respond to the summons of the Spirit in the world. Ministers, in short, must always be "part of" not "apart from" the communities they serve. They must be alert to the stirrings of grace in the lives of members of those communities; they do not relieve those members of the opportunity to make their own response to the Spirit, but seek to empower these responses. Equally, ministers are recipients of the prayer, support, and challenges that come from their fellow pilgrims.

The fundamental identity of all ministers, lay and ordained, is as baptized believers. When reflections on the ordained priesthood are inattentive to this designation—when they begin with the effects of ordination or the differences between priests and other Christians—they obscure the identity of the priest as a member of the one pilgrim people, called to the one fulfillment in the God and Father of Jesus Christ. It is likely that much of the dysfunction evident in various aspects of the history of the ordained priesthood has roots in this form of separation.

Vatican II's recovery of the primacy of baptism reshaped the landscape of ministry—indeed, it did so beyond anything that the bishops at the council could have anticipated. The primary expression of this reshaping is the emergence of lay ecclesial ministers, who work alongside ordained priests to form disciples for mission. The cohort of ministers in today's Catholic Church encompasses women and men, single, married, and divorced, as well as gay and straight. The current demographics of ministry are startling compared to what prevailed before Vatican II, but they resemble the dynamics of communities of faith in the apostolic period of the church. This echo is emblematic of the council's retrieval of the neglected richness in the church's history.

The developments in ministry in recent decades have certainly raised a range of questions about the particularity of ordained ministry. Answers to these questions often prioritize what makes the ordained priest "different" or "unique." Likewise, the answers may focus on what "only the priest can do," sometimes implying that the priest has an exclusive relationship to Jesus Christ or possesses "powers" that are independent of the life of the church. Such accounts sever the priesthood from the ministerial and ecclesial ecosystems, thereby impoverishing even its connection to the mission of the Trinitarian community.

As an alternative to such strategies, "To Serve the People of God" concentrates on the ecclesial identity of the ordained. The text depicts the priest not as an autonomous figure but as a member of the community of faith, a baptized disciple among baptized disciples, and a minister among ministers. Just as a focus on the Trinity does not diminish what is particular to each of the three persons who constitute it, so beginning with the ecclesial community—its shared mission and its range of ministries—does not lessen the priesthood nor deny its specificity. It does underscore, however, that all efforts to clarify and enhance the priesthood must begin with the ecosystems that form and shape the ordained ministry.

The many issues constellating around the ordained priesthood today may make it tempting to bypass the opening section of "To Serve the People of God" and head immediately to the material on the theology and practice of the priesthood. Doing so would narrow unduly the base on which to construct a contemporary understanding of priestly ministry. For the sake of those broader possibilities, the first section of the document directs readers to the three ecosystems—the Trinity, the church, and ecclesial ministry—that help to situate the priesthood.

All ecosystems share the most fundamental defining characteristic: they are living realities. For the church and its ministry, being alive means being part of a history that continues to change, that is always different from the endless repetition of "the same." The inability to change, or the unwillingness to do so, is fatal for all living things. The God whose life is inexhaustible empowers change and growth in the life of the church.

The grace of the Spirit enables the ecclesial community to face questions it had not anticipated and to develop responses that express what "has seemed good to the Holy Spirit and to us" (Acts 15:28). This possibility applies to the church's ordained ministry as much as to all other aspects of ecclesial life. There can be no doubt that the questions and challenges that confront the church in relation to its ordained ministry are broad and deep, especially in the wake of the clerical sexual abuse crisis. These questions and challenges are not for priests alone, but are for the whole church to address. Creative responses that may generate a healthy future for the ordained priesthood require the church's grounding in God, its communal mission, and the role of ministry in service of that mission. In short, that healthy future requires a renewed appreciation of the ecosystems on which the ordained priesthood depends.

Questions for Reflection

1. How do you understand the relationship between the mission of the baptized community and the specific nature of ecclesial ministry?

2. In what ways is the Trinity a model of the relationships between the various ministers of the church?

2

A Profile of a Well-Formed Priest

Richard R. Gaillardetz

At the heart of the document "To Serve the People of God" is a section dedicated to the profile of a well-formed priest. That profile proceeds from a set of theological presuppositions, principal among which is a thoroughly relational understanding of priestly ministry. In this chapter, we consider three key features of such a theology—the baptismal, Christological, and pneumatological foundations of a theology of the priesthood.

The Baptismal Foundations

A theology of the ministerial priesthood adequate to both our great tradition and the demands facing the church today must begin not with holy orders but with baptism. As the early Christians understood, baptismal commitment brought each person into a new form of existence, a new understanding of the human vocation. In baptism, we are initiated into Christ's body and discover ourselves fully, our truest identity, within the relational life of the church. For the apostle Paul, life in Christ meant life in the Body of Christ, the church. By baptism into the Christian community, one participated in a new reality; one was a new creation. As French theologian Yves de Montcheuil stated, "It is not Christians who, in coming together, constitute the Church; it is the Church that makes Christians."[1]

Baptism also constitutes the most basic "ordering" of the church. When we consider the sacraments of initiation as a unity, we recognize that Christian initiation offers its own anointing, "laying on of hands," and entrance into eucharistic communion. To be initiated into the church is to take one's place, one's "*ordo*," within the community, the place of the baptized.

---

[1] Yves de Montcheuil, *Aspects de l'Église* (Paris: Cerf, 1949), 51.

37

As Eastern Orthodox metropolitan and theologian John Zizioulas writes, "There is no such thing as non-ordained persons in the church."[2] To be baptized is to be ordained into a very specific ecclesial relationship along with all who profess the lordship of Jesus Christ.

If baptism constitutes the church as an ordered communion, ordination to the ministerial priesthood represents an ecclesial *re*-ordering, or repositioning of the ordinand within the relational life of the church. By virtue of his ordination, the ordinand is called to be *in and for* the church in a new, public way. At the same time, entrance into this new ecclesial relationship does not erase one's relationship within the church established in Christian initiation. The demands of baptism and Christian discipleship continue for the ordained.

If ordination effects an ecclesial repositioning, we can no long consider ordination as simply the conferral of sacramental powers on a solitary individual (a standard scholastic approach within Catholicism) or as the mere delegation of authority from the community to the individual (a perspective common to some Protestant traditions). Ordination does, of course, confer ministerial power, but it is not the conferral of power that makes the ordained minister; it is the reconfiguration of the person within a new ministerial relationship that requires an empowerment necessary for the fulfillment of that ministry. This "empowerment" is a function of the new ministerial relationship. Karl Rahner observes, for example, that the most fundamental (but not sole) identity of the priest is to be a pastor. "He must, then, have all the powers which necessarily belong to such a leader of a Church in a particular locality in the light of the theological nature of the Church as such."[3] "Power" follows from his particular ecclesial relationship.

This shift to a more relational theology of the priesthood does not deny the distinctive sacramental reconfiguration established at ordination. It does challenge, however, any theology of holy orders that relies on a more individualistic, interiorized understanding of sacramental character, one that would focus on the distinctive powers conferred upon the *ordinand* and, therefore, on the distinctive ecclesial status of the *ordinand* over against the rest of the baptized.

---

[2] John D. Zizioulas, *Being as Communion* (Crestwood, NY: St. Vladimir's Seminary Press, 1985), 215–16.

[3] Karl Rahner, "Pastoral Ministries and Community Leadership," in *Theological Investigations*, trans. E. Quinn, vol. 19 (New York: Herder & Herder, 1983), 73–86.

The Christological Foundations

Just as Christian initiation has a Christological character in that baptism draws us into a new relationship with Christ and his church, so too does the new ecclesial relation constituted by priestly ordination have its own properly Christological character. According to Vatican II, all Christians, by their baptism, can be said to "act in the person of Christ" as priest, prophet, and king (*Lumen Gentium*, 9–17). Yet the council also taught that, in a distinctive manner, the ordained priest acts "in the person of Christ the head" (*in persona Christi capitis*) (*Presbyterorum Ordinis*, 2). What might be missed here is the theological significance of the council's choice of the "*in persona Christi capitis*" formulation. Baroque Catholicism had frequently described the priest as an *alter Christus*, "*another Christ*." This "*alter Christus*" language generally presupposed a much more static, individualistic, and sacral/cultic view of the priesthood. From this Christological formulation proceeded the conviction that the priest was perched on a higher wrung of the ecclesiastical ladder, exercised dominating power over the people, was objectively superior to the laity in holiness, and merited the kind of unquestioning deference and privilege that has helped sustain a pernicious clerical culture.

Theologian and ecumenist James Puglisi has helpfully teased out the theological implication of the council's preferred Christological formulation.[4] He draws our attention to the Latin verb *agere*: the priest is not Christ in some static and essentialist fashion; rather, the priest *acts* in the person of Christ. The priest's ministry is always active in the service of Christ's body. This emphasis on the fundamental relationality and ecclesial nature of presbyteral ministry is rooted in ancient liturgical custom and practice. The ordination rituals found in the third-century *Apostolic Tradition* often associated with Hippolytus, for example, affirmed that when gathered for liturgical prayer, "all celebrated but one presided." In both ancient and modern eucharistic *anaphoras* (Eucharistic Prayers), the priest prays in the first-person plural in all but the words of institution. Ignorance of this ancient liturgical insight has given rise to problematic popular references to "father's mass."

This more dynamic and relational Christological formulation was further expanded by Pope St. John Paul II, for whom the priest acts "in the

---

[4] James F. Puglisi, "Presider as *Alter Christus*, Head of the Body?," *Liturgical Ministry* 10 (2001): 153–58.

person of Christ as head *and shepherd*" (*Pastores Dabo Vobis*, 21). Although not without its own shortcomings, this formulation at least has the merit of foregrounding the essential ecclesial nature of the priesthood. There can be no priest acting "as head" without the engagement of the ecclesial body; there can be no priest acting "as shepherd" without an ecclesial flock. Properly interpreted, the assertion that the priest "acts in the person of Christ as head and shepherd" can encourage a fresh consideration of the ministry of the priest as preacher, liturgical presider, public representative, and practitioner of pastoral charity and the work for justice; these are all aspects of a ministry, which manifests itself not as dominating power and privilege but as a service to the people of God.

The Pneumatological Foundations

The Christological foundations of the ministerial priesthood, when read in a relational key, still require an adequate pneumatological complement. The council's tentative reappropriation of a more pneumatological ecclesiology represented an advance beyond the mystical body ecclesiology that emerged in the late nineteenth and early twentieth centuries, and which Pope Pius XII affirmed in his encyclical *Mystici Corporis Christi* (1947). Pope Pius presented the role of the Holy Spirit as the animating soul of the ecclesial body. However, this schema tended to position the Spirit as a secondary adjunct to Christ; the Spirit is the Trinitarian person who comes along later to animate what Christ has already established. A more adequate theology recognizes what Yves Congar referred to as the "co-instituting" character of both Word and Spirit in the life of the church.[5]

Vatican II's nascent pneumatology is reflected in its assertion that the Spirit "guides the church in the way of all truth and, uniting it in fellowship and ministry, bestows upon it different hierarchic and charismatic gifts, and in this way directs it and adorns it with his fruits" (*LG*, 4). In this passage "hierarchic gifts" refers to stable church office, and "charismatic gifts" refers to those many charisms the Spirit distributes among all the faithful. In the council's teaching, baptismal charism and ordained ministry are not opposed to one another since both have the Spirit as their origin. Church office could not function properly unless it was empowered by the Holy Spirit, and charisms could not survive unless they were subject to an

---

[5] Yves Congar, *I Believe in the Holy Spirit*, vol. 2 (New York: Seabury, 1983), 7.

ordering that sought the good of the whole church. The council avoided any competition between charism, lay ecclesial ministry, and clerical office by stressing their mutual dependence on the power of the Holy Spirit.

This conciliar teaching was explored in more depth in a much-overlooked Vatican document, *Iuvenescit ecclesia* (2016). There, the Congregation for the Doctrine of the Faith (CDF) noted the danger of setting up a charismatic church in opposition to an institutional church. It insisted on the complementary—and noncompetitive—relationship between hierarchic gifts and charismatic gifts:

> They have the same origin and the same purpose. They are gifts of God, of the Holy Spirit, of Christ, given to contribute, in diverse ways, to the edification of the Church. He who has received the gift to lead in the Church has also the responsibility of keeping watch over the good exercise of the other charisms, in such a manner that all contribute to the good of the Church and to its evangelizing mission, knowing well that the Holy Spirit distributes the charismatic gifts to whomever he desires. (*Iuvenescit Ecclesia*, 8)

This noncompetitive, pneumatological framework illuminates our understanding of the priest as collaborative leader.

In the parochial life of the church, many of us have encountered an unproductive "turf warfare": the newly ordained parochial vicar claims his presbyteral privilege over against that of the permanent deacon; the deacon, in turn, claims his clerical privilege over against the lay director of adult formation, who claims privilege over the lay volunteer. The council's portrait of the work of the Spirit in the life of the church draws us away from ministerial "turf wars" and toward a noncompetitive vision of the church's ministry.

Yet, according to the council, the priest is to recognize, order, and enable the charisms and ministries of all the baptized. It falls to pastors "not to extinguish the Spirit" but rather "to make a judgement about the true nature and proper use of these gifts" of the baptized (*Apostolicam Actuositatem*, 3). Priests are to "uncover with a sense of faith, acknowledge with joy and foster with diligence the various humble and exalted charisms of the laity" (*Presbyterorum Ordinis*, 9). This exercise of pastoral leadership is further strengthened by the appropriation of a more productive, relational understanding of authority.

For too many people, authority is thought of as a reality that resides in a person: the president, law enforcement officers, a CEO, or a bishop. But properly understood, authority abides not in a person or office but in a trusting relationship in which one freely assents to be influenced by another, both for the sake of their flourishing and for the furtherance of the common good.

Anglican theologian Victor Lee Austin, drawing inspiration from Thomist political theorist, Yves Simon, helps explain this perspective on authority.[6] Austin distinguishes ways in which individuals within a community can both *materially* and *formally* will the common good for that community. To be a productive member of a community, one is obligated to formally will the common good. As such, the members of an orchestra should all be concerned about the orchestra's performance of a particular piece of music. They are *formally* concerned with the overall performance. *Materially*, however, their attention will naturally lie with their specific duty to perform their own part well. The conductor, however, exercises authority by being both formally *and* materially concerned with the overall performance of the work. To offer another example, as a faculty member of a Catholic Jesuit university, I am *formally* committed to serving the university's mission. At the same time, I accomplish this *materially* by dedicating myself to the practice of theology and the initiation and formation of our students into that practice. It is for those directly responsible for the leadership of the university, not only formally but also materially, to will the achievement of the university's mission.

This account of authority suggests that authentic authority is not a matter of domination but of acting in such a way as to best bring about, materially, the common good of the community through the empowerment and coordination of those in the community who are working to achieve a vast array of particular goods. This account is suggestive for the priest's authentic exercise of pastoral leadership. To transpose the council's teaching into Austin/Simon's terminology, we might say that the ordinary believer is *formally* concerned with the common good of their local church, but *materially*, they pursue that by the exercise of their particular charisms. Church leaders are not only *formally* concerned with the common good of their community, they make this their *material* concern, directing the exercise of

---

    [6] Victor Lee Austin, *Up with Authority: Why We Need Authority to Flourish as Human Beings* (London: T&T Clark, 2010); see also Yves R. Simon, *A General Theory of Authority* (South Bend, IN: University of Notre Dame Press, 1962).

particular charisms in ways that build up the church in the pursuit of its mission. Concretely, the priest pursues the common good of the community by identifying, empowering, and ordering the exercise of individual charisms toward the church's larger mission.

Conclusion

What does this baptismal, Christological, and pneumatological account of the priest as pastoral leader say about our current approach to the work of encouraging and forming priestly vocations? I belong to a generation in which to come into adulthood as a single male who was also a practicing Catholic was to be peppered with questions about the possibility of a priestly vocation. These questions simply presupposed a particular theology of priestly vocation and a set of church structures (e.g., the office of the vocation director, seminaries) that supported that theology. This theology of vocation presumed that a vocational calling was primarily a personal, interior reality and that, once it was juridically validated and ecclesiastically cultivated, the recipient would be granted ministerial power by way of sacramental ordination.

Our current structures and policies for both discerning and forming priestly vocations certainly presume this reductive theology of priestly vocation. When a young (or not so young) man presents himself to a diocesan vocation director with the claim that he might have a vocation to the priesthood, there usually follows an initial investigation into whether there are canonical impediments to his ordination. There will also be, one hopes, some assessment of the candidate's sanctity and basic mental health. If no obstacles present themselves, the candidate will likely be accepted into the seminary. Now, let us presume that over the course of his period of seminary formation he passes all of his courses, dutifully attends daily mass, sees his spiritual director and confessor regularly, and does not manifest heretical or "dangerous" views in his academic work, preaching, pastoral counseling, or field education. Even if this candidate manifests no aptitude for genuine pastoral leadership, is there any doubt that this candidate would be ordained? In other words, our current vocational system is constructed more to discern impediments to ordination than the existence of a charism or aptitude for the exercise of genuine pastoral leadership or pastoral ministry of any kind. The theology of the priesthood that we sketched out earlier challenges much of this model.

The relational model developed in "To Serve the People of God," by putting a premium on the recognition and cultivation of a gift or aptitude for pastoral leadership, requires a dramatic expansion of the pool of candidates for ordained ministry. The church can no longer afford to ignore the thorny disciplinary, doctrinal, and theological commitments that limit the pool of candidates to celibate males. The quality of church leadership can only suffer when the pool of candidates is artificially limited.

Effective reform also requires a move away from the traditional emphasis on personal sanctity, rigorous doctrinal orthodoxy, and the mere identification of impediments. The church needs to cultivate ecclesial structures that focus our attention on the identification of charisms for pastoral leadership among the faithful. One would expect such a charism to be manifested in a discernible aptitude for recognizing, empowering, and celebrating the gifts of others.

Finally, this more relational theology of the priesthood challenges the current practice of forming priests in the seclusion of a seminary modeled on the life of the monastery. Surely, we cannot form someone for pastoral leadership without exposing the person regularly to the daily life and concerns of ordinary believers.

In this chapter, we have explored three features of a relational theology of the priesthood that is both faithful to our tradition and more adequate to the needs of the church in the present moment. That theology begins with the way baptism constitutes the fundamental ordering of the life of the church. Priestly ordination constitutes entrance into a new ecclesial relation. Through the anointing of the Spirit, the priest acts in the person of Christ as head and shepherd in service of God's people, particularly in preaching the Word of God, presiding over the corporate worship of the local church, and representing the church before the world—and in the exercise of pastoral charity and the work for justice. The work of the Holy Spirit liberates the priest from a competitive ministerial framework, encouraging him to collaborate with all the baptized by identifying, empowering, and ordering a "symphony of charisms" in service of the church's mission. In conclusion, we briefly considered some implications of these three theological features for our understanding of priestly vocations and priestly formation ministries. Without a significant reimagination of how the church calls forth candidates for priestly ministry and attends to their adequate formation, the people of God will continue to suffer under leadership inadequate to the demands of our time.

Questions for Reflection

1. What are some concrete ecclesial practices that might help us break out of the competitive turf wars so many encounter in our parishes?
2. If the church were to call forth candidates for presbyteral ministry who have an aptitude for identifying and celebrating the gifts of the baptized, what kinds of local church structures might help identify those candidates?

3

SHAPING THE FUTURE

Liam Bergin

I have spent thirty-seven years living in seminaries. In fact, from the age of twelve to the age of fifty-one there were only two years when I did not live in a seminary. I attended minor seminary, in the shape of a diocesan boarding school, for five years; college seminary for four; major seminary for five. Then I was successively a faculty member, formation director, vice rector, and finally rector of the Pontifical Irish College in Rome for ten years. I got parole in 2011 and, you will be happy to learn, I have been in regular contact with both my spiritual director and my therapist ever since!

I don't regret any of it. I met wonderful people who were generous and sincere. I worked with young people, helping them to discern God's will and how they might best serve the church. Many were open and honest, genuinely seeking to do what was right and true. One, Ragheed Ganni, was martyred with three subdeacons after celebrating mass in Mosul, Iraq, in 2007. The cause for his beatification is moving apace. I had fine faculty colleagues who allowed us to function effectively as a formation team, and I had the privilege of collaborating with others beyond: Sr. Katarina Schuth gave us workshops, and Father Joe Tobin conducted retreats and recollection days.

In the Service of Pastoral Charity

Since 1992, *Pastores Dabo Vobis* has been the Magna Carta of formation.[1] Its focus on the four pillars of human, spiritual, academic, and pastoral formation provided a structure for the seminary endeavor that promoted pastoral charity as the goal of the process. This suggested that it did not particularly

---

[1] Pope John Paul II, *Pastores Dabo Vobis*, 1992, http://www.vatican.va.

matter if a candidate was liberal or conservative, a prodigy or a plodder, introvert or extrovert. What truly mattered was that he would develop those qualities that would allow him to treat people—women and men, young and old, poor and rich—with dignity and respect, and that he would love and serve them with the heart of a shepherd.

But something changed from the mid-1990s. There was a marked retreat from the street to the sacristy, from what was a broader pastoral ministry to a narrower cultic service that represented a more old-fashioned reading of *Pastores Dabo Vobis*. This change found expression in the documents that were issued during the "Year for Priests" in 2009. These underlined the personal dignity that the gift of priesthood bestows on the individual and emphasized what distinguishes the priesthood of the ordained from that of the baptized. There was a growing ambiguity not only around the articulation of a theology of priesthood but also around the practical dynamics of formation.

Two documents from the Congregation for Catholic Education, which then had responsibility for seminaries and formation (Pope Francis transferred the responsibility for seminaries to the Congregation for Clergy in 2013) added to the equivocation and confusion. The 2005 "Instruction Concerning the Criteria for the Discernment of Vocations with Regard to Persons with Homosexual Tendencies in View of Their Admission to the Seminary and to Holy Orders" declared that persons who "practice homosexuality, present deep-seated homosexual tendencies or support the so-called 'gay culture'" (article 2) cannot be admitted to the seminary or to Holy Orders.[2] The outcome was a "don't ask, don't tell" culture where an open and honest discussion around issues of affective and psychosexual maturity was rendered very difficult.

The second document, "Guidelines for the Use of Psychology in the Admission and Formation of Candidates for the Priesthood," was promulgated in 2008.[3] It acknowledges that the "priestly vocation involves an extraordinary and demanding synergy of human and spiritual dynamics"

---

[2] Congregation for Catholic Education, *Instruction Concerning the Criteria for the Discernment of Vocations with Regard to Persons with Homosexual Tendencies in View of Their Admission to the Seminary and to Holy Orders*, 2005, https://www.vatican.va.

[3] Congregation for Catholic Education, "Guidelines for the Use of Psychology in the Admission and Formation of Candidates for the Priesthood," 2008, http://www.vatican.va.

(article 2), yet there was a hesitancy around the mandatory psychological screening of applicants or seminarians. This was to undermine the importance of human and psychological development in the formation process.

In 2016, the Congregation for the Clergy published *The Gift of the Priestly Vocation*, the new *ratio fundamentalis* for priestly formation.[4] Reflecting the teaching and personal example of Pope Francis, it reminds us that priests never stop being disciples of Jesus Christ in the ecclesial community. Much of the ambiguity of recent years has been resolved. That is why the reception of this document by national episcopal conferences and by each seminary is critical. Indeed, the pastoral reception of the magisterium of Pope Francis in the United States has recently been questioned by significant commentators, including the papal nuncio.

Inquiry among the Christian People

During the ceremony of ordination to the priesthood, there is an important dialogue between the ordaining bishop and a priest designated by the bishop, generally the seminary rector. The priest requests, "Most Reverend Father, holy mother Church asks you to ordain these, our brothers, to the responsibility of the priesthood." The bishop asks in reply, "Do you know them to be worthy?" The priest responds, "After inquiry among the Christian people and upon the recommendation of those responsible, I testify that they have been found worthy."

This "inquiry among the Christian people" represents those undergirding ecclesiological principles of our Boston College document, "To Serve the People of God," that are essential at every stage of the process: discernment before seminary, formation during seminary, and ongoing formation after ordination. Part 3 looks to the future and suggests concrete strategies for formation at these three stages for effective ministry. It makes the case that the multifaceted and multistaged formation of effective priests must be a priority for the whole church, not only for bishops and priests. Three points emerge.

First, the choice of candidates for formation is critical, particularly as the numbers presenting themselves decrease. The damage that unsuitable candidates can inflict on seminary life is painfully documented. The community

---

[4] Congregation for the Clergy, *The Gift of the Priestly Vocation*, 2017, http://www.clerus.va.

of faith must seek out and encourage from their midst candidates for priest-hood who have shown themselves to be dedicated to the service of God and others. A broad canvas of those who know the individual is indispensable to form a comprehensive picture of the candidate. Does this candidate possess the basic human qualities to become "a bridge and not an obstacle for others in their meeting with Jesus Christ" (*PDV*, 43)? Does this person manifest a sincere desire to love God and others? Do candidates indicate a willing-ness to collaborate with their baptized sisters and brothers and to give of themselves, to follow Jesus Christ, and to imitate his life and passion so as to witness to God's saving presence among us?

Second, the link between the seminary and the wider Christian commu-nity is crucial. Certainly, sometimes vocational discernment is enhanced by silence and retreat, but this must not lead to isolationism. "To Serve the People of God" encourages shared learning between candidates for diocesan priesthood and lay and religious candidates for ministry. Not only would this benefit the intellectual and pastoral programs that the seminary offers, it would also offer verification and challenge to the human and spiritual formation of the candidates. A formation that is collaborative, inclusive, and open to the contemporary reality of cultural diversity is thereby facilitated.

Third, the ongoing formation of ordained priests has been undertaken with limited success since *Pastores Dabo Vobis* first promoted its importance. While many priests engage individually in spiritual direction and coun-seling, there is little enthusiasm for the group programs offered by dioceses, generally to those in the first years of priesthood. Among the reasons cited are formation fatigue, a lack of time due to other commitments, and the perceived irrelevance of subjects treated. Here again, the involvement of a wider group of women and men who collaborate in pastoral ministry would provide incentive and foster responsibility in this lifelong process.

A Synodal Church

At the beginning of the final session of Vatican II, Pope Paul VI announced his intention to establish the Synod of Bishops as a permanent structure that would gather to reflect on issues of concern to the church and the world. Since his election, Pope Francis has increasingly highlighted the role and influence of the Synod of Bishops both in the articulation and in the subse-quent reception of his own teaching. In 2015, on the fiftieth anniversary of the institution of the Synod, Francis noted that "it is precisely this path of synodality that God expects of the Church of the third millennium."[5]

In a press conference announcing an international symposium on a fundamental theology of priesthood slated for Rome in 2022, Cardinal Marc Ouellet, the prefect of the Congregation for Bishops, offers a timely description: "Synodality basically means the active participation of all the faithful in the mission of the Church, it describes the united march of the baptized towards the Kingdom. . . . [It] requires a life of faith and close collaboration between lay people, priests and men and women religious, for the proclamation of the Gospel to the world through the attractive witness of Christian communities."[6] Central to the ministry of the priest, then, is the ability to live and foster synodality in the Christian community that he is called to serve. What are the characteristics that might shape the features of such a priest? The 2018 International Theological Commission's document, *Synodality in the Life and Mission of the Church*, offers four pointers.[7]

Spirituality of Communion

Fundamental to formation for synodal living is the spirituality of communion that recognizes the primacy of the "we" over the "I." Baptized in the name of the Father, the Son, and the Holy Spirit, the Christian community lives and journeys as a people in which the gifts of all are cherished and placed at the service of the ecclesial community. The eucharistic gathering is the source and model of the spirituality of communion. As we celebrate together, we learn what church is. Gathered by the invocation of the Trinity, the assembly paves the path for communion by means of reconciliation with God and our sisters and brothers. Listening to the Word of God, we hear God's voice that illumines our path. We don't receive Holy Communion at our seats but we are called to leave our places and walk toward the altar. We perform a movement that reminds us that we are a pilgrim people who

---

[5]   Pope Francis, "Ceremony Commemorating the 50th Anniversary of the Institution of the Synod of Bishops," October 17, 2017, http://www.vatican.va.

[6]   Cardinal Marc Ouellet, "Intervention: Press Conference to present the International Theological Symposium 'For a Fundamental Theology of Priesthood,' organized by the Congregation for Bishops (Rome, 17–19 February 2022)" (April 12, 2021), https://press.vatican.va.

[7]   International Theological Commission, *Synodality in the Life and Mission of the Church*, 2018, http://www.vatican.va.

are nourished by sacred bread for our journey. The Communion procession expresses this truth: shoulder to shoulder gathered by the Spirit, in the company of Jesus, we journey to meet our God and Father. To break the Word and the eucharistic bread demands that the priest be familiar with the joys and sorrows, the hopes and challenges that face the particular community that he serves.

Standing before the eucharistic minister, we raise our arms and open our hearts to receive the consecrated bread. We open our hands as a people who desires to receive a gift. The gesture reveals an inner attitude of vulnerability and trust. We don't take it but receive it from another who places it into our open hands, teaching us that all we have is saving gift freely given by the Father. The minister of the Eucharist holds out the consecrated host and says, "The body of Christ," and as we respond, "Amen," we not only agree with the saving truth that it is the real, sacramental presence of the Body and Blood of Christ, we also affirm who we are and whom we are called to be. The mass takes its name from the final dismissal: "Ite, missa est" (Go, you are sent forth). We gather to be sent. We receive the body of Christ so that we can be the Body of Christ in the world. The priest not only sends the congregation forth but is part of the tide of charity that flows from the eucharistic assembly. These are some of the wonderful things the liturgical gathering learns by actually doing them.

Listening and Dialogue for Communal Discernment

The synodal life of the church is built on genuine listening and dialogue for communal discernment. Again, the dialogical structure of the eucharistic liturgy provides a model: genuine listening to each other is preceded by a shared listening to the Word of God. Communal discernment calls for institutional conversion that abandons attitudes and practices that have not been renewed by the ecclesiology of communion. Any monopolizing of charisms by pastors is to be challenged as the baptismal dignity and co-responsibility of all are acknowledged and promoted. Synodality prospers when each one has the courage to speak and is listened to with dignity and respect. It thrives when consensus is prized over factional victory. It flourishes when humility and vulnerability overcome pride and defensiveness.

Pope Francis has spoken repeatedly of clericalism as a perversion of the church and its mission. It infantilizes the laity and distorts ordained ministry. It stifles the breath of the Spirit as it ultimately denies that Christ's saving mandate has been entrusted to the entire church. By contrast, a priest in a synodal church is called, as Pope Francis says, to contemplate the Word and to contemplate his people. As servant not master, he enters into meaningful dialogue with his sisters and brothers, is attentive to the concrete needs of the living community—particularly its poor and marginalized members—and facilitates the gifts of all in proclaiming the gospel and building up the Body of Christ in that place. Evidence of an openness and capacity to cultivate these human and spiritual qualities should be identified in any candidate for ordained ministry.

Journeying with Other Christians

Synodality demands a renewed ecumenical commitment to walk more closely with our separated brothers and sisters in Christ. While significant strides were taken in the aftermath of Vatican II, a lack of motivation and enthusiasm is developing for ecumenical engagement and dialogue as the memory of the achievements of the council recedes.

The 2011 English translation of the Roman Missal is a case in point. In the aftermath of Vatican II, contact with other Christian churches resulted in agreed liturgical texts for common prayers used in the liturgy. *Liturgiam authenticam*, the 2001 document from the Congregation of Divine Worship on the preparation of vernacular translations of liturgical texts, put an end to this with the extraordinary statement that "greater caution is to be taken to avoid a wording or style that the Catholic faithful would confuse with the manner of speech of non-Catholic ecclesial communities or other religions, so that such a factor will not cause them confusion or discomfort" (40).[8] Before the 2011 translation, many Christians had common texts for the *Gloria*, the Creed, and the *Sanctus*. This is no longer the case. This unilateral Catholic decision is a serious ecumenical step backward that has caused embarrassment in Catholic circles and hurt in non-Catholic quarters.

A not insignificant number of the people presenting themselves as candidates for priesthood show a predilection, if not a preference, for the extraordinary form of the mass. This represents more than a linguistic or aesthetic choice. Liturgy shapes the church and molds the self-identity

---

[8] Congregation for Divine Worship and the Discipline of the Sacraments, Liturgiam authenticam: *On the Use of the Vernacular Languages in the Publication of the Books of the Roman Liturgy*, 2001, http://www.vatican.va.

and the mission of the Body of Christ in the world. As Pope Paul VI often noted, to opt for the Tridentine liturgy is to promote an ecclesiology that is suspicious of conciliar reforms such as religious freedom and ecumenical engagement. This is contrary to the synodal way and poses great challenges to the effectiveness of the church's life and mission. It unveils attitudes that simply should be challenged in members of the ecclesial community, particularly in candidates for priesthood.

Promoting Social and Ecological Justice

Deeply rooted in scripture and tradition, Catholic social teaching continues to evolve in the modern period from Leo XIII's *Rerum novarum* of 1891 to Francis's *Laudato Si'* of 2015. It stands on the conviction that working for justice is an integral part of the church's mission to proclaim the reign of God. The central themes it proposes include human dignity and the right to life, solidarity, the universal destination of goods, subsidiarity, common good, integral ecology, and the priority of the option for the poor. Catholic social teaching acknowledges the interdependence of the human family and the imperative that the church walk with each woman and man as sister and brother in Christ Jesus. Catholic social teaching calls for constructive dialogue with people of different religious confessions and traditions to bring about a culture of encounter. As it breaks down barriers between the sacred and the profane, the religious and the secular, it draws the priest from the security of the sanctuary to the uncertainty of the public square.

"To Serve the People of God" ends with a reference to Pope Francis's oft-repeated reference to "boldness." It is a boldness given by the Spirit to all God's people. It is a boldness that is necessary for candidates to ordained ministry as they serve their sisters and brothers in heralding "a kingdom of justice, peace and joy" (see Rom 14:17).

Questions for Reflection

1. What concrete strategies for formation toward effective ministry do you envisage as we seek to promote a vision of priesthood that serves the needs of our time?

2. What are the human and spiritual qualities necessary in a candidate for ordained ministry to serve the people of God as together they walk the synodal way?

4

Renewing the Conversation on Priestly Ministry

Reinhard Cardinal Marx

It is an honor for me to be asked to contribute some after-dinner remarks to this conference.[1] I will not speak about the current situation of priesthood. All of you know that it does not look good. The scandal of sexual abuse by priests aggravated this situation of priestly ministry. But in order to contribute to the latter and give impulses, I will try to list five short points that are absolutely necessary if we want to give new perspectives to the profession of our priests.

Of course it needs prayer, trusting intercession, and hope in the work of the Holy Spirit. But prayer alone does not release us from the task of putting all our power into making this success happen. May the aspects presented here help to determine what to do. These aspects have become clear when considering the future of priesthood in Germany, and they are current subjects of consultation in the Synodal Way that we have just started there. You may find some congruence with your text "To Serve the People of God: Renewing the Conversation on Priesthood and Ministry."

This congruence makes clear how strongly we are associated within the one church. However, maybe our German perspective can shed another light on your American thoughts. So, I invite you to listen to five short impulses.

---

[1] Taken from Reinhard Cardinal Marx, Archbishop of Munich and Freising, postdinner comments at the conference on "To Serve the People of God: Renewing the Conversation on Priesthood and Ministry," Boston, Massachusetts, January 2, 2020.

The True Spiritual Profile of Priesthood

Despite all the theological meanings of priesthood, all the estimation of its service, and all its moral quality, it is not helpful to exaggerate this profession. In fact, it is really dangerous to elevate the profession of a priest to the sphere of the sacred, the everlasting holiness, the supernatural detached from the world. From a sacramental perspective, it is even wrong to sacralize priesthood. Ordination, as well as the ministry, is part of the basic sacramental structure of our church. It is an effective sign of God's proximity to humankind—a proximity that at the same time means salvation. But it is not salvation itself.

The church, as the Mystical Body of Christ, remains the pilgrim people of God. It has not reached its destination, but is still on a pilgrimage through time and history. In this perspective, the church has always been understood as a community of fallible and limited humans, who try to give space to the gospel in their everyday lives. The priest is also part of this community of the baptized and confirmed, and the grace of his ordination does not free him from human banality. Like every other sacramental grace, the grace of ordination is God's offer to humankind that it must accept and respond to, so that this offer may become prosperous in the life of the church.

The priest is a man on his life journey. He has planned and obligated himself to this service. This means hard labor and effort—the adversity of human life does not spare him. It is not really helpful to use, in the context of ordination, language that is more appropriate for beatification and canonization. If aspects of a life dedicated to God, of heroic virtue, and, last but not least, of vocation and closeness to God are overemphasized with reference to priests, these aspects will lead to difficulties. Expectations will be exaggerated, the well-grounded candidates for priesthood will shy away from the moral pressure, and unsuitable types of personality will be attracted by the institutionally safeguarded and spiritually elevated position; an inadequate understanding of priesthood and ministry will develop.

Bearing in mind the current small number of candidates for priesthood, the church must take care not to feed wrong ideas. Would it not be better to name the really interesting aspects of this service in a more outspoken way, and to stimulate the professional service of the priest: to provide demanding pastoral care, to be in contact with people searching for the meaning of existence, to stand by them even in difficult situations, to support them in pastoral care and liturgy without exaggeration, and so to show them the love of our God? Comprehensively, priestly ministry is about priests offering their lives in service, which specifically means: living with love; giving and sharing time; and being there for others, also in prayer. How the people are yearning for such men, who have subjugated their own desires. This is the true spiritual profile of priesthood, now and also in the future.

Protecting the Priest against Overload

The second impulse is that, in times of a shortage of priests, it must be a major interest of each bishop to protect his priests against an overload of tasks. In theory, it is completely obvious and easy. If a priest must be excellent in pastoral care, liturgy, and homily, he cannot simultaneously manage a medium-sized social company with schools, hospitals, senior-living homes, community centers, and nurseries. Moreover, he cannot be the engine of all committees in a huge parish with thousands of parishioners.

If a priest must be able to provide demanding pastoral care, he needs corresponding external conditions: time for conversations, time for reflection and meditation, and strength and support for helping with difficult situations in life. The time needed here is filled up with management tasks and the lifestyle of a top manager. The tasks of spiritual leadership, and administrative supervision must be differentiated and adapted to one another, so that the priest does not become just some spiritual helper on the periphery, or a stressed manager substitute.

I know how difficult and delicate it is to structurally unburden priests, especially the few efficient ones, without giving them the feeling of losing significance. But without a cultural change regarding responsibility and the self-understanding of our priests, we will not achieve a renewal of priestly services. Ordination does not grant universal competence or power, nor does celibacy guarantee overall responsibility.

Access to the Priesthood

Talking about the future of priesthood also means thinking about the conditions for access to this ministry. The classic biography of a priest, which includes school, directly followed by university and seminary formation, then diaconal consecration and ordination and service as a priest, no longer exists. At least, this biography does not correspond with a normal career.

The new pastoral reality shows men with job experience, or men who still need further schooling, or those who developed intense contact with the church or priesthood via church groups. With our educational concepts, we try to take these different individual biographies into account. The Amazon Synod (2019) made clear that we must also take into account the ordination of married men, "*viri probati*," which is not a substitute for celibate priesthood, but perhaps an additional element under certain circumstances. We will have to think and speak about this.

Bearing in mind the historical developments and challenges of present times, one must also point out that the church—especially regarding the critical views of its members—must discuss the possibility of opening access to consecration for women. No matter how we will judge this topic theologically, there is no doubt that a simple statement that the discussion has been closed already by the magisterium will not be sufficient. The fact remains that the discussion is obviously not closed.

A Sound Formation

A fulfilling biography and demanding work in pastoral care will not be possible without a solid formation. Nowadays, faith and Christian tradition are no longer a matter of course. Therefore, I do not have to point out the meaning of a sound theological formation. It must make the priest eloquent and informative on matters of personal faith. No one will be convinced by preformulated statements and theological clichés.

Today, the social and human sciences are an indispensable part of a formation curriculum. Priests who want to support people competently in their complex lifestyles need useful theoretical tools. Of course, the formation must be backed up by pastoral practice. This especially means focusing on working in a pastoral team. The times of a priestly lone ranger are definitely long gone. However, it is not only spiritual care but also reflection and psychological health that must be practiced in professional communication with others. Premises that are valid for all other professions in the psychological and social areas must be similarly adopted in the working fields of pastoral care and priesthood. I doubt whether the *ratio fundamentalis* for priestly formation programs provides enough adequate orientation. Here, further consideration is required, with a view to the priesthood of the future.

Preventing the Isolation of the Priest

All those who—like me—consider celibacy as a strong opportunity for radical discipleship of Christ will agree that more suitable external conditions must be in place to realize this way of living in a lifelong, fulfilling way. The few priests whom we still have today must be supported with great care and circumspection, so that they do not fall victim to loneliness and social incompetence. A priest who is ordained today does not have the backing of his fellow priests—those who were ordained with him in the same year and who, in former times, played an important role in a priest's life. We need a suitable substitute for this, which does not arise by itself.

From the beginning, the candidates must learn to develop their own personal network and a strong social network. They must learn to separate—but also unite—professional and private matters. They must know whom they can contact with professional, religious, and personal questions and problems. Moreover, they need support and backing with their life planning and planning for their old age. Thus, we need strengthening of the celibate lifestyle. Living a life of celibacy—including in old age—does not mean living without relationships, since "It is not good that the man should be alone" (Gen 2:18). However, should not, and must not, there also be a perspective for how unmarried and married priests can together represent the future of priesthood? Is this possible in a good way?

All these items are not easy to realize. Some require significant efforts. But only if we succeed in making the service of a priest into a real profession and life concept will we then have a chance to captivate people with this fascinating mission and vocation. I firmly believe that there are more vocations for priestly service than there are currently seminarians in our seminaries. And are there not also vocations among married men?

Questions for Reflection

1. How can we maintain the sacred function of priesthood without falling into "exaggeration and false sacralization"?
2. Do you favor or oppose the proposal to ordain *viri probati* to priesthood (mature men, married or celibate)? Why?

Part II

Responses

5

CRISIS AND HOPE

Catherine E. Clifford

It is no mean task to reflect on "the best hopes for the future of the priesthood" while a grave pandemic rages worldwide, having already claimed millions of lives. While there is light at the end of the tunnel as the population gains access to lifesaving vaccines, these are dramatic, indeed apocalyptic times. The term "apocalypse"—often associated with a time of catastrophic destruction—is derived from a Greek word meaning "revelation" or "uncovering." The present global health crisis has shone a harsh light on the cracks and fissures of our society, revealing profound inequities, including humanity's inability to respect the order of God's creation and systemic failures to care for the vulnerable in our communities and in our nation, and among the nations. There is no avoiding the fact that we are living through a time of dramatic decline, a time of reckoning.

Context

Prior to the onset of the pandemic, there were also dramatic signs of ill health, crises, and failure in the life of the church. The reality of clergy sexual abuse emerged in both Canada and the United States in the early 1980s. After a generation of efforts to minimize the crisis and claims that this was but a problem of a "few bad apples," the true scope of the scourge of abuse and of the systematic betrayal of survivors by bishops who prioritized the protection of the clergy and the institution over the protection and care of victims has come to light. In country after country, Catholic leaders have been shamed—often by secular media and civil authorities—into recognizing the scale of the problem and of their own failures. The shock of each new revelation has left committed and well-meaning Catholics with

61

a deep sense of betrayal and their overworked pastors demoralized. For many, ordained priesthood is no longer a "respectable" vocation. How, they wonder, can trust be restored?

Pope Francis has courageously committed the whole church to address the roots of the sexual abuse crisis. He has rightly identified a culture of clericalism as a significant factor contributing to the church's failure to place the victims of abuse at the center of concern. That same culture enabled the pathology of abuse to persist unchecked—including the abuse of power, the abuse of conscience, and sexual and financial abuses. Canadian pediatrician Nuala Kenny characterizes the culture of abuse within the church as an "endemic" condition, a "pervasive and multigenerational" state of ill health that has spread throughout the body until "the affected community experiences the sickness as normal."[1]

Clericalism is a sad distortion of priesthood, an attitude of exceptionalism that conceives of the ordained as belonging to a separate caste, untainted by the quotidian holiness of ordinary Christian discipleship. As Francis describes it, clericalism tries to "replace, or silence, or ignore, or reduce the People of God to small elites." In his 2013 Apostolic Constitution *Evangelii Gaudium* (*EG*), "On the Joy of the Gospel," Pope Francis links the pathology of clericalism to the vice of "pastoral acedia"—the despondency and paralysis of a church turned in on itself, more preoccupied with its own comfort or survival than with its essential mission to care for others (*EG*, 81–82).[2] He recalls that the ministry of the ordained is at the service of the laity, "the vast majority of the people of God" (*EG*, 102). The abuse crisis has laid bare a wide-ranging crisis of leadership and ministry across the Catholic Church. For the church, too, this is a dramatic time of reckoning. The old ways of proceeding no longer hold. In this context, where can one find hope?

Reflecting on the nature of Christian hope, Karl Rahner argued convincingly that the Christian is not given to facile optimism. In his view, the virtue of hope must be accompanied by a spirit of "Christian pessimism."[3] By this he meant that the Christian is a realist, unafraid to

---

[1] Nuala Kenny, *Still Unhealed: Treating the Pathology in the Clerical Sexual Abuse Crisis* (New London, CT: Twenty-third Publications, 2019), 14

[2] Pope Francis, Post-Synodal Apostolic Exhortation *Evangelii Gaudium*, "The Joy of the Gospel," 2013, http://www.vatican.va.

[3] Karl Rahner, "Christian Pessimism" *Theological Investigations*, vol. 22, trans Joseph Donceel (New York: Crossroad, 1991), 155–62.

face squarely the ambiguity and incomprehensibility of the human condition, including the humiliation of his or her own sinfulness. With St. Paul, we can say that we are "afflicted" and "perplexed, but not driven to despair" (2 Cor 4:8). Mindful that the treasure of the gospel is borne in earthen vessels, we can lay bare the dark side of our humanity before God's merciful light with the unshakable confidence that redeeming grace can transform our wounds.

It is in this sense that I have hope for the future of the ordained priesthood and for the whole church, the priestly people of God. The way forward lies, I believe, in a theology and practice that will restore the ordained ministry to a location squarely within, and at the service of, a community of saints and sinners called to transform the world. The future lies in a return to the Christ-centered teaching of the New Testament—a vision that the Second Vatican Council sought to embrace—that remains an abstract ideal not yet reflected in the concrete structures and practices of the church.

Elements for a Renewed Theology of Priesthood

A culture of clerical exceptionalism is manifested among many recent ordinands who—whether from seminary courses or the parallel online universe—have imbibed a theology of ordained priesthood that emphasizes their being set apart for the practice of cultic worship. As a young professor, I once witnessed a seminary colleague and formation director address a class of candidates for ministry a few weeks before their ordination. They were told in no uncertain terms that the conferral of the sacrament of orders would transform each of them into a "new person" —a clear allusion to the "ontological change" that would enable them to act henceforth *in persona Christi*. The focus on identification was not balanced, as the teaching of both Pope Pius XII (*Mediator Dei*) and Vatican II's Dogmatic Constitution on the Church (*LG*, 10) from which it is apparently derived, by the corollary of praying and acting "in the name of the church." This naïve theological line of reasoning finds support in magisterial teaching that has sought to underline the "essential" difference between the priesthood of the ordained and the common priesthood of the baptized in an unproductive, and less-than-traditional, zero-sum game.

Vatican II's teaching offers significant elements for a renewed theology of priesthood that have yet to be fully received. The council fathers sought to move past the clericalism and juridicism of reigning ecclesiologies by realigning the understanding of holy orders in accord with the New Testament and patristic traditions. In his effort to receive the council's vision of the church more fully, Pope Francis has grasped its potential to inform the life of a more synodal and dialogical church, an "inverted pyramid" where the ordained minister is "located beneath the base," supporting and sustaining a community of missionary disciples.[4] A renewed theology of priesthood must build upon Vatican II's recovery of the biblical image of the priesthood of Christ, of the priority of the priestly people of God, and of ministry as service. Such a vision will better reconcile the liturgical and diaconal life of the church, a community that exists to serve the world.

The One Priesthood of Christ

Vatican II's teaching reflects the priority given in the New Testament to the unique and unrepeatable priesthood of Christ and to the corporate priesthood of the whole church. The centrality of Christ's priesthood is often neglected or taken for granted in our thinking. Nowhere in the New Testament does Jesus present himself as a priest. Nor is the ministry of the apostles associated with the Jewish temple cult. "Priest" is a term reserved for Christ (see Heb 4:14–5:10; 9:11–10:14) and for the baptized people of God (1 Pet 2:4–10). Indeed, the term *sacerdos* would not be applied to ordained ministers of the church until after the fourth century, when Christianity became the official religion of the empire and the roles of clergy and laity became more sharply defined.

Christ, our high priest—who, according to the Letter to the Hebrews, has accomplished "once for all" (Heb 9:26; 10:10) the perfect offering— is the model of all Christian priesthood. His sacrifice is not in the cultic mode of the Jerusalem temple, where the priestly class of the Jewish people presided over the burnt offerings of animal sacrifice to restore communion with God. Rather, Jesus's gift of self even in the face of violent rejection, torture, and death is the fulfillment of the prophetic tradition that looked to the fullness of God's covenant in sacrificial living and in the work of social justice. The paschal pattern of Jesus's passion and death is not found in the repetition of ritual sacrifice, but in the unreserved offering of his whole self, an act of self-giving love. Christians are called to reproduce

---

[4] Pope Francis, "Address of His Holiness Commemorating the 50th Anniversary of the Institution of the Synod," October 17, 2015, http://www.vatican.va.

the pattern of his self-offering, the sacrifice "pleasing to God" in lives of mutual love and service, in "good works and the sharing of resources" (Heb 13:1–16).

The Priestly People of God

The first document promulgated by the council was the Constitution on the Sacred Liturgy (*Sacrosanctum Concilium*), which rightly presents the liturgy as "enacting the priestly role (*Sacerdotalis Muneris*) of Jesus Christ." Christ is the primary actor and minister of the liturgy: "offering," "baptizing," and "speaking when scripture is read" (*SC*, 7). "In the liturgy . . . the mystical body of Jesus Christ, that is, the head and its members, is together giving complete and definitive expression to its worship" (*SC*, 7). The ecclesial body, together with Christ, the head, form what Augustine would call the *totus Christus*, the whole Christ. The "right and duty" of the baptized faithful to participate in the priestly offering of Christ flow from their dignity as members of "the chosen race, the royal priesthood, the holy nation, the people of whom God has taken possession (1 Pet 2:9; see 2:4–5)" (*SC*, 14). Against this horizon the council speaks of the common priesthood of the baptized and the priesthood of the ordained as different participations in the one priesthood of Christ (*LG*, 10).

Paul calls every Christian to imitate Christ by offering themselves "as a living sacrifice, holy and acceptable to God," to make their whole lives a "spiritual sacrifice" (Rom 12:1–2). By reproducing the pattern of Christ's self-giving love—in their roles as spouses and parents; in caring for their neighbors, coworkers, and the poor and vulnerable; and in working for the transformation of society—the baptized faithful grow in holiness. This is how they live out what *Lumen Gentium* calls the universal call to holiness. Pope Francis has drawn our attention again to the gracious gift of holiness that God has bestowed on even "the humblest members" of God's faithful people and is reflected in the small gestures of the saints "next door."[5] He understands that neglect of this fundamental insight into the dignity of the baptized faithful has a disempowering effect, marginalizing their contribution to the decision-making and pastoral activity of the church (*EG*, 102).

---

[5] Pope Francis, Apostolic Exhortation *Gaudete et Exsultate*, "Rejoice and Be Glad: On the Call to Holiness in Today's World," 2018, http://www.vatican.va.

The Priesthood of the Ordained Minister

In a nod to the New Testament's priority of the corporate priesthood of the baptized, the documents of Vatican II generally reserve sacerdotal language for the common priesthood, preferring the biblical term "presbyter" for the ordained minister. The council's "Decree on the Life and Ministry of Priests" describes the goal of the ordained ministry as enabling the daily self-offering of the priestly people of God: "Through the ministry of priests (*presbyterorum*) the spiritual self-offering of the faithful is celebrated in union with the sacrifice of Christ, the one mediator, in that by their hands it is offered in the name of the whole church" (*PO*, 2). The *Catechism of the Catholic Church* expresses this idea more clearly as it explains the essential distinction between the common and ordained priesthood: "The ministerial priesthood is at the service of the common priesthood. It is directed at the unfolding of the baptismal grace of all Christians" (CCC §1547). For this to happen in practice, the link between life and liturgy needs to be better understood and to become more evident in the life of those gathered and of the presider. The offering of the Eucharist is a sacramental representation of who and what the baptized Christian is called to be each day. In the words of Augustine, the presbyter is to assist us to "receive what we are" and "become what we receive."

From Alterity to Closeness

A priesthood that has lost contact with the lives of ordinary Christians has no future. To become the instruments of that humble, listening presence that Pope Francis envisions in a church that looks more like an inverted pyramid requires candidates for ordained ministry with a strong sense of belonging to the priestly people of God. Their ministerial identity will be less rooted in the piety of difference or otherness than in solidarity with a people on the way and bearing a common mission. They will come to know themselves as "brothers among brothers with all those who have been reborn at the baptismal font . . . members of one and the same Body of Christ, the building up of which is required of everyone" (*PO*, 9). For this to happen, a renewed theology of ministry must be met with new models of seminary formation and training.

Pope Francis has spoken of the need for pastors who follow the pattern of Christ's "closeness" in the art of accompanying others in the journey of Christian life, for a ministry characterized by "respectful and compassionate listening" (*EG*, 171, *et passim*). To develop the virtue of "closeness," candidates for ordination must be formed in a context where they naturally interact with the people they are called to serve. Models of seminary formation that set men apart or separate them geographically from the churches they serve have not prepared them well for the realities of effective pastoral leadership. By failing to integrate theological education programs for ordination candidates with those preparing women and men for various lay ecclesial ministries, churches have missed an important opportunity to prepare ordination candidates for genuine collaboration in ministry.

Building a truly synodal church, where pastors walk together on the way with their parishioners, requires the formation of ordained ministers with a strong set of people skills, including the ability to consult and seek advice from competent lay persons, to welcome their ideas and gifts, and to channel them for the upbuilding of the community and the accomplishment of its mission. Turning the pyramid on its head requires pastors who are open to differing perspectives, who model the habits of respectful listening, and who are willing to work with others to arrive at consensus. In a mission-driven church, they will be especially attentive to the poor and the marginalized.

Some of these skills can only be acquired through lived experience. The church could consider new models of living in small faith communities during the period of theological and pastoral formation. Sharing in the daily responsibilities of food preparation, household chores, and shared decision-making can strengthen and test one's capacity for empathy and compassion. Immersion experiences of solidarity with and pastoral activity among groups that are excluded or on the margins of economic, social, and ecclesial life can reeducate unfounded suppositions and undo many unconscious defense mechanisms. They provide opportunities to deepen one's understanding of God's preferential love for the poor and the church's mission to reflect God's "closeness and compassionate gaze" (*EG*, 169). Formative experiences like these bear fruit when they are accompanied by good spiritual direction and a strong program of personal integration for ministry led by experienced professionals.

I have attempted to lay out the seeds for a renewed theology of ordained priesthood in the ecclesiology of the Second Vatican Council that until now have laid dormant. Their reception in a renewed theology of priesthood will be essential to the formation of ordained ministers who understand themselves as placed squarely within the heart of God's prophetic people, a people sent to serve and transform a broken world. New models of formation for ministry will be required to form presbyters who serve the people of God as brothers, who are unafraid of getting a little mud on their shoes as they walk alongside their fellow disciples (*EG*, 45). The challenge ahead is great, but together the community of disciples will discern and set the course of the future.

Questions for Reflection

1. How do you understand your vocation as a baptized Christian, and how is this related to your belonging to the priestly people of God?
2. How do you understand the relationship between your participation in the liturgical celebration of the Eucharist and the reality of daily life?

6

RECLAIMING THE PARISH DIMENSION

John Kartje

As the rector of a seminary that serves multiple dioceses, I have had the privilege of attending numerous ordinations. On these occasions, I am usually the one asked by the bishop whether the ordinands have been found to be "worthy." At this point, I recite the scripted response: "After inquiry among the Christian people and upon the recommendation of those responsible, I testify that they have been found worthy." Despite my confidently scripted answer, I am often haunted by the questions: Have I adequately inquired among the Christian people? To whom should the inquiries have been directed? Did they respond honestly and in good faith, and were they adequately informed to proffer a wise decision? Whose recommendations should I have even sought? It is generally assumed that the seminary faculty should offer their formal recommendation, and they do. But the language of the rite does not restrict the responsibility of recommendation only to them.

If I were derelict in my preparation for answering the bishop's question, the sacrament of ordination would likely still be valid, but its ecclesial integrity would be seriously compromised. This deceptively simple exchange between bishop and rector ought to be understood as a culminating moment in the entire process of seminary formation. It highlights the critical importance of the role of the laity to the success of priestly formation. I believe that diocesan seminaries have yet to integrate that role fully and properly into the structure of their mission. In this chapter I hope to outline what such an integration might look like, focusing particularly on the contribution of parishes to the overall formation process.

East of Eden

The word "seminary" is derived from "seedbed," which conjures up the image of a carefully tended plot of land in which fragile seeds can be nurtured and developed—in short, a garden or vineyard. And yet, in the Bible, gardens and vineyards are often not portrayed as the idyllic settings one might expect. Even in Eden, where every conceivable need was satisfied, the one small call for humanity's obedience was met with rebellion. One might also think of Isaiah's famous song of the vineyard (see Isa 5:17), which describes how the Lord's careful tending of the land yields nothing but rotten grapes. One could also add the murderous coveting inspired by Naboth's vineyard (see 1 Kgs 21:1–16) or Judas's betrayal of Jesus in Gethsemane.

By contrast, the normally dangerous wilderness or desert is not infrequently portrayed in the Bible as a site for renewal and safety. Although Adam and Eve are expelled from paradise, it is only outside the garden—where farming and childbirth are hard—that they actually carry out the Lord's injunction to be fruitful and multiply. Hagar flees with Abram's unborn son to the desert for safety, where she is met by an angel and given her place in Israel's salvation history (see Gen 16:6–12; cf. Rev 12:6). It is out into the wilderness that Yahweh plans to lure Yahweh's unfaithful spouse, Israel, to rekindle their covenantal love (see Hos 2:16–25). And Jesus himself is driven into the desert after his baptism where his identity as the Father's beloved Son is powerfully affirmed (see Matt 4:1–11).

In a similar vein, when Jesus takes on the role of preparing his disciples to follow after him, he explicitly does so by sending them away from himself, on their own. He guarantees that they will struggle—take no money, sack, extra tunic, or sandals, and so on—and he sends them "like sheep among wolves" (Matt 10:16). In short, their preparation as disciples is designed to be challenging and at least partially disorienting. But what they always have is the assurance of Jesus's reception when they return to him and his confidence in their ability, which often exceeds their own confidence.

So, perhaps the image of a protective seedbed does not fully capture the biblical sense of how one is to be prepared to grow closer to the Lord and carry out the Lord's mission. With respect to the needs for priestly formation, I suggest that we take up the wider biblical perspective and broaden our understanding of where and how formation is accomplished.

Parish Roots of Priestly Formation

In Chaucer's celebrated *Canterbury Tales*, several men and women from religious life are numbered among the pilgrims. They are all corrupt, with the exception of the parish priest ("the Parson"), who is described as a virtuous and holy man. Modeling his life after that of Jesus and his apostles, living simply yet generous toward his poorer parishioners, he willingly puts their needs before his own and makes every effort to reach out to them. He is a good preacher and teacher as well as a learned scholar. In modern seminary parlance, he is very well formed in all four dimensions—human, pastoral, intellectual, and spiritual! It raises the question as to where and how he acquired his priestly formation.

Chaucer began writing the *Tales* around the year 1390, about 150 years before the start of the Council of Trent. As a student, this parson would likely have lived at the cathedral church or at another large parish in his diocese and studied with a mentor priest who was expressly appointed by the bishop. In this environment, the presence of the people was always close at hand. The parson would have prayed with them and walked among them, even as he was finding time to devote to his studies. It is not hard to imagine that such regular, daily interactions throughout the parish could contribute to a sense of humility and compassion. To be sure, Chaucer's parson represents an ideal case, and we have many recorded complaints about the woeful preparation of the medieval secular clergy. Nevertheless, it is noteworthy that while the poet takes pains to portray friars, monks, nuns, and prioresses as greedy, lecherous, and vain, he takes a markedly contrary view of the cleric, who was formed and lived among the people he served.

The Council of Trent called for the establishment of seminary institutions separate from the parish church, with well-trained faculty dedicated to the formation of priests. That system has largely served the church well for centuries. But in today's culture, in which many seminarians have not grown up with a strong experience of parish life, and in which the pervasive virtual opinions of social media can easily supplant the role of interpersonal interactions in a young person's development, key elements of priestly formation can only be supplied by reclaiming the parish's rightful place within the seminary system of formation.

The Heart of the Diocese

The Second Vatican Council's document on priestly formation identified the seminary as the "heart of the diocese" (*Optatam Totius*, 5). This implies a vital link between the seminary and the parishes to which the newly ordained priests are sent. A heart in isolation from the body does little good; both heart and body will quickly die. The seminary and the parishes are meant to form one intertwined community as the Body of Christ.

This means that the laity in the parishes have a *responsibility* to assist in the formation of their future priests, just as the seminary faculty have a *responsibility* to embrace the role of the parish in providing content and guidance that is integral to what they themselves provide in the classroom, the chapel, or the spiritual director's office. My hope for the future of priestly formation is that this dual responsibility will increasingly be seen as a joyful opportunity for creative collaboration rather than as one more burdensome task for pastors to shoulder or for seminary personnel to fear as robbing their precious face time with the students.

Let me be clear: I am not advocating for the dissolution of seminaries and the full-time placement of seminarians into parishes. So what might this model look like? Such models have been tried and have significant advantages and challenges. By learning from those experiences, we are uniquely poised in the church to draw upon the best practices of seminary-based and parish-based formation. Some elements of formation are best served by focused time away from parish life—for example, in intensive academic units or on a prolonged retreat—just as some elements are doubtless best served by immersion among parish priests, staff, and lay parishioners, such as learning to become more self-aware in the face of difficult pastoral scenarios. A hybrid model, with part-time residence in a parish—or parish cluster—and part-time in a traditional seminary may provide an optimal solution. Most seminaries already integrate a full parish immersion semester or pastoral year into their curriculum, and those months in the parish typically produce a remarkable degree of growth in the seminarian's formation. Why should the benefits of such immersion be limited to only a fraction of the entire seminary tenure?

My intention here is not to attempt a detailed outline of the elements of such a hybrid formational model, but rather to call for a focused and serious exploration of what that model might entail. For example, one could easily imagine the need for higher-quality and better-integrated methods of distance learning with which, due to the pandemic, nearly every seminary has gained some experience. It would also require the diocese to assign quality priests and staff to serve as formators at those parishes where the seminarians were in part-time residence. Regarding time management, there is no reason why the calendar for priestly formation must follow the traditional academic calendar. A year-round formation program could introduce significant flexibility and would more closely track the actual schedule of parish priests. One could imagine several five- or six-week units spent at the seminary, interspersed with time in the parish, possibly supplemented with distance-learning modules or online seminars.

But we should not be naïve. Such a vision demands a significant reimagining and reworking of what it means to be seminary and parish. Seminary faculty and formators would have to be prepared for a more focused experience and tighter time frame than the typical semester-long itinerary permits. Furthermore, they would need to adapt their pedagogy to leverage better the real-life experiences of church that their students would regularly be bringing into the classroom. Parishioners, for their part, would require their own formation to appreciate more fully the goals of priestly formation and how they provide a unique contribution to that process.

The Benefits

The primary benefit of greater interaction between the seminary and the parish is the gift of *encounter*. The experience of encountering the other provides the foundation for all four dimensions of priestly formation. When a seminarian encounters someone in the parish, it brings a different level of engagement than he would typically experience in the seminary, where he is surrounded by familiar faces and scenarios. Whether through the intensity of a hospital visit, the potential awkwardness of having dinner with a parish family he has never met, or the tension of listening to a disgruntled parishioner rant after mass about the pope, a seminarian in the parish is continually experiencing interior thoughts and feelings that are not likely replicated in the seminary classroom or chapel.

A well-trained formator, either in the seminary or in the parish, can skillfully help a man grow in self-awareness and process what he is feeling and how he is reacting in such situations. These formation conversations, which can sometimes lead to counseling sessions, are invaluable for helping a seminarian to integrate such critical qualities as his psychosexual development, his way of relating to women, his capacity for compassion, his desire and ability for collaboration, and his respect for authority.

A seminarian who is willing and able to undergo such integration will grow in affective maturity, an essential quality for successful priestly formation. In *Pastores Dabo Vobis*, St. John Paul II writes that "affective maturity, which is the result of an education in true and responsible love, is a *significant and decisive factor* in the formation of a candidate for the priesthood" (*PDV*, 43; emphasis added). As the phrase implies, affective maturity encompasses the ability of a man to acknowledge responsibly the emotions he is feeling in any given situation (joy, fear, awe, etc.) and to manage them constructively without being controlled by visceral reactions.

While the inability of a man to develop affective maturity should clearly preclude him from pursuing priesthood, such inability is sometimes only exposed via the man's interactions with others in unfamiliar surroundings. For example, a seminarian's rigid resistance to collaborative ministry may never surface within the seminary walls, where direct obedience is demanded, but may quickly manifest itself once the man is asked to codirect a parish project with a staff member.

Regarding the hybrid model discussed earlier, a benefit of having seminarians spend part of each year living together in parish communities within their home dioceses is fostering the growth of authentic presbyteral unity. Seminarians from the same diocese living together within a parish setting have the opportunity to build lifelong relationships that are difficult to duplicate within a seminary population of one hundred to two hundred men, gathered from many disparate dioceses. Furthermore, they can maintain closer ties to their bishop, become more familiar with the people of the diocese, and nurture their relationships with the actual presbyterate they will one day join.

Finally, the five central aspects of priestly ministry that were highlighted in the document "To Serve the People of God"—preacher, worship leader, collaborative leader, public representative of the church, practitioner of pastoral charity—can all be enhanced if future priests were to have greater interaction with parishioners throughout their seminary years. For example, while every seminary offers classes in homiletics and students are given opportunities to preach in front of their peers and teachers, nothing can replace the experience of actually preaching before a parish congregation, especially if they have been prepared to offer constructive, nonevaluative feedback. Similarly, as a seminarian becomes more comfortable interacting with the diverse population he is likely to encounter in a parish, compared to the largely homogeneous demographics of a seminary, his ability to focus more on the grace of the Holy Spirit and less on himself when he is leading at prayer is greatly improved. Furthermore, the only way to develop collaborative leadership skills is actually to share a leadership role with others. No amount of role-playing in a seminary classroom can reproduce the intellectual and emotional challenges that one faces when public choices have to be discerned among two or more.

As we approach the sixtieth anniversary of the opening of the Second Vatican Council with its recognition of the proper charism of the laity, I am hopeful that the future church will more fully integrate that charism into its mission of priestly formation, and that it might do so in the place where that charism is most fittingly lived out: the parish.

Questions for Reflection

1. Do you agree that parishes have a responsibility to share in the formation of future priests? If so, how should that responsibility be exercised?
2. What qualities do you think many parish priests lack that they could have acquired when they were seminarians from greater interaction with lay parishioners?
3. What have been your personal experiences of interactions with seminarians? Describe your impressions of them. How might they more readily learn from parishioners?

7

THE PRIEST AS SACRAMENTAL MINISTER

John F. Baldovin, SJ

I have been involved in the education of candidates for the priesthood and other ministers for more than thirty-seven years. I began teaching liturgy and sacramental theology at the then Jesuit School of Theology at Berkeley (JSTB) in 1984 and subsequently switched coasts (but not jobs), moving to the Weston Jesuit School of Theology in Cambridge in 1999. In 2008, Weston moved to Boston College to join with the Institute of Religious Education and Pastoral Ministry and to found a new school, the Boston College School of Theology and Ministry. Needless to say, I have experienced a good deal of change during that time, especially in the attitudes of students and in styles of pedagogy.

 I consider myself relatively moderate and centrist when it comes to the celebration of the church's liturgy. In recent years, from necessity, I have become a champion and apologist for the post–Vatican II liturgical reform. I say "from necessity," because it seemed that the reform was very much taken for granted when I began at JSTB, even though there were signs of caution and retrenchment that increased with the pontificate of Pope John Paul II in 1978. Likewise, I have considered myself somewhat of a moderate when it comes to theological questions, although there I would put myself a little left of center. I have had the opportunity and privilege of teaching courses on priesthood and on ecclesial ministry over these past three decades. Much of my research and writing has centered on the role of the priest in the celebration of the Eucharist, trying to negotiate the delicate relation between Vatican II's vision of full, conscious, and active participation by all the baptized who are assembled and the crucial role of the ordained.

76

A Shift in Mood

What has changed over time? When I began, most of our Jesuit students and by and large the Franciscan students from their Santa Barbara Province as well as the Dominicans from their Southern province, and the seminarians from the Congregation of Holy Cross, tended to be progressive. Our faculty at JSTB was very solid in all areas, with several of my colleagues pushing the edges of theology and practice. By the mid-nineties, I could observe a discernible shift in student attitudes. The priesthood candidates were much more cautious in their approach to theology. Their attitudes toward religious life were much more conservative than in the eighties. In the eighties, attitudes toward sexuality tended to be somewhat free-wheeling. Straight and gay ordination candidates were, for the most part, open and accepting. Much of that started to change after the first Vatican seminary investigation of 1987, which seemed to aim a warning shot at progressive theologates. In addition to a certain chill in the church, especially over matters concerning sexuality, many of our students were (understandably) defensive given the indifference if not hostility of many of their peers to matters religious.

These trends continued in the first decades of the twenty-first century. At times, even among the Jesuit students, we have had some who were decidedly traditionalist and legalistic in their approach to theology and liturgy: "Just teach us what the church teaches [i.e., repeat the *Catechism*] and how to do the rubrics." Though our priesthood candidates continue to value the tradition somewhat more than students did when I began teaching in seminary formation, the traditionalist edge seems to have abated, only to have a small but energetic lay cohort take its place. Of diocesan seminaries, I have only second-hand knowledge and impressions. Frankly, those impressions are of a very buttoned-up system that expends an enormous amount of energy in training for celibacy and tends to be very conservative both in theology and liturgy.

My Hopes for Sacramental and Liturgical Ministry

Since my field of teaching and study has been in sacraments and liturgy in both theory and practice, I concentrate here on my hope for sacramental and liturgical ministry. By no means do I intend to suggest that the liturgical role can be isolated from the prophetic and pastoral dimensions of priestly ministry. On the contrary, the so-called *tria munera*, or three offices of

Christ's priesthood—shared in different ways by the baptized and ordained alike—need to be balanced in priestly ministry.

Let me start with some theological observations. It has frequently been observed that the documents of Vatican II failed to integrate the council's initial vision so strongly expressed in the Constitution on the Sacred Liturgy (1963) which insisted (§14) on the centrality of the full, conscious, and active participation of all the baptized in the church's liturgy with its treatment of the priesthood especially as articulated in the council's last (and apparently hastily composed) document on the Ministry and Life of Priests (1965). A good example of this failure can be illustrated by the following section from the Constitution on the Church:

> Though they differ from one another in essence and not only in degree, the common priesthood of the faithful and the ministerial or hierarchical priesthood are nonetheless interrelated: each of them in its own special way is a participation in the one priesthood of Christ. The ministerial priest, by the sacred power he enjoys, teaches and rules the priestly people; acting in the person of Christ, he makes present the Eucharistic sacrifice, and offers it to God in the name of all the people. But the faithful, in virtue of their royal priesthood, join in the offering of the Eucharist. They likewise exercise that priesthood in receiving the sacraments, in prayer and thanksgiving, in the witness of a holy life, and by self-denial and active charity. (§10)

But how precisely do these two manifestations of the one priesthood of Jesus Christ differ "in essence and not only in degree"? The *Catechism of the Catholic Church*, after repeating the difference between the two iterations—though this time emphasizing the distinction and not the inter-relation—explains that "the ministerial priesthood is at the service of the common priesthood" (*CCC* §1547).

So far so good, but when applied specifically to the liturgy, a problem is manifested by the council's desire to affirm the fact that the people offer the eucharistic sacrifice in concert with the priest:

> Taking part in the Eucharistic sacrifice, which is the fount and apex of the whole Christian life, they offer the Divine Victim to God, and offer themselves along with it. Thus, both by reason of the

offering and through Holy Communion all take part in this liturgical service, not indeed, all in the same way but each in that way which is proper to himself. (Constitution on the Church §11)

At this point, the constitution echoes Pius XII's 1947 Encyclical on the Liturgy (*Mediator Dei* §82) minus that pope's very strong emphasis on the distinction. I would maintain that the tension between the insistence on maintaining the distinction between the manners of offering (or celebrating) the Eucharist and the liturgy constitution's strong commitment to the communal dimension of the liturgy as the act of Christ's priestly people is still alive and well today. The tension is manifested most clearly in the teaching that the priest acts *in persona Christi* (in the person of Christ) in the liturgy when repeating the words of the Lord, "This is my body," and so forth. That teaching was strongly emphasized in Pope John Paul II's postsynodal exhortation on the priesthood, *Pastores Dabo Vobis* (1992, §§15, 21). To be fair, John Paul II did try to contextualize the ministerial priesthood in relation to the common priesthood of the baptized (§17), but his insistence on the priest acting in the person of Christ *the head* (*in persona Christi capitis*) tends to exacerbate the tension we continue to experience by stressing difference over communal participation.

Another piece of this theological puzzle is relevant to both our theological understanding of the priesthood and pastoral experience. Over the past century, many sacramental theologians have questioned the theology of a "moment of consecration" (namely the institution narrative) in the Eucharistic Prayer. That attitude—one could call it an obsession—regarding the moment of consecration arose only in the twelfth century. Prior to that, it can be argued that the whole Eucharistic Prayer or even the entire prayer-action was considered to be consecratory. As long as the actions of the priest during the institution narrative are maintained, however, very few people, including priests themselves, will be able to appreciate this theology. I am by no means suggesting that we can change the liturgy on our own, but perhaps ecclesial authorities can eventually be persuaded to rethink how we enact the Eucharistic Prayer as an integral assembly of the baptized. I am under no illusion that, on the one hand, what I am arguing for would cause a sea change in Catholic piety. On the other hand, our preaching and catechesis on the Eucharist as the action of the church have been inadequate, and helping Catholics to understand better the role of the priest vis-à-vis the assembly would be a great step forward.

Why spend so much space on eucharistic theology in a chapter intending to lay out hopes for the future of the ministerial priesthood? Simply because theology, and the way it is enacted in the liturgy, has profound practical consequences in both the attitudes of priests and also the rest of the assembly. The way we enact the Eucharist (e.g., at the eucharistic narrative of institution) will not likely change any time soon, but I can hope that seminary formation can help tomorrow's priests understand that they do not stand—sometimes literally—so much *over and against* as *with* the assembly. As I have often told my presiding classes, we should always refer to *the rest of the assembly* because we ourselves are part of it.

In addition, I hope that we can instill in priests the attitude and conviction that the liturgy as reformed after Vatican II is a team effort. In addition to discouraging the so-called private mass, which at the very least is an anomaly (see *General Instruction of the Roman Missal* §254), seminary formation needs to instill an attitude of cooperation that is vital to the enactment of the liturgy as a communal exercise of Christ's priesthood. This attitude should extend beyond the Eucharist to liturgical rites like baptism and the anointing of the sick, which call for the exercise of other ministers. For example, although anointing sometimes needs to be done quickly and somewhat privately in an emergency, our preference should be to involve family members, friends, and caregivers as much as possible (see Constitution on the Liturgy §27).

The contemporary rites of the church call for far more than mere adherence to the rubrics (Constitution on the Liturgy §§11, 16–18). They call for priests to be imbued with the spirit of the liturgy itself. Of course, this requires that they receive sufficient education and training in theory and practice.

The "Extraordinary Form"

Unfortunately, in terms of the future, I also need to address the popularity of the pre–Vatican II liturgy: the so-called Extraordinary Form. Pope Benedict's stated rationale for liberalizing the use of the old rite was to provide for the pastoral care of small groups of Catholics who could not accept the post–Vatican II liturgy. Whether this was disingenuous is not my call, but it certainly did act like a dog whistle for a number in the church who wanted to return to the church's "traditional liturgy." The movement for this older liturgy has attracted a good number of young people and younger priests in particular. One occasionally even sees notices of the newly ordained celebrating their "First Mass of Thanksgiving" in the older rite. The attractiveness of this older rite is understandable, because it can represent a beauty and a choreography sometimes lacking in the post–Vatican II liturgy, especially as it is often celebrated.

Nevertheless, this movement, especially among younger priests, should be regarded as nothing less than a disaster. Why? Despite the fact that the pre–Vatican II liturgy served as the rite of the church since the Early Middle Ages (not only after Trent, as some suppose) and despite the fact that it supported the profound holiness of Catholics throughout the centuries (as many traditionalists claim), it is difficult to maintain that this rite—including the Eucharist and other sacramental celebrations—can authentically be faithful to the aims of the Constitution on the Liturgy as outlined earlier. The full, conscious, and active participation of the baptized in the liturgy is not well served by the older rite. No doubt many who worship in the older forms do so attentively and with great piety, but the older rite's very form encourages the kind of theology and spirituality that unduly stress the difference between clergy and laity as outlined earlier.

Furthermore, although some claim that their preference for the older rite has to do solely with their liturgical piety and spirituality, this claim does not hold up. The preference for the older liturgy is completely in line with a wholesale rejection of Vatican II; its theology of the church; its openness to other Christians and other religious faiths, especially Judaism; its affirmation of religious freedom; and its support of the engagement of the church with the modern world in general. There is a nostalgia among the traditionalists for a world that no longer exists, unless we want to opt for an Amish-like separation from modern society and culture. We need to ask ourselves honestly: is this really how we see the church moving forward into the future to which God calls us? If not, it is time to discourage the use of the older rite, especially in seminary formation.

This has now been made abundantly clear by Pope Francis's July 16, 2021, motu proprio *Traditionis custodes*. The pope has judged the movement to celebrate the traditional Latin mass and other liturgies associated with it as divisive. To what extent individual bishops enforce the literal mandates and the spirit of *Traditionis custodes* remains to be seen. Clearly, however, Pope Francis wishes to discourage new and younger priests from celebrating the older rites. They must now receive their bishop's explicit permission, and the bishop must grant that permission in consultation with Rome. At the very least it is incumbent on bishops to forbid instruction in the older rite in their seminaries.

The Ordained among the Common Priesthood

As I mentioned earlier, and I think all can agree, the role of the ordained is to support the common priesthood of the baptized. The priest as sacramental leader is not so much deputed to stand between God and the church but rather to enable the church to worship authentically in spirit and truth.

In the pastoral realm and very much in tune with the present situation of the church coming out (please God) of the restrictions forced upon us by the coronavirus pandemic, it seems that priests should be helped to reinforce and reinvigorate our experience of the post–Vatican II liturgy. People need to be catechized about the importance of our assembling together as church week by week. They need to be instructed in the symbolism behind and the value of sharing in the precious blood—although, after the COVID-19 pandemic, it will be particularly challenging to encourage people to return to the common cup—Communion in the hand, the song of the assembly, and of the exchange of a sign of peace. Each of these practices supports the communal nature of our sacramental life and places the priesthood of the ordained in proper perspective.

In the wake of the Second Vatican Council, we experienced a wave of departures from the priesthood and, in some parts of the world, a great drop in vocations to priesthood and religious life. Beginning in the late 1970s with the papacy of John Paul II, there was a strong movement to reinvigorate the priesthood by means of strengthening the separate identity of the priest. In many ways, this movement has gained even more support after the sexual abuse crisis of the past twenty years. Once again, strengthening the identity of the ministerial priesthood is an understandable and worthy goal. But should it be done at the expense of our contemporary appreciation of the common priesthood?

Now more than ever, we need well-formed priests, skilled in the role of liturgical leadership, not to mention the qualities of pastoral and prophetic leadership that I have noted. My hope is that today's and tomorrow's priests can dedicate themselves to the inspiring pastoral vision proposed by Pope Francis, a vision that has nothing to do with clerical privilege or overemphasizing the sacramental role of the ordained. For that to occur, my hope is also that more and more bishops exercise courageous leadership in promoting the authentic vision of the contemporary church and will, in particular, choose seminary formators who are thoroughly committed to that vision.

Questions for Reflection

1. What is the appropriate balance between the necessity of ordained leadership in our sacramental/liturgical life and the common priesthood of the baptized?
2. How might seminary formation be improved so that candidates can integrate their formation in liturgical leadership with pastoral sensitivity?
3. How can today's and tomorrow's priests help the rest of the Christian people to understand how important full, conscious, and active participation in the liturgy is for the vitality of the church?

8

Faithful Pastors and Fellow Pilgrims

Bishop John Stowe, OFM Conv.

In our diocese, when a pastor's tenure draws near its end, he is asked to appoint a transition committee. Members of the committee, representing a cross-section of the parish, are tasked with, among other responsibilities, describing the kind of priest they think their parish needs at this time. It is easy to joke that not even Jesus himself would meet the standards set for their dream priest. I often find myself musing about whether parishioners think I have a warehouse of priests from which I can draw the one that best meets their unique needs. Nonetheless, the people of God do express their expectations for their next pastor with the trust that these will somehow be factored into the equation, and, in doing so, describe what they think are the essential qualities of a good priest.

Parishioners almost inevitably want a priest who wishes to be in their parish, not someone stuck there by the luck of the draw. They want someone who seeks to know and understand them, hoping that he will grow to love them. They want someone to come with fresh energy and ideas, but with the wisdom not to impose them too quickly nor to fit their parish into a mold created for another place. They want someone who is able to be collaborative in ministry and to awaken the gifts found already among the people he is called to serve. Frequently, the ability to minister with women is particularly noted. The new priest will be expected to be a unifier, not to play favorites. Often, he should be able to speak Spanish.

For the most part, the ideal priest described by the expectant community will be a competent manager and able to raise the funds necessary for the parish to flourish. He will be attentive to the sick and the needy, will provide strong leadership when building projects and major changes are needed, and will be eager to engage the youth. Rarely does the description include the importance of being a man of prayer, hopefully, because it is taken for granted! Too infrequently does the description include being an inspirational and effective preacher—perhaps too unrealistic—nor do these descriptions ever describe the priest's ability to lead the parish in prayer or form them in a deeper understanding of their Catholic tradition. Sometimes in our part of the country, where there are few Catholics, the committees explicitly ask for someone to be involved in the local ecumenical scene. I still look forward to reading the form that says, "The successful pastor will be able to draw easily from the rich sources of Catholic social teaching and challenge us to work for the transformation of society and make it more closely resemble the reign of God."

The Contemporary Priesthood

If the teaching church is also to be a listening church, as Pope Francis has stated, the expectations of the priesthood from the people of God must be heard and discerned. If the church is to be the faithful witness and proclaimer of the paschal mystery in concrete historical circumstances, the priesthood cannot be limited only to the perceived, and real, present needs as articulated by the people to be served. Priests must be about calling the community to live their Christian faith more abundantly and to transcend the tendency to focus on the needs and comfort of its members at the cost of outreach and evangelization.

A particularly frustrated friend of mine once told the parish he pastored that what they really wanted was "a full-time festival promoter and a part-time sacramental provider"—and that he was no longer interested in the position. A similarly exasperated parishioner in another place told me that she was glad that their pastor exhibited all the saintly qualities of the Curé of Ars, like the desire to spend hours in the confessional, but couldn't figure out how he could be so oblivious to the fact that no one was coming to confession and that attendance at mass was dwindling.

How do we move from the "classified ad" description of the need for a pastor to a contemporary understanding of the priesthood and what that ministry should look like going forward? It should be noted that there are and have always been multiple models of priesthood existing simultaneously: ordained monks and apostolic religious priests, priests whose primary function is teaching or administration, priests in a new mission or developing church, priests inserted in poor and marginalized communities, priests engaged in ministry in affluent circumstances, and many other particular incarnations of Catholic priesthood. While searching for general descriptions of the essential priesthood of the future, the dominant emphasis here is on the role of the priest engaged in pastoral ministry to a particular community.

Evolving Images of Priesthood

In the decades since the Second Vatican Council, we have seen the functional role of the priesthood evolve. We have also witnessed the pendulum swing from one perspective—with the priest being just like everyone else but set aside for service by ordination—to the opposite perspective emphasizing the ontological difference between the ordained and the laity, insisting upon the role of the priest as a spiritual father who knows best and must lovingly discipline his children. We have explored images such as the priest as conductor of a symphony who brings the music on the page to life only through the various musicians and their respective instruments playing their parts in relation to one another and creating a harmonious sound. In reality, the image has often looked like the lone priest on the parish staff as the CEO with the final word, but one removed from the nitty-gritty of daily operations. In another model, a business manager performs the organizational work of the parish nominally overseen by the pastor, who is focused on preaching and worship; he is engaged in pastoral care but shares those responsibilities with lay persons appropriately formed for ministry. Frequently the latter model allows a priest to pastor multiple communities, although the quality of shepherding multiple communities simultaneously varies considerably.

Within these understandings of priesthood, some people emphasize their unique role and demonstrate reluctance to engage in other, less sacramental activities. Others are eager to empower the laity to engage their baptismal priesthood in shared opportunities for pastoral care, teaching the faith, outreach to the poor, and occasionally leading worship and reflecting on the Word of God. To these variations, we would add priests who are invited from other parts of the world to serve people who worship in their language and sometimes share in their culture. There are also priests recruited from other countries to supplement the local presbyterate out of necessity. These priests are formed in an entirely different environment and are often given little introduction or support to be able to navigate their way in foreign ecclesial and cultural surroundings. How can they be expected to serve their people, proclaim a hopeful and meaningful homily to them, teach the faith, and provide leadership in circumstances still foreign to them? Many do so admirably, but it is the rare exception when it happens without a considerable and difficult period of adjustment for both priest and parish.

No discussion of the contemporary priesthood can avoid mention of the challenges of declining numbers of priests and the various proposals to address it that the institutional church has either not been willing to consider until now—such as the ordination of married men—or claims that it does not have the authority to consider—such as the ordination of women. Nor can any conversation about the priesthood of the future fail to consider the irreparable harm done to the church by the sexual abuse of youth and vulnerable adults that has been perpetrated by priests and bishops, and by the clerical culture that too often ignored the cries of victims while protecting predators. Although considerable and effective steps have been taken to correct that betrayal of the church's mission, the wounds are still profound and the church's credibility, especially that of the ordained ministry, has been substantially reduced.

Priests and Liturgy

According to the Second Vatican Council, because the celebration of the Eucharist is the source and summit of the church's life, that celebration must be led by a priest and because the vast majority of the faithful come into contact with priests primarily through the mass, it is vitally important to consider the liturgical ministry of priests in the discussion of the priesthood now and in the future. The decision by Saint John Paul II to permit the limited celebration of the mass in its preconciliar form and the subsequent decision by Pope Benedict XVI to expand its availability and permit priests to celebrate the Tridentine mass, now called the "Extraordinary Form," has introduced new difficulties in the relationship between priests and people. While the same liturgical constitution, *Sacrosanctum Concilium*, that emphasized the supreme importance of the mass also called for full, conscious, and active participation in that mass, the document refers to the mass being offered by the whole people of God led by their priest. When the priest's liturgical preferences clash with the liturgical preferences of the people, the question arises as to whose preference takes precedence.

The Extraordinary Form of the mass allowed for those communities still attached to that older form and requires that priests be prepared to celebrate in that form. Intentionally or not, this situation has resulted in priests who, without any personal experience of the preconciliar church, now prefer the preconciliar mass and, in some cases, even impose it on the people who had already adapted well to the *novus ordo* or who have had no previous familiarity with the older form. Where it is not possible for these priests to implement fully the preconciliar mass, they import elements of it into the "ordinary form" from the use of outmoded vesture to adopting some of the priest's gestures in the old mass and even celebrating the mass *ad orientem*, facing the altar rather than the people. Since the church teaches that our worship expresses our beliefs and our beliefs inform our worship, a clash of understandings of the faith can take place between the priests and people rendering pastoral ministry difficult or incoherent. When priests emerge from seminary formation without an appreciation for the significance of the Second Vatican Council in the church's contemporary life, there is bound to be a discrepancy between the pulpit and the pews because the faithful have, by and large, acquired a practical integration of the council in their Christian lives.

The Future Priesthood

The Joy of the Gospel

The 2013 election of Pope Francis initiated a new chapter in the postconciliar history of the church. Unlike his immediate predecessors, Pope Francis was not actually present for the deliberations and declarations of Vatican II. He nonetheless lived the experience of a church transformed and renewed by that pastoral council, because he ministered in the Latin American church where the council produced profound effects and great fruits through the Conference of Latin American Bishops—which created a community of local churches united in their preferential option for the poor, committed to the new evangelization of the American continent, and forming a church of missionary disciples.

Pope Francis brought the experience of that evolving Latin American church to the center of the universal church when he was elected. During his pontificate, he has tirelessly encouraged the church to go to the margins, to find Christ on the peripheries, and to redevelop a missionary spirit and fervor. He has expressed his vision of a poor church for the poor and his magisterial teachings in a very accessible way. He is a visible pastor, who has spent his life as a shepherd in the midst of the sheep; he preaches with vivid images and in language that he describes as comparable to a mother speaking to her children, and he writes in ways that can engage everyone. As the church's universal pastor, he teaches by example and is particularly eager to provide a model of priestly ministry.

Francis began his pontificate shortly before Holy Week in 2013, and while he still enjoyed the curiosity and attention of the press, he celebrated his first Holy Thursday Mass of the Lord's Supper in a detention facility, where he washed the feet not only of women but of Muslims. He delivered for the world an unmistakable lesson in the role of ordained ministry imitating Christ the Servant, expanding the pastoral outreach and care of the church, transcending liturgical directives, and making Christ present to the marginalized. He has repeated this practice except for the years when the COVID-19 pandemic made it impossible.

The homilies that Pope Francis has preached at the other Holy Thursday celebration, the Chrism Mass, have employed memorable images, such as the need for priests to have the "smell of the sheep" on them, and that of the people extracting oil from priests who do not give it generously. He has reflected with priests on the joyful exhaustion that they should experience in ministry and has challenged them not to be bound by schedules but to be open to the experiences God places before them in the present moment. He urges them to make themselves accessible and not to function like bureaucrats with layers of gatekeepers. The pope expresses his preference for a church that is wounded and dirty from being out in the streets, rather than sick from confinement. Priests must first be missionary disciples—for only as disciples can they be genuine teachers, only by an ongoing encounter with the living Christ can they meaningfully sanctify, only by listening can they be genuine preachers, and only by acquiring the smell of the sheep can they effectively guide and govern.

From the pastoral ministry of Francis, characterized by the joy of the gospel, we can discern a future model of priesthood that is neither a radical departure from the past nor a new invention, but a share in the ministry of the High Priest Jesus Christ as it has evolved through the ages and conforms to the example of the Good Shepherd willing to lay down his life for his sheep.

Priests within the Pilgrim People

There can be no retreat from the Second Vatican Council's renewed emphasis on the priesthood of the faithful and baptism as the foundational sacrament. The priesthood has a special role within, but not above, the pilgrim people of God on the way to the kingdom. Ordination means being consecrated for service, a service performed in concert with the priestly people of God and for their benefit. While the charism of leadership is an aspect of this consecration for service, it is vital that the priest call forth the gifts of leadership from within the community. With their extensive education and formation, normally provided for them by the people of God, the priests should be eager to use their learning and knowledge to build up the community and patiently teach and guide them to a deeper understanding of their faith.

Among the ministries of pastors, including bishops, the Second Vatican Council gives high priority to the role of preaching. God is continuously revealing God's self to us, and we have inherited a rich record of that revelation in scripture and tradition. That revelation must be proclaimed, shared, and applied to the signs of the times—the real circumstances in which the people of God live. The ancient words recorded are to be given a breath of new life in such a way that they resound and echo in the hearts of the hearers, inviting them to ever deeper intimacy with the God who speaks.

As mediators of God's word, priests must conform to the example of the Word made Flesh, whose revelation was performed in deed as much as in word. Jesus's teachings came alive because they were accessible and addressed the real needs of the hearers, both affirming them and challenging them to greater lives of virtue and service to each other. The Word made Flesh got his hands dirty in his interactions with those he considered brothers and sisters; even those labeled as sinners, outcasts, dirty, and contagious were embraced with his touch and transformed by his words.

The priest entrusted with breaking open the Word of God is also entrusted with breaking the Bread of the Eucharist. Empowered by ordination, the priest calls on God's Holy Spirit to transform the offerings of bread and wine, symbolic of the people and their work, into the body and blood of Christ and to transform the assembly into the Body of Christ by their share in the sacrament. They must lead the people in prayer in ways that are engaging, orienting them toward God, inviting their prayers of supplication, and making them his own. He should lead them in celebrating all that God has done in history and in their own lives in that great prayer of thanksgiving in which Jesus becomes present anew. The priest's own prayer life should be evident and manifest if he is truly to function as mediator, in the role of Christ, inspiring them to lead lives of prayer. The celebration of the mass cannot be *his* celebration, nor can his preferences dictate its form of prayer, but he must lead the people to the Father with one heart and one voice.

It is essential that the priest who preaches and presides must also lead the community in putting that word into action and sharing the fruit of communion with the world. Again, never alone but with the priestly people, the priest should be eager to engage them in encountering Christ outside the walls of the church and especially in the marginalized and outcast.

Demonstrating the church's care and fraternal love, the people of God should share their material goods in charity as generously as their spiritual goods and be eager to represent the needs of the most vulnerable and voice-less in society as their own. Priests must help the people of God make the connection between what happens at the altar and what happens in their daily life, emphasizing the encounter with Christ in the Eucharist and the encounter with Christ in the poor.

This aspirational description of a future priesthood is far from compre-hensive, but is within the tradition handed on from Jesus and the apostles. The fruits of the Second Vatican Council are in abundance, especially visible in the people of God who have taken their rightful place in the full, conscious, and active celebration of the Eucharist and have learned the responsibility that is theirs from baptism. They have opened their hearts and minds to the Word of God in scripture and grown in familiarity with those sacred texts. They have grown in charitable fraternity with Christians of other denominations and people of other faiths and continue on the pilgrim journey as the people of God. They have a right to faithful pastors, to priests who lead them on this journey but always as fellow travelers.

Questions for Reflection

1. Imagine being invited to describe the kind of priest that your parish needs at this time. What qualities would you be sure to name?

2. As priesthood continues to evolve through the centuries, what do you imagine are important features in the future?

9

Imagining New Optics for Catholic Priesthood

Jacqueline M. Regan

Five years ago, I responded immediately to Thomas Groome's invitation to participate in a seminar at Boston College on the future of the priesthood. In addition to my work in ministerial formation at the Boston College School of Theology and Ministry (STM), I brought over thirty years of experience working alongside a diverse group of priests, seminarians, and lay ministers in various forms of educational and pastoral ministry. The lived experience of priests, the theology of priesthood, and the emerging theology of ministry were topics I knew and understood well. Because of my close association with Catholic priests, I had also become a keeper of stories told by lay people through the years—at family parties, on long runs with friends, and in conversation with STM students and alumni from around the world—about their experiences, positive and negative, with ordained clergy. I was eager to contribute to the conversation on the future of the priesthood and share some of my hopes, based on collaborations that spanned the better part of four decades.

What became known as the "Boston College Priesthood Seminar" and the document and conference that followed, "To Serve the People of God: A Contemporary Theology of Priesthood," were often a source of personal and ecclesial hope for what priesthood in the Catholic Church can and should be. The composition of both the seminar group and the January 2020 conference—lay women and men, diocesan and religious priests, bishops and cardinals, theology faculty and students, vowed religious and married persons, pastoral ministers and other administrators—embodied powerfully the ecclesial communion and model of collaboration that the seminar and its documents promote. It is a model rooted in the best of

Catholic theology, the testimony of the Gospels, and descriptions of the earliest Christian community.

As familiar an experience as this might have been for many of the participants, the image of a diverse group of men and women gathered together as ecclesial leaders has not seeped into public perceptions of Catholic ministry. One regret of the January 2020 conference is that we did not take photos. It would have been a powerful optic—a picture telling the story that such groups can and do exist within the church. Some might claim that these experiences of collaboration are rare, confined to elite spaces. I suggest, however, that contrary to being a rarefied experience, this form of ecclesial leadership characterizes healthy and vibrant Catholic schools, parishes, and other apostolates worldwide.

With this positive image of the church as its background, this chapter offers three hopes for the future of the priesthood. Drawing on these hopes stemming from the Boston College Priesthood Seminar, the second half of the chapter considers five factors that characterize the priesthood.

Hopes for the Priesthood

The first hope for the future of the priesthood, and the hope that underpins this chapter, centers on the priest's role in communities of faith. The hope is that priests, as the appointed leaders of communities of faith, will always view themselves as presbyteral leaders in relationship with other ministers *and* with the people they are called upon to serve.

If formation for ordained ministry prioritizes the role of priests as collaborative leaders in all aspects of their ministry, there is, of course, a better chance that this model will become the norm for Catholic faith communities, rather than the exception. On a systemic level, this means giving priority to the needs and concerns of God's people, not the self-interest and preservation of priesthood, by accepting candidates for priesthood who possess the human qualities, relational capacity, and skills for the realities and demands of ministry in the twenty-first century.

For the past several years, Father John Baldovin, SJ, my colleague at the STM, has invited me into his class on the priesthood to speak to the men preparing for ordination about collaboration. During one Q&A session, a Jesuit scholastic asked, "What do you see as the most important quality in a priest?" When I responded that "he needs to have and show a genuine like for people," the group erupted in laughter. I interpreted this as confirmation that they too had experienced what others and I have too frequently encountered: priests and ordination candidates who might, in theory, have a deep love for God and God's people, but lack the interpersonal skills that enable them to express it adequately.

This deficit is not simply a matter of different personality types; it is the inability to connect with and show concern for people. One advantage of integrated formation programs in which seminarians study with lay students—programs that the final document of the Priesthood Seminar promotes—is the challenge that such programs offer to candidates who are socially awkward, fearful of women, or reluctant to interact with anyone other than their ordination-track peers. Although integrated formation programs exist for a larger purpose—preparing people for ordination and other ecclesial ministries for the sake of the church's mission—daily interactions with lay students and faculty ensure that a lack of people skills does not go unnoticed. Whether it is properly addressed, especially in times of a scarcity of seminarians, is a larger question.

My second hope is that, as leaders of the Body of Christ, those who will be ordained will move us closer to the vision of the church expressed in the Acts of the Apostles 4:7–32 and in 1 Corinthians 12. Moving the church forward as a body in which all members contribute to its mission requires fuller recognition and acceptance of the way in which ecclesial ministry has broadened and expanded in the past fifty years.

Even as the number of priests and women religious continues to decline, the number of permanent deacons and lay ecclesial ministers—80 percent of whom are women—continues to grow. The teaching ministry of the church and the frontline work of evangelization and social justice in Catholic schools, colleges, and universities depend on lay teachers and ministers. The church's ministry of healing would falter without lay chaplains serving throughout the world in hospitals and other healthcare settings. We can continue to gloss over the troubling statistics detailing the decline in the number of priests, or we can harness the energy, talents, and resources of lay women and men who offer themselves in committed service to the church. After forty years of fretting about numbers, can ordained leaders start to plan and think creatively about what collaborative and inclusive ministry might look like in the next decade, and then strategize to support it, both canonically and financially?

In addition to highlighting the urgent need to reckon with the deep roots of systemic racism in our nation and church, the global pandemic has brought into relief the value, necessity, and competence of women in leadership. The mutuality of women and men working together during the pandemic as heads of government, healthcare professionals, researchers, educators, business leaders, and essential workers has been on full display. Men and women working together in our church is the reality in many apostolates, as it was at the January 2020 conference, but it is one that needs more structural support and encouragement from bishops and priests.

My third hope for the future is that priests and bishops will move beyond *thinking about* ways in which women can be involved and represented in the church's leadership. They must take concrete steps toward ensuring that women are represented and visible as Catholic faith leaders and decision-makers on every level, especially in the communities of which they are a part. In this way, the church will more fully reflect the vision and image of the triune God who made us.

Advancing the Church's Mission

This section draws on the five central aspects of priestly ministry identified in the Boston College document. My aim in this section is to illustrate how priests, while maintaining their own distinctive identity, can take steps to enact the hopes sketched above and advance the church's mission.

The Priest as Preacher

Through the gift of the Spirit conferred at baptism and confirmation, and continuously nourished by the Eucharist, all Catholics are called and sent to "Go, and announce the gospel" in the experience of their daily lives. Preaching the gospel in the liturgical assembly, however, is at the heart of priestly ministry and the primary duty of priests.

In the summer of 2020 my appreciation for the work of good preaching was renewed when I was asked to prepare a reflection for the website Catholic Women Preach. It takes an enormous amount of time, creativity, knowledge, and skill to prepare an engaging, challenging, and relevant homily. Digital media like Catholic Women Preach, *America Media* podcasts, *Give Us This Day*, and the work of Catholic lay theologians not only provide spiritual wisdom for homilies but they also serve as a way to include, refer to, and acknowledge the voices, experiences, and ideas of women and lay men in Catholic liturgy. It is essential that priests use and reference these resources in liturgical spaces, so that they draw upon the knowledge, ideas, insights, and witness of women—not only in their role as mothers and sisters—until we are able to hear women speak and preach for themselves.

Encouraging opportunities outside of the eucharistic liturgy, for example, the Liturgy of the Hours, is an obvious way to expand women's contribution to the church's ministry of prayer, worship, and preaching, while highlighting the multiplicity of gifts in the ecclesial community. When priests are able to participate in prayer groups, spiritual exercises, and retreats as one of the baptized, it broadens their own perspective and highlights their identity as disciples among disciples on the Christian journey. Expanding the ministries and ministers of the faith community also gives priests the time and space to experience how the leadership of women serves the proclamation of the gospel.

The Priest as Leader of Worship and Prayer

One of the great gifts of Catholic liturgy is that its efficacy is not dependent on the priest's personality. The priest as leader of worship and prayer gathers the prayer of the assembly and directs our attention to God rather than himself. Although eucharistic liturgy—and Sunday Eucharist, in particular—is the source and summit of our prayer and worship, the many ways in which Catholics have gathered for prayer and worship during the pandemic have demonstrated that it is not, nor should it be, the only form of prayer and worship.

Opportunities for virtual family liturgies and lay-led prayer services have empowered the laity and reinforced the value of communal prayer outside of Sunday Eucharist. Emerging from the pandemic, these opportunities, which simultaneously reflect the continuity and change embedded in the Catholic spiritual tradition, should be encouraged by clergy. The sharing of voices and roles, a hallmark of lay-led liturgies, should also be present in the church's public worship, especially in its major celebrations. As we return to embodied worship, the optic of all-male ceremonies puts Catholic liturgy at greater risk of becoming more distanced and less relevant to people's lives.

As we listen to and learn from marginalized groups in our struggle for greater social justice in our church and world, we know that representation does matter and presents an image of demonstrable commitment toward justice, equity, and inclusion. Priests as leaders of prayer and worship should always be thinking creatively of ways to include lay people, especially underrepresented women, in the liturgical rites. When there is a sense of collective effort in liturgy, when members of the assembly see people who look like them sharing its leadership, the optic conveys a fuller sense of the Body of Christ.

As such, do the gatherings of ministers in sacristies or lower church halls prior to liturgical celebrations show the depth and richness of our liturgical team? Are sacristies spaces of welcome for those involved in preparation of liturgy, or do they appear to be places reserved for the boys' club? Do priests encourage parishioners and lay faithful to accept lay leaders of prayer in spaces where they are permitted, for example, the prayer of committal at the graveside? Often, the church's most solemn and high-profile liturgies are also more masculine, reinforcing the perception of the exclusion of women. Can we launch a universal effort to change the optics?

The Priest as Collaborative Leader

At the end of their three years of study toward the MDiv at the STM, students, both lay and on the path to ordination, gather for a final evening of shared prayer and reflection. A recurring theme in these communal gatherings across the years is the formative impact of the collaborative experience. As equals in the classroom, in study groups for comprehensive exams, at school liturgies, and as co-leaders of retreats, men and women, lay and *ordinandi*, reflect on the fruits of listening and learning from each other, and working together in ministry. The mutuality mirrors many of their experiences of life outside the STM and prepares them for their future ministries as ordained priests, lay campus ministers, teachers, and hospital chaplains. This dynamic consists of much more than lay people adding value to the experience of priestly formation.

Integrated formation programs provide many opportunities for experiential learning of co-responsibility and the collaborative, servant leadership needed for today's church. Most view this model as a welcome and necessary approach to ecclesial leadership for both theological and pragmatic reasons;

some are fearful. Some candidates for ordination view co-responsibility and collaboration as a threat to the distinctive identity of the priest and are cautious about "clericalizing" the laity. Good leaders, community organizers, and parents, however, know that providing clear expectations of different roles while also sharing responsibility and inviting participation creates cultures with a deep sense of mission, identity, and purpose. The church's doctrine of the Trinity reminds us that relationality enhances, rather than diminishes, uniqueness.

As all Catholic apostolates become increasingly complex, multicultural organizations that depend upon a variety of ministers to serve the needs of the community, the collaboration of priests with lay ecclesial ministers, and the formation of teams of ministers, becomes essential. It cannot be merely a stopgap for the priest shortage or a matter of splitting ecclesial leadership into spiritual and temporal spheres with priests overseeing the spiritual, and lay people responsible for the administrative work. It is particularly important for ordination candidates to realize that whether they see themselves as leaders or not—whether they hold positional or symbolic leadership—as Catholic priests, they will always be viewed as leaders. Leadership consists of many skills that can be learned. Learning to lead collaboratively will enhance the ministry of priests and the church's mission.

The rite of ordination does not magically and mechanically turn a priest into a leader, or into anything else that he is not already. The charisms, human qualities, and most importantly, the capacity for relationship should all be manifest in priest candidates before they are ordained. Priests must become familiar with styles of leadership that enable them to think and act with humility—to know what their role is and what it isn't. In February 2019, Sr. Veronica Openibo, SHCJ, when speaking to leaders of episcopal conferences in Rome, testified to the pervasive, harmful effects of priestly formation that separates priests from the people they are called to serve:

> It worries me when I see in Rome, and elsewhere, the youngest semi-narians being treated as though they are more special than everyone else, thus encouraging them to assume, from the beginning of their training, exalted ideas about their status.[1]

---

[1] Veronica Openibo, "At Abuse Summit, Sr. Veronica Openibo Calls for Complete Transparency," *National Catholic Reporter*, February 23, 2019, https://www.ncronline.org.

As part of the human formation required for ordination, formation programs need to focus on the skills required for effective leadership in today's world. Formation that emphasizes the special status of priests, thus encouraging clericalism, must end—now! So, too, priests must be prepared to challenge the clerical attitudes of people they serve, offering gentle correction in the moment ("Father, you know better than I/we do") and through sustained catechesis on the role and dignity of all the baptized.

The Priest as Public Representative

An integral part of the leadership of priests is their responsibility to represent the church to the people of God and to the wider public. My hope for the future of the priesthood in this context is to see priests representing the church publicly in areas of need and with the most vulnerable, not only—and certainly not predominately—with the prosperous and those whose lives are secure. To be a church with and for the poor takes an intentional commitment to live simply, to resist the values of consumerism, and to be careful about accepting favors that might weaken our witness to the gospel.

As more people rely on the internet for information, opportunities abound to present a fuller and more diverse picture of what present-day Catholic leadership looks like. This may occur more naturally in school settings, hospitals, and nonprofit settings that are lay-led and employ large groups of people. Knowing the power of images, parish websites featuring photos of parish pastoral teams, not just the ordained, and the listing of lay ministry in parish and diocesan directories can be powerful tools in presenting to parishioners as well as to the wider world an alternative vision of Catholic leadership.

The Priest as Practitioner of Pastoral Charity

The 2014 film *Calvary* presents a compelling portrait of life in a post–sexual abuse crisis Catholic parish in a small village in the west of Ireland. The parish priest, Father Lavelle, is imperfect. Parishioners are cynical and distrustful. Still, they turn to him for wisdom as they struggle to find some inkling of God's presence in the brokenness of their lives. These small moments of mercy, however fraught they may be, serve as the tendrils that keep parishioners connected to the vine of their Catholic faith.

Far removed from the small-village church experience, many parish priests rely on the work of lay ministers and hospital chaplains to extend the church's pastoral care, especially to the sick, dying, and grieving. These are lay people who are comfortable with intimate conversation, sit patiently and listen without judgment, reach for a hand, offer a tissue when tears begin to fall, and lead family members in prayer. Priests are called in to anoint and offer the sacraments after the resident chaplains and pastoral ministers have tilled the soil for the encounter. Many of the people with a true charism for this ministry are not ordained. Inviting the priest to step in and anoint without any previous relationship with the sick and dying splits the church's healing ministry in two. The priest becomes a dispenser of sacraments. Is there a way to bridge this divide in the future so that lay ecclesial ministers can extend the church's sacramental care to the sick?

Much of what I have presented here is not new. It is rooted in the theology of Vatican II and the church's theological developments since then. It has been translated into action in many settings, but widespread implementation remains uneven. Images of an all-male church hierarchy still dominate perception of ecclesial leadership. As we move toward making these hopes a reality, I encourage priests, the next time they are invited to pose for a photo following a parish, diocesan, or school liturgy, to ask themselves, "Who needs to be in this picture?"

Questions for Reflection

1. The presence of lay ecclesial ministers is often viewed as a luxury affordable only to well-resourced parishes. How can the church make this form of ministry a reality for communities that are most in need?

2. The bright, talented lay students who enter theology and ministry formation programs are often considered a threat, rather than a gift, to the church's ministry. What would enable a better integration of lay ecclesial ministry into the church?

10

Transforming Priestly Identity and Ministry

Bradford E. Hinze

The Boston College seminar document on priesthood, "To Serve the People of God," achieved its two main goals: "to deepen the theology of priesthood that began to emerge at the Second Vatican Council" and "to offer a theological framework adapted to the pressing pastoral questions facing the contemporary church." The authors offer a seasoned articulation of the theology of priesthood, drawing on documents of Vatican II and subsequent official teachings and directives, and on the contributions of respected theologians and people involved in priestly formation programs to delineate their central pastoral implications and applications.

Without denying these accomplishments, the document mentions neither the relevance of the praxis and theology of synodality, nor the church's work for justice. Nor does it consider how these two facets of the church should influence priestly identity and mission. To address these lacunae requires analysis from historical, theological, and practical perspectives that I attempt to do in this chapter based on the contributions of Vatican II and Pope Francis.

The Praxis and Theology of Synodality

Synodality is a central unfinished agenda of Vatican II and a defining feature of the papacy of Pope Francis. The term "synodality" is derived from Vatican II's teaching on the college of bishops, the Synod of Bishops, episcopal conferences, and various forms of councils—plenary, regional, diocesan, and at the parish level.[1] Since his election, Francis has resolutely worked to advance synodality in all areas of the church.

In July 2013, at a meeting with members from the Latin American bishops' conference, with whom he had collaborated in preparing the 2007 Aparecida document, Francis posed this rhetorical question: "Is pastoral discernment a habitual criterion through the use of diocesan councils? Do such councils . . . provide real opportunities for lay people to participate in pastoral consultation, organization, and planning?" His response was clear: "I believe that on this score, we are far behind."[2] Speaking several months later to a group of priests, religious, and lay members of diocesan pastoral councils in Assisi, he repeated the point: "How needed pastoral councils are! A bishop cannot guide a diocese without pastoral councils. A parish priest cannot guide the parish without the parish council. This is fundamental!"[3]

Francis's judgment applies not only to parish and diocesan pastoral councils but also to presbyteral councils, diocesan synods, and other canonical forms of councils and synods in the church. Francis's stance raises certain pressing questions about priestly formation and practice, including: How can learning the praxis of synodality be incorporated into training for priests and bishops? How might this formation elicit the willingness to heed the sense of all the faithful people of God, promote lay partnerships and leadership, and nurture missiological discipleship?

On the fiftieth anniversary of the institution of the Synod of Bishops in 2015, Francis acknowledged, "From the beginning of my ministry as Bishop of Rome, I sought to enhance the Synod, which is one of the most precious legacies of the Second Vatican Council. . . . It is precisely this path of synodality which God expects of the Church in the third millennium."[4] Priestly identity and ministry are constitutive ingredients in Francis's synodal vision of the church and marked by building communities and partnerships of discernment with all the faithful. Synodality demands courageous, honest speech and priestly power-sharing with the faithful

---

[1] International Theological Commission, "Synodality in the Life and Mission of the Church," March 2, 2018.

[2] Pope Francis, "Address to the Leadership of the Episcopal Conference of Latin America," July 28, 2013, http://www.vatican.va.

[3] Pope Francis, "Address to Clergy, Consecrated People, and Members of Diocesan Pastoral Councils," October 4, 2013, http://www.vatican.va.

[4] Pope Francis, "Address at the Fiftieth Anniversary of the Institution of the Synod of Bishops," October 17, 2015, http://www.vatican.va.

people of God in their shared efforts to advance sacramental communion and missiological discipleship.

If the need to learn the ways of synodality is thus warranted by Vatican II and Pope Francis, what exactly does this call for in the formation of priests, bishops, and lay people? Since Vatican II, those who have employed councils and synods have gone through phases of learning and experimentation with such methods as *Robert's Rules of Order* used in political and business contexts, various forms of group process and dynamics, methods of community organizing, and approaches used in certain organizational management programs, such as in worker cooperatives. After Vatican II, many religious institutes, especially of women religious, developed group discernment methods to assist in group decision-making. The prospect of following canon law requirements for synods often deters bishops and their staffs from choosing to conduct a synod.

Learning the skills of dialogue and the use of discernment in group decision-making is important if seminarians, priests, bishops, and lay leaders are to learn how to foster synodality in building faith communities. People must cultivate a range of communication skills such as listening and speaking, and learning to talk about their own and their communities' pressing needs, criticisms, and aspirations—and also about how leaders and group members can engage their imaginations in developing strategies for addressing communal problems and conflicts, developing community goals, and facing differences of views and areas of strong disagreement.

Work for Justice

Justice advocacy became increasingly pronounced in modern Catholic social teaching beginning with Pope Leo XIII's *Rerum Novarum*—subsequently taking different forms, for instance, in Catholic Action's promotion of the "see, judge, act" method, and in the documents prepared by the Conference of Latin American Bishops.

"To Serve the People of God" says nothing about the work for justice of the priest, the parish, or the diocese. It does, however, speak about "the priest as practitioner of pastoral charity" (TSPG, 45). This expression has become commonplace when describing seminary formation and priestly ministry in documents issued by the Congregation of the Clergy, such as the periodically updated *Ratio Fundamentalis Institutionis Sacerdotalis* that describes the constitutive ingredients in priestly formation and in the application of this document for specific national episcopal conferences, such as in US contexts in *The Program of Priestly Formation*. It is also found in the recent document "The Pastoral Conversion of the Parish Community in the Service of the Evangelizing Mission of the Church."[5]

The expression "pastoral charity" could be intended in the Boston College text to include work for justice. Or perhaps witnessing for justice is included when the Boston College document describes "the priest as a public representative of the church." It quotes Pope Francis on the need for the church to make a concerted effort to care for the poor and marginalized, but without a word on the priests' role, particularly concerning preaching on issues of justice, or about their involvement in civic engagement with the people of God in public witness on justice issues. The text speaks of the church's involvement in the wider world, particularly on "social, educational and economic [issues] . . . and also [in] debates about race, gender, marriage, and climate control" (TSPG, 8). But it is not clear about how the identity and pastoral ministry of priests entails collaborating with the people of God at moments of crisis and conflict when such a witness in word and deed for the promotion of justice is urgently needed.

The evangelical obligations of Catholics to work for justice, which received increasing attention during the late nineteenth and the first half of the twentieth centuries, were corroborated by Vatican II's *Gaudium et Spes*, and thereafter increasingly embraced by episcopal conferences and lay social justice movements. This program of work for justice also found expression in John Paul II's endorsement of the populist Solidarity movement, and was obliquely referenced in Benedict XVI's remarks on the economics of the gift, which gave credence to worker cooperatives in Europe and in the United States.

The recent edition of the *Ratio Fundamentalis*, known in English by the title *The Gift of the Priestly Vocation*, was issued in 2016 and ratified by Pope Francis,[6] and, like John Paul II's 1992 Apostolic Exhortation *Pastores Dabo Vobis*, explicitly endorsed both pastoral charity and work for justice in the formation of seminarians. Three notable formulations are offered

---

[5] Congregation of the Clergy, "The Pastoral Conversion of the Parish Community in the Service of the Evangelizing Mission of the Church," July 20, 2020, http://www.vatican.va.

[6] Congregation of the Clergy, *Ratio Fundamentalis Institutionis Sacerdotalis* (The Gift of the Priestly Vocation), 2016, http://www.vatican.va.

in this more recent document: seminarians need to cultivate "a constant concern for justice" (*RF*, 63); they should be trained in the social doctrine of the church on the values of justice and peace (see *RF*, 172); and the strongest formula states that seminarians should "become sincere and credible promotors of true social justice" (*RF*, 111). The authors of the Boston College document may have assumed that work for justice was included in their mention of social charity, but preparation for justice advocacy, and how to pursue it in collaboration with the faithful people of God in the church and with other people of goodwill—merit much greater attention in the formation of seminarians, newly ordained priests, and the training of bishops.

Pope Francis has written of the need for the people of God to work for justice in official teachings such as *Evangelii Gaudium* (2013) and *Laudato Si'* (2015). His most compelling appeals about the importance of work for justice, however, have been in his numerous addresses to popular social movements. As archbishop of Buenos Aires, Jorge Bergoglio reached out to people who were suffering during the Argentinean economic crisis taking place at that time. This initiated a long period of his involvement with popular social movements in Argentina and nurtured his commitment to collaborate with poor and marginalized people, whether they were Catholic or religious at all, to foster their roles as social poets and active protagonists in their own social destiny through protests and work for social change. Francis's example exhibits a particular way that priests and bishops as pastors can and should be outspoken, standing with the poor and those who are marginalized, advocating for their rights, and pushing back against destructive powers and economic forces in civil society.

This development of modern Catholic teachings and forms of engagement in works for justice must be matched by programs for those preparing for priestly or episcopal ministry, but such training should also be a basic part of the initiation of all the faithful in the requirements of missiological discipleship.

Sources of Constraint

Why do some priests and bishops not respond to the clarion call for synodality and work for justice issued by Vatican II and Pope Francis? Let me identify two obstacles that can be traced back to the council.

Most bishops at Vatican II rejected an older theology of priesthood that theorized the cleric as a distinctive class and status in the church in contrast to the nonordained. This older theology authorized an institutional structure and clerical culture marked by paternalism and the infantilization of the lay faithful, and misogyny toward women. In the place of this theology, Vatican II sanctioned a doctrine of equality of all the faithful that supported their full and active participation and partnership through baptism in the priestly, prophetic, and kingly offices of Jesus Christ through the power of the Spirit of God.

The council distinguished the common priesthood of all believers from the ministerial priesthood in terms of the *sacra potestas* (sacred power) bestowed on priests at ordination. This formula is juxtaposed with the three-fold theological offices of priest, prophet, and king. However, this threefold theological formula represents a nineteenth-century juridical division that distinguished sacramental ministry, governing, and teaching (*ministerium, regimen,* and *magisterium*) of the ordained in contrast with the common priesthood. Yet the council neither employed nor evoked a much older jurid-ical distinction between the *potestas Ordinis* (power of orders) and *potestas jurisdictionis* (power of jurisdiction), which had been used to differentiate the priest's exercise of the power of orders in sacramental ministries, and which also entailed exercising governing authority in the parochial context, whereas the exercise of the power of jurisdiction was associated with the juridical power to teach and govern reserved to the episcopacy.[7]

Karl Rahner predicted that the failure at the council to work through these diverse frameworks—theological and juridical—would give canon lawyers trouble and problems for some time.[8] More perniciously, however, the operative categories combined with the still-lingering juridical distinc-tion of sacred power of orders and power of jurisdiction seem to have a history of effects and receptions in subsequent actions to limit the laity's ability to participate in certain ways in sacramental ministry and in decision-making in synodal and conciliar collaboration with priests and bishops. The power of orders and power of jurisdiction may no longer be invoked, but they hover and lurk behind the scenes, continuing to disable the empow-

---

[7] Ormond Rush, *The Eyes of Faith: The Sense of the Faithful and the Church's Reception of Revelation* (Washington, DC: Catholic University of America Press, 2009), 185–93.

[8] Karl Rahner, "The Changing Church," in *The Christian of the Future* (London: Burns & Oates, 1967), 9–38.

erment of lay people by means attributed to the sacred powers reserved to priests and bishops.

During the papacy of John Paul II, the distinctive character of priests and their unique status in worship, teaching, and decision-making were accentuated, especially in a 1997 statement released by eight Vatican offices that damaged the full and active participation of the people of God in lay leadership.[9] These policies build on the new Code of Canon Law promulgated in 1983, in particular, the "consultative-only" clause, which authorized lay people to participate in certain councils and synods, but with no role in actual decision-making.

A further difficulty has both hindered the active role of the lay faithful in synodal and conciliar decision-making and undermined the active role of priests and bishops in work for justice. Vatican II distinguished the sacred realm and the secular realm, correlating ministerial priesthood with the sacred realm and the mission of the laity with the secular realm.[10] On the one hand, this contrast enhanced the power of priests in sacramental worship, preaching, and decision-making in the sacred realm, understood as comprising church-related matters, while undermining their public role particularly in work for justice in the civic realm. On the other hand, this distinction challenges the baptismal calling of all the faithful to share in the priestly, prophetic, and kingly offices of Jesus Christ, through the gift of the Spirit in the church and in the world. These conflicting theoretical models underwent further official reinterpretation and application during the papacies of John Paul II and Benedict XVI, culminating in what too often became a restoration of an older theology of priesthood to the detriment of the church's embrace of synodality and work for justice.

Questions for Reflection

1. Instead of concentrating on older ways of demarcating how sacred power has been associated with the identity and ministry of priests, how can we create synodal processes that make possible

---

[9] "Instruction on Certain Questions Regarding the Collaboration of the Non-ordained Faithful in the Sacred Ministry of Priests," August 15, 1997, http://www.vatican.va.

[10] Wolfgang Beinert, "Priestly People of God," *Irish Theological Quarterly* 85 (2020): 3–15.

the sacred empowerment of lay persons as active participants, in group discernment and decision-making, in the creative promotion of missiological discipleship? On what issues do lay people long to be active, decision-making participants in the synodal church today? What kind of training is required to equip priests to foster synodality by building Christian communities and cultivating lay leadership?

2. Can we intertwine the sacred and the secular dimensions of all the realities enfolding the church and the world? How might such a social imaginary enable peoples of the earth to encounter the divine by attending and responding to the cries of the poor; the marginalized, precarious forms of life; and the wounded earth through works of mercy and work for justice? How can we let the cries for life and those shouting out for the dignity of human life and freedom be better heard and expressed by our priests, so that along with women, people of color, marginalized communities, LGBTQ people, and the poor in our communities, they can challenge the faithful to stand up, speak out, and thereby promote work for justice?

11

"Animators According to the Spirit"

Boyd Coolman

Throughout the course of the Second Vatican Council, a small number of bishops inspired by Pope John XXIII's evocation of a "church of the poor" met regularly at the Belgian College in Rome while the council was in session. These bishops were persuaded of the need to engage in a more evangelical ministry inspired by direct gospel imperatives. In the fall of 1965, as the council drew to a close, some forty bishops gathered in the Domitilla Catacombs outside Rome where they celebrated the Eucharist and signed a pact that would come to be known as the "Pact of the Catacombs." The original document is no longer extant, and the only record of it comes from a transcript provided in the chronicle of the council by Franciscan bishop Bonaventura Kloppenburg. He titled the document "Pact of the Servant and Poor Church."[1]

This remarkable pact included a pledge in which the bishops committed themselves to adopt a particular modus vivendi. It included renouncing "ambition and presumption," living "according to the ordinary manner of our people," eschewing "the appearance and the substance of wealth," forgoing "names and titles that express prominence and power," and avoiding "everything that may appear as a concession of privilege, prominence, or even preference to the wealthy and the powerful." The bishops involved in the pact also committed themselves to a particular approach to their ministry that entailed "sharing our lives in pastoral charity with our brothers and sisters in Christ, priests, religious, and laity, so that our ministry constitutes a true service"; making "an effort to 'review our lives' with them"; and finally, seeing all the members of their flock as "collaborators in ministry

---

[1]   See https://www.pactofthecatacombs.com/the-document.

so that we can be animators according to the Spirit rather than dominators according to the world."

Not only is this profile of episcopal and priestly ministry compelling, it contains much of what is central to my hopes for the future of the priesthood. One particular phrase captures my imagination, namely, "animators according to the Spirit." Today it seems that we are at a loss trying to define priestly ministry in relation to the faithful under his charge. We cast about, often borrowing terms and concepts from other spheres of contemporary life: Is a pastor a leader, a manager, a facilitator, a healer, therapist, a counselor, a life coach? In my opinion, "animator according to the Spirit" has rich potential for identifying the soul (*anima*)—pun intended—of priestly ministry.

At the outset of his extended discussion of the gifts of the Spirit in the life of the church in the First Letter to the Corinthians 12–14, the apostle Paul observes, in a remarkably proto-Trinitarian statement, "Now there are varieties of gifts, but the same Spirit; and there are varieties of services, but the same Lord; and there are varieties of activities, but it is the same God who *activates* all of them in everyone." A few verses later: "All these are *activated* by one and the same Spirit, who allots to each one individually just as the Spirit chooses" (1 Cor 12:4–6, 11; emphasis added).

The verb "activates" in these verses translates the Greek "*energōn*" and the Latin "*operatur*." The Spirit, we might say, "energizes," "operates," "enacts" its gifts (*charismata*) in individuals within the community. In the very next verse, though, Paul, situates this discussion within the notion of the church as the Body of Christ, a Body made alive by the Spirit: "For just as the body is one and has many members, and all the members of the body, though many, are one body, so it is with Christ. For in the one Spirit we were all baptized into one body . . . and we were all made to drink of one Spirit" (1 Cor 12:12). So the Spirit's energizing and operating "activation" of its gifts within the church could fittingly be described as the animation of the church—the Spirit is the Animator of the Body of Christ.

For the "Pact of the Catacombs" to characterize priestly ministry in this way—namely, as participating in the Spirit's animating work in the Body—is to suggest a richly pneumatic and charismatic account of priestly ministry. Of course, Vatican II's "Decree on the Ministry and Life of Priests" (*Presbyterorum Ordinis*) affirms this pneumatic account of priestly ministry by viewing the sacrament of ordination as the reception of the "anointing of the Holy Spirit," which, as a participation in Christ's own anointing with the Spirit (*PO*, 2), enables priests to "act in the person of Christ the Head" (*PO*, 2).

Let us now sketch briefly a profile of priests who are "animators according to the Spirit," in that they share in the anointing of Christ.

Animated

From this perspective, being himself animated by the Spirit is a precondition for a priest sharing in the Spirit's animation of the Body of Christ; this must also be a personal participation in the anointing of Christ the Head himself. The anointed life of Jesus himself, then, provides the pattern and indeed the source for the priest.

"The Spirit of God descending like a dove and alighting on him" (Matt 3:16): the public ministry of Jesus was launched with an anointing of the Spirit at his baptism. As Paul reminds us, though, our own baptism is a participation in Christ's death, a participation in his own sacrificial self-offering: "all of us who have been baptized into Christ Jesus were baptized into his death" (Rom 6:3). Accordingly, Paul later urges believers to offer themselves as "a living sacrifice, holy and acceptable to God, which is your spiritual worship" (Rom 12:1–2). I hope for priests whose public ministry is grounded in, and thus emanates from, a vital participation in the baptismal anointing of Jesus, by which they themselves become *living sacrifices* who offer *spiritual worship*.

"Jesus, full of the Holy Spirit, returned from the Jordan and was led by the Spirit in the wilderness" (Luke 4:1). The Spirit-empowered ministry of Jesus begins in the desert, to which he is led, even driven, by the Spirit. I hope for priests, who have been led and driven by the Spirit into the wilderness. The wilderness is the place where one is forced to wrestle with the demonic temptations that beset every believer who would be a faithful disciple. I hope for priests whose Spirit-led lives bear the mark of having experienced the desert.

"Many crowds would gather to hear him and to be cured of their diseases. But he would withdraw to deserted places and pray" (Luke 5:16). The desert is also a place of prayer—serious, agonizing prayer—"He offered up prayers and supplications, with loud cries and tears" (Heb 5:7). The apostle Paul describes the prayer of one who is led by the Spirit and who is living in the Spirit as sharing in the deep cosmic intercession of the Spirit—"that very Spirit intercedes with sighs too deep for words" (Rom 5:26). I hope for priests whose ministries are not too busy for regular, Spirit-animated prayer, whose lives bear the mark of the Spirit's groaning in the labor of the world's redemption.

One could argue that the ancient Christological heresies (e.g., docetism and monophysitism) are perennial temptations to our "theological imaginary" regarding Jesus: "He learned obedience through what he suffered" (Heb 5:9). In other words, though in theory we affirm that he was fully human, in practice we draw back from completely embracing that fact. A parallel temptation besets our conception of priesthood. We tend to imagine neither Jesus nor his ministers wrestling with the demands of faithful obedience and discipleship with existential anguish, with loud cries and tearful supplications. Yet scripture invites us to imagine Jesus thus; the church invites us to imagine a priesthood that conforms to Christ's suffering in this way.

"There he was transfigured before them. His face shone like the sun, and his clothes became as white as the light" (Matt 17:2). If Karl Rahner was right to predict "the devout Christian of the future will either be a 'mystic,' one who has experienced 'something,' or he will cease to be anything at all," all the more must it be so of those who minister.[2] I hope for priests in whom I can see the limp of Jacob, who have experienced the "wound of knowledge."[3] I hope for priests who also know what it means to "suffer divine things."[4]

"But the fruit of the Spirit is love, joy, peace, patience, kindness, generosity, faithfulness, gentleness, and self-control" (Gal 5:22–23). Much could be said about each of these traits, and perhaps in the context of the recent past, self-control might garner special attention. But taken as a whole, the profile of one whose life bears these fruits is at once *inwardly* grounded and integrated (love, joy, peace), as well as *outwardly* disposed (patience, kindness, generosity, faithfulness, gentleness, self-control). In a word, "graceful," in both the literal and fulsome sense of the term, captures the idea. A genuine humanness radiates in one so graced. I hope for priests who

---

[2] Karl Rahner, "Christian Living Formerly and Today," *Theological Investigations*, vol. 7 (New York: Crossroad, 1977), 15.

[3] Rowan Williams, *Wound of Knowledge: Christian Spirituality from the New Testament to St. John of the Cross* (Boston: Cowley Publications, 2003).

[4] Williams, *Wound of Knowledge*, 131.

are charismatic in precisely this sense: endowed with a certain Spirit-born winsomeness—a magnetic wholeness and infectious generosity.

Animators

There is, of course, a danger in sacramental ministry of a dead and deadening formality, a "form of godliness" devoid of the power (*dunamis*) of the Spirit (see 2 Tim 3:5). The sacraments do their work irrespective of this personal anointing, of course, but it is no lapse into Donatism—a view of ministry that links its efficacy to the personal holiness of the minister—to hope for priests on whose heads the flame of the Spirit rests, who are redolent of the unction of the Spirit that flows down from Christ their Head, and whose ministry is thus life-giving, animating.

In the synoptic accounts of Jesus's ministry, two "notes" continually resound: compassion—*he was moved with compassion* (Matt 9:36, 14:14, 15:32; Mark 6:34, 8:2–3; Luke 7:13)—and authority—*he taught them as one having authority* (Matt 7:29, 9:6, 28:18; Mark 1:27; Luke 4:32–36, 20:1–8; John 17:2). Both seem to be signature markers of Jesus's messianic identity—that is, his anointing; both are crucial markers of those who share in his *unctio* and who minister in his *persona*.

Anointed, Animating Pastoring

As Pope Francis had reminded us, the "biblical term 'compassion' recalls a mother's womb. The mother in fact reacts in a way all her own in confronting the pain of her children. It is in this way, according to Scripture, that God loves us."[5] This is a maternal longing, ache even, for a child's well-being and flourishing, along with the corresponding pain evoked by any absence of that well-being. It is a participatory desire for the as-yet-unrealized, but longed-for good of another. And it involves the remedial action elicited by that co-suffering. The compassion of Jesus recalls the Spirit's groaning and maternal travail noted earlier, as well as the maternal imagery Paul invokes to talk about his pastoral relationship to the believers in Galatia: "I am in labor pains until Christ is formed in you" (Gal 4:19). So, Francis says, "The mercy of Jesus is not only an emotion; it is a force which gives life that raises man!"[6] In a word, animating!

---

[5] Pope Francis, *Angelus*, June 9, 2013, http://www.vatican.va.
[6] Pope Francis, *Angelus*, June 9, 2013.

There is a seldom-noted flip side to the *compassio* of Jesus in the Gospels to which Pope Francis also draws attention, namely, joy—more precisely, the "co-rejoicing" (literally *congratulatio*) over the good of another:

> God is joyful! And what is the joy of God? The joy of God is forgiving, the joy of God is forgiving! The joy of a shepherd who finds his little lamb; the joy of a woman who finds her coin; it is the joy of a father welcoming home the son who was lost, who was as though dead and has come back to life, who has come home. Here is the entire Gospel! Here! The whole Gospel, all of Christianity, is here![7]

Strikingly, the Gospels portray this joy in Jesus, with reference to the Spirit: "Jesus rejoiced in the Holy Spirit and said, 'I thank you, Father, Lord of heaven and earth, because you have hidden these things from the wise and the intelligent and have revealed them to infants'" (Luke 10:21).

The crucial point here is that such pastoral dispositions are profoundly animating to those who receive them. To have someone genuinely sympathize with your suffering and sincerely rejoice in your well-being is deeply empowering. I hope for priests who "weep with those who weep and rejoice with those who rejoice" (Rom 12:15).

Anointed, Animating Preaching

"The Spirit's been kicking my butt with this Gospel all week!" So began the young priest's homily one Sunday morning at the large midwestern Catholic parish where I was visiting. He immediately had my attention as he unfolded the radical demands of discipleship contained within the passage. What remained compelling throughout was the penitential posture of one who stood under the Word whose words he was preaching, of one who understood himself to be, first and foremost, a disciple judged and found wanting by his Master.

The homily was personal but not autobiographical; it was not a sneaky way to make it all about him. As he probed the applications of the text, it was compellingly clear that he was inviting us to join him in repentance and renewed discipleship, in hearing and heeding the voice of the One whom

---

7   Pope Francis, *Angelus*, September 15, 2013, http://www.vatican.va.

we both called Lord. The anointed authority of those who preach in Jesus's name is a derivative, even borrowed, authority of one who is not himself the Word but who stands *under* that Word, himself judged and claimed *by* that Word, and thus in service *to* that Word.

If one of the tasks of the Spirit is "to convict the world of sin" (John 16:8), then anointed preaching begins with, and emanates from, a Spirit-convicted preacher. Herein lies such preaching's power to animate: it not only *moves* the members of the Body to repentance, it *moves* them to discipleship—it *moves* them to action, to service and witness in the world. I hope for priests whose anointed preaching is "not with plausible words of wisdom, but with a demonstration of the Spirit and of power" (1 Cor 2:4).

Anointed, Animating Fruit-Bearing

If pastors are shepherds, then they must emulate *the* Shepherd, who "lays down his life for the sheep" (John 10:11). While actual martyrdom is not likely necessary in the West (not yet), the "death to self" that life in the Spirit demands is always necessary. There is a subtle temptation to make a priestly vocation into a self-serving enterprise—"*my* vocation," "*my* work," "*my* ministry"—and thus the work (the "business") of serving the church and of the church's work in the world becomes subtly an extension of the priest's own identity and even personal ambition.

Part of this priestly death to self is about a single-minded commitment to the Body, to the church: "Did you not know I had to be about my Father's business [work]?" (Luke 2:49). I hope for priests who are genuinely *ecclesial* priests. Another part is to forgo the seduction of praise and admiration. "For you love to have the seat of honor in the synagogues and to be greeted with respect in the market-places" (Luke 11:43). The praise, admiration, and honor of others are seductive and ruinous in priests.

In his autobiography, St. Augustine, the great pastor of Hippo, confessed that his own desire for adulation and admiration was his greatest weakness and temptation: it "has not ceased to trouble [him], nor during the whole of this life can it cease."[8] Love of praise, the need to feel admired and loved by others, still caused him to be "roasted daily in the oven of men's tongues" (in

---

[8] Augustine, *Confessions* 10.36.59, trans. Peter Brown, rev. ed. (Berkeley: University of California Press, 2000), 201.

the felicitous translation of Peter Brown). "No one," he confessed, "who has not declared war on this enemy can possibly know how strong it is." I hope for priests who minister for only one compliment: "Well done, good and faithful servant" (Matt 25:23; Luke 19:17).

In an age awash in virtue signaling of all kinds and on all sides, caution must be exercised in valorizing symbolic gestures, but Jesus's exemplary act of washing his disciples' feet, about which he could not have been more explicit ("I have given you an example"), remains a perennially potent emblem of priestly ministry. What is crucial, of course, is a priestly practice that goes beyond lip service and gesture, a model of priesthood that truly is an "inverted pyramid": "Their rulers lord it over them. . . . But it is not so among you" (Mark 10:42–43). I hope for priests who are indeed *servus servorum Dei*—"we are unworthy servants" (Luke 17:10)—the very posture advocated by the Pact of the Catacombs.

But such priestly ministry is in the service of animating the Body; such priestly "death to self" is not an end in itself, for "if it dies, it bears much fruit" (John 12:24). Rather, these are the conditions for fruitful ministry, for ministry that bears fruit, fruit "that remains" (John 15:16). The fruitfulness here is the fecundity of the members of the Body; it is not the individual fruit of the priest, but the flourishing of the community. In this way, it is animating—it shares in, cooperates with—the Spirit's energizing and activating work in the Body; its fruit is the identification, activation, and deployment of the Spirit's gifts in the members of the Body. I hope for anointed animating priests whose death to self is fruit-bearing.

Questions for Reflection

1. What are your best hopes for priests who are "animated by the Spirit"? Name some features that would distinguish their ministry.
2. Reflect on the image of priests as "animators" of the Spirit in other people's lives. What would be some distinctive services they would render? For example, would their ministry reflect that "the joy of God is forgiving" (Pope Francis)? And what else?

12

PRIESTS AT THE SERVICE OF GOD'S PEOPLE

Raúl Gómez-Ruiz, SDS

Priests have to be formed to be at the service of God's people. And though they are key to church ministry, they are part of a larger reality that requires them to work well alongside a variety of ministers. This includes permanent deacons and trained laity. Based on my experience, this view of priestly ministry is slowly coming into focus, and various efforts are under way to advance it.

My experience includes being a faculty member and administrator for over twenty-four years at Sacred Heart Seminary and School of Theology in Wisconsin. At Sacred Heart, we chiefly focus on what are often labeled "older" or delayed vocations—those who range in age from twenty-three to sixty-five years old. Additionally, we educate laity at the graduate level from the local archdiocese for service in the church. Our faculty also helps prepare permanent deacons through the archdiocesan diaconate program. We have had much success in these efforts.

My reflection begins by addressing the current situation. Then I outline the ideals of what I envision a priest to be as we move into the future. I continue with a plan of formation that I believe will help incarnate that vision and, finally, propose some questions for reflection to continue the conversation.

The Horizon

Since the 1970s, the number of priests in the United States has greatly diminished. This is often attributed to the so-called vocation crisis. The notion of crisis is related to the fact that the ratio of priests to laity has decreased, thereby limiting the availability of priestly ministry and raising the question of its centrality to Catholicism. Some attribute the decrease in vocations to the reforms of Vatican II. Whether this is true or not, there has been a marked reduction of numbers of seminarians and priests while the number of Catholics has continued to grow. This is primarily due to the increase of Catholics of Hispanic, Asian, and African origin. Many of these immigrants view priests as absolutely necessary for both sacramental and pastoral ministry. They also often express the need for priests of their own ethnic, cultural, or racial origin. Yet for many reasons, recruitment of candidates from these groups has been mostly ineffective. Consequently, currently the majority of seminarians consist disproportionately of those labeled as "Anglo." Thus the need for diversity among the clergy is evident. In some cases, priests from related countries of origin have been imported for ministry in the United States. In addition, dioceses and religious orders have recruited foreign seminarians to meet the demands of the growing ethnic, cultural, and racial groups.

Another factor is the age of priestly vocations. According to the latest statistics gathered by the Center for Applied Research in the Apostolate (CARA), the average age of seminarians today falls in the mid-thirties.[1] Even so, we are finding at Sacred Heart Seminary that many of the dioceses that used to entrust their seminarians to us have opted to focus their recruitment efforts on candidates in their early twenties. They largely are being recruited either while in college or soon after having completed their undergraduate studies.

The reduced number of priests and seminarians has widened the way for the permanent diaconate. It has also opened the way for lay persons to be theologically and pastorally trained. Both the diaconate and lay ministries are currently seen as ways to supplement ordained priestly ministry. Though permanent deacons and lay ministers are becoming more accepted as ministers in their own right, they are still seen by many as placeholders for priests. Pope Francis's recent move to institute laity as catechists is a step forward in seeing ministry as not being limited to priests. In addition, the reconsideration of a diaconate for women opens the horizon for rethinking priestly ministry even more broadly. Nonetheless, priesthood is integral to Catholicism in terms of both our baptism as well as those ordained for specific priestly ministry.

I firmly believe priestly ministry will not disappear. Why? Because priests actualize the priesthood of Jesus Christ, they make it evident, they

---

[1] See https://cara.georgetown.edu/StatisticalOverview201819.pdf.

prolong it in history, and they concretize an encounter with Christ through the sacraments that are transformative because of their participation in the ministry of the church in a particular and designated way (see Eph 4:11–12). I am convinced that the ministerial priesthood is the continuation of Christ's earthly ministry and integral to his work of salvation. Priests, as humans themselves, also actualize the human reality of the Galilean Jew, the Divine Savior.

Ideals for the Future

The qualities of priesthood upheld today for this specific ministry are encased in the Program of Priestly Formation, a document by the United States Conference of Catholic Bishops that is now in its sixth edition (PPF6) and waiting for confirmation by the Holy See.[2] The PPF6 is the US bishops' adaptation of the Holy See's *Ratio Fundamentalis Sacerdotalis Institutionis* (2016). Once confirmed, it will be implemented and adapted by seminaries in the United States within a set time frame, usually the following academic year. My citations of selected articles from the PPF6 throughout this chapter are examples of the ideals of who a priest is—ideals to which I ascribe.

The PPF6 points to the human dimension of formation as the foundation of the other dimensions. It stresses that Christ's own humanity in its fullness is the starting point (PPF6, 176, citing *Pastores Dabo Vobis*, 1992 [*PDV*, 5]). Does this imply that being fully human is the starting point for the candidate also? It clearly avers that "the human personality of the priest is to be a bridge and not an obstacle for others in their meeting with Jesus Christ the Redeemer of the human race" (PPF6, 177). The list includes such qualities as leadership, abiding faith, and service (see PPF6, 41, 178). The PPF6 also acknowledges the need for an increased cultural diversity of candidates (see PPF6, 21, 51, 275–76). Pastoral experiences, albeit controlled and limited in scope, are also required (PPF6, 348–54).

The goal is an integrated formation that includes human, spiritual, pastoral, and intellectual dimensions (PPF6, 132). I agree with and affirm all of these qualities. However, this implies that priestly formation, to a certain extent, is to be adapted and adjusted for the individual because personal

---

[2] See USCCB Committee on Priestly Formation, *Program of Priestly Formation*, 6th ed. (Washington, DC: USCCB Publishing, 2019).

growth, integration, and conforming oneself to Christ are not just matters of accomplishment—that is, meeting the benchmarks as given for each stage of priestly formation in the PPF6. This process unfolds over time. For this to happen, the PPF6 stresses the need for accompaniment and community (e.g., PPF6, 10–16, 33, 48, 117–18, 144–48), but within the seminary setting much more than outside of it.

The overriding image of what a priest is today comes from the ideal of the Good Shepherd (see *PDV*). This could be understood as a shift from the priest as the head of the Christian community who shares in Jesus Christ as the head of the body of the church, the Body of Christ (see Eph 1:22–23; Col 1:18). This image, however, does not eliminate the priest's governance role, nor is it diametrically opposed to the priest's cultic role. The latter is especially important in terms of the celebration of the sacraments, particularly the Eucharist and reconciliation.

Most importantly, it takes seriously the Gospel passages in which Jesus stresses that those whom he calls are to imitate him, he who came not to be served but to serve (see Matt 20:26–28; Mark 10:35–45). These are some of the facets of who the priest is, like a diamond that has various facets that shine forth when the light hits them. My hope is that all these dimensions will be strengthened, integrated, and celebrated. In this way, priests will truly be at the service of God's people and not at the service of their own ambitions and desires for power and authority.

Even so, the priest as a human being is incapable of doing it all. We have our limitations, defects, and deficiencies. We also have our gifts, abilities, and talents. Both aspects contribute to our successes or accomplishments. Our deficiencies as well as using our intelligence and surrendering ourselves to God's grace often impel us toward improvement and going beyond ourselves. And like all human beings, a particular priest will excel at some things and not at others.

For that reason, one of my hopes for the priesthood is that priests will be trained so that they will see they are part of a bigger picture and will have adequate self-knowledge to identify their strengths and weaknesses. Hopefully, they will capitalize on their strengths and address their weaknesses for the welfare of the people they serve.

To be able to have adequate self-knowledge, to know how to work with others and minister alongside others, there must be sufficient and significant life experience—the wisdom, knowledge, and intelligence that come from having studied, worked, lived, and learned from the school of hard knocks.

Though much of this is acquired throughout life, there seem to be specific periods in one's life when life-changing experiences take place. These experiences contribute to knowing oneself better, to understanding the human condition better, and to entering more fully into the mystery of God, the mystery of grace, the mystery of mercy, the mystery of someone greater than oneself forming us into a people.

I refer to the time when a person has to make one's own way through life—when one has to learn to cook for oneself, clean for oneself, be responsible for oneself, to find work, to pay one's bills, and to fulfill one's obligations. It is also a time when one has to come to terms with one's faith, one's vision of the world, one's political and ideological leanings, one's ability to face the incoherencies and inconsistencies of one's life—and with the reality of suffering and evil and one's participation in it. Some of this occurs during college, but often that period of time is also a protected or sheltered time, especially if that college is a seminary. Often college, whether a seminary or not, involves structures and obligations that surely help one mature, but a certain maturity occurs only when one has to live outside of that structure.

The maturity I envision is one marked by humility, prayerfulness, becoming other-centered, and having the ability to dialogue openly and honestly. It is a maturity marked by kindness gained from the experience of forgiveness and mercy. This involves having listening skills and possessing the ability to address and resolve conflict, to empower others, and to identify the needs that are presenting themselves and finding the solutions to them without thinking that one has to do it all alone.

Therefore, my hope for priesthood is that priests will have adequate human, theological, and practical formation for pastoral ministry. I also hope that priests will be able to recruit and work well with men and women from various realms in order to minister well to the needs of the people they have been sent to serve. My hope is for priests who are able to relate to, understand, and speak to the hopes and dreams, fears and troubles of the person in front of them, because the priests have experienced these themselves.

Priestly Formation

What kind of formation is needed for this kind of priest? The PPF6 holds the right ideals indicated earlier. The central operating theme of the program is that priestly formation is a *journey*—a process over time (PPF6, Preface,

n. 4). Furthermore, priestly formation is to be grounded in community and missionary in spirit (n. 4). Clearly, this reflects Pope Francis's magisterium. However, the PPF6 also envisions mostly taking young men in their early twenties, without much life experience, and beginning to form them while still in college. It envisions them living in a house of formation sponsored by a diocesan bishop where they will engage in discernment and learn the basics of Catholic doctrine and practices, while also working or studying according to their situation.

This so-called propaedeutic year is to take place outside of a seminary setting. It is then to be followed by *entrance into a seminary* where the study of philosophy and the basics of Catholic theology are taught in addition to helping candidates understand themselves as "disciples" who are learning and deepening their vocation to configure themselves to Christ the priest. This stage can take place in a college seminary or after college, but a period of two to four years of formation is envisioned. It can be followed by a "spiritual year" or type of diocesan novitiate marked by deep prayer and reflection preparing the candidate to enter the *configuration stage*, which includes theological studies, as well as deepening the traditional dimensions of priestly formation begun earlier. A period of three to four years is envisioned.

The last dimension of priestly formation envisioned is the *pastoral synthesis stage*. The candidates, once certain of being called to priestly ministry and giving evidence of configuring themselves to Christ as affirmed by their priestly formators, are ordained deacons and placed in a pastoral setting for a year outside of the seminary. This whole process as envisioned can take from eight to ten years prior to ordination as a priest.

One can imagine the costs of implementing such a program of priestly formation. The principal cost is the end product. If candidates enter the process at age twenty-three, ordination would take place at thirty-three, perhaps not by coincidence. However, the candidates have had little chance to live outside of a protected and highly structured environment where struggles with faith, sexuality, human relationships, and exploring one's abilities to integrate them for the purpose of pastoral ministry are greatly handicapped. Candidates emerge with a very narrow experience of life. Their ability to relate to the people they encounter in a parish of any kind will have been filtered by controlled forays into the lives of those people through pastoral experiences. Would it not be better if there were an approach that better prepared them for the reality of people's lives?

I propose rethinking the whole of seminary formation and thus of preparation for priesthood. It involves starting with candidates who have significant life experience outside of a seminary setting. In broad strokes, ideally one would not be considered an apt candidate until one has at least one year of working and living on one's own. This would be followed by a year or two of accompaniment by a vocation director and include online or in-person courses providing rudimentary Catholic doctrine and philosophy (traditionally labeled "pretheology")—enough to prepare the candidate for graduate-level theology and priestly formation. The candidate would then enter a seminary for a three-year period to receive what is needed for ordination to the diaconate.

Once ordained, deacons would be assigned to parish and other types of ministries for a three-year period. One or two courses (online or in person) would be required each semester, and they would be guided by a priest mentor who would help them engage in deep theological reflection on their experiences and what they mean for priestly ministry. Theological reflection would take place with a group of deacons and a facilitator. Online courses over the journey of priestly formation could be taken from a variety of seminaries, thus broadening the horizons of the candidates.

During this diaconal period, the candidates would earn the requisite degree for ordination (currently the MDiv or STB). Deacons would also return periodically to the seminary for short-term in-person sessions for reflection, consultation, prayer, and community-building with peers. Once ready as determined by the bishop or religious superior, individual candidates would be ordained to the priesthood. However, during the first five years, the newly ordained priest would be required to engage in ongoing education, taking courses online or in person to supplement or deepen the topics currently seen as essential for effective priestly ministry. Topics would build on the dimensions of human, spiritual, pastoral, and intellectual formation. After ordination to the priesthood, the priest would be required to do a semester-long ongoing formation experience every five years in order to continue developing skills in and understandings of priestly ministry.

This type of formation program affirms the intuition underlying the PPF6 that becoming a priest is, first, a process and not a matter of accomplishment. It is a journey that begins at baptism (PPF6, 10) and is aimed at conforming the heart to the heart of Christ (PPF6, 12). Second, configuring oneself to Christ is a lifelong activity shared not only by those ordained but by all Catholics who are to be missionary disciples (PPF6, 14). It means conforming the world to the heart of Christ. Third, this type of formation responds to the times just as the seminary system envisioned by the Council of Trent did, a system that remains basically intact to the present. Whereas the Trent model of an ideal, protected seedbed (*seminarium*) replaced the original apprentice model of priestly preparation with its limitations and abuses, the proposed model that I envision here reintroduces a modified apprentice model joined to the best of the seminary model. It also incarnates the ideals of the PPF6 and the process model envisioned by the *Ratio*.

The seminary, in turn, takes on a new role. It not only provides periods of formation in all of its dimensions but also provides resources to dioceses and religious orders through a well-prepared faculty. It will also need to reenvision who its students are, since in order for priesthood candidates to be able to live and work with deacons and laity prepared to complement their priestly service, permanent deacon candidates and lay ministry candidates need to be in class with seminarians. Instructors and formators also need to include well-prepared and experienced deacons, lay men, and lay women, as well as priests.

Another key element is who and how vocation directors recruit candidates. A related factor is how seminary administrators and formators take seriously the need to accompany individual seminarians to help them grow into the ministerial priesthood envisioned. All of this depends on when candidates are recruited, how their program of priestly formation is focused, and a philosophy of formation that builds on the candidate's gifts rather than one that sees the person as clay to be molded into the ideal priest. This requires the formator to be primarily a mentor: a bold vision for some, but worth considering.

Questions for Reflection

1. How do we reform seminary formation to build on life experience and include the preparation of deacons and lay ministry candidates?
2. How do we shift seminary formation from molding candidates to mentoring them into servant priests?
3. What is required to adapt formation for the individual candidate?

13

PRIESTHOOD AS DISCIPLESHIP FOR MISSION

Emily Jendzejec

Holy Thursday is my favorite day of the liturgical year. However, this was not always the case. I remember when I was in high school and was slightly annoyed because my parents wanted us to go to church on Thursday, Friday, and Saturday of Holy Week! Begrudgingly sitting at the mass of the Lord's Supper, we were invited to the sanctuary to have our feet washed by members of the community, just as Jesus washed the feet of his disciples. It was an awkward encounter, yet in this moment I started to pay more attention. Certainly I had heard that story many times, but that time, as a sixteen-year-old, Jesus washing his disciples' feet hit me in a new way. Jesus's humble and bold act was countercultural, uncomfortable, and powerful. Leading by example, he showed the way for the disciples to act and serve when he would no longer be with them physically. As I reflect on my best hopes for the future of Catholic priesthood, I am brought back to John 13:1–17. Jesus washes the feet of his disciples with a clear commission: go and do likewise.

   I am grateful to have been a part of the conversation on a renewed theology of the priesthood sponsored by Boston College's Church in the 21st Century Center. Over the course of the three-year project, I was serving as a Catholic chaplain at a women's college and studying as a PhD student in theology and education at Boston College, and also gave birth to two children. My vocations as chaplain, theologian, and mother inform my hopes for the future of priesthood. I have a deep personal commitment to the community of the faithful. This chapter offers my reflections based on the three main sections of the document "To Serve the People of God" (TSPG): "Ministry in the Life of the Church," "A Profile of the Well-Formed Priest," and "Shaping the Future."

"Ministry in the Life of the Church"

The document asserts that Catholic priesthood must be located within a contemporary understanding of the church, and of the church's purpose in the world. While exploring our hopes for the priesthood, we must continually situate the conversation within the question of how the church is to be an effective sacrament of God's reign in the world. The document emphasizes that the church is "a community for mission" (TSPG, 19).[1] The document draws from the example and writings of Pope Francis, who has empowered all the faithful to take seriously a call to live out our faith not just on Sundays, but in the streets, in our homes, and in our communities. Francis explains that "an evangelizing community gets involved by word and deed in people's daily lives. . . . It embraces human life, touching the suffering flesh of Christ in others" (*EG*, 24). A crucial part of engaging with the challenging realities of the world is by touching the suffering flesh of Jesus Christ. Francis continues to order priests out into the streets and into the world, to meet people where they are, especially in their suffering.

Francis's theological understanding of priesthood—to grow in holiness—is not to retreat from the world but to engage in it. He urges priests to lead not from a place of purity or righteousness but from a posture of humility and service. TSPG fittingly quotes Pope Francis's address to priests during the Chrism Mass on Holy Thursday in 2013. Francis urges priests to be "shepherds with the 'smell of the sheep'" (TSPG, 4). Francis's own powerful example from Holy Thursday was when he washed the feet of people who were in prison, breaking from the tradition of his predecessors, who washed the feet of priests within the walls of the Vatican.

Priests must be equipped theologically and practically to address the suffering in the world within globalized and localized contexts. A renewed theology of the priesthood should allow the mission of the church not to become stagnant or irrelevant but rather open for constant renewal and engagement within our present context. Priests, alongside all the faithful, are constantly called to discern what it means to live as disciples of Jesus in the world. Ordained priesthood is at the service of the priesthood of all believers—enabling all the baptized to play their vital function in the

---

[1] References to TSPG refer to paragraph numbers in the document reproduced at the beginning of this volume.

mission and ministry of the church to the world. As the document points out, "Ministers, priests included, are to serve the community of the baptized disciples in its responsibility for the one mission of the church in the world" (TSPG, 28). Priests are called to be disciples who play an interdependent role with their community of faith in carrying out the mission of the church to the world. Priesthood in the service of a missional church must not be focused inward but outward. First and foremost, disciples of Jesus, priests, like all of the faithful, must be constantly discerning how the church can act and be in solidarity with the most vulnerable in our society, leading the faithful especially in the works of compassion and justice.

"The Profile of a Well-Formed Priest"

TSPG articulates five essential characteristics of priestly ministry that must be explicitly grounded in a posture of humility and discipleship. While *in persona Christi* has been dangerously misconstrued to mean that priests are more holy and closer to God than lay people, priests instead should take seriously the servant leadership style that Jesus modeled. Priests should lead from a posture of humility and service, and with particular outreach to those most vulnerable within their communities.

While the five characteristics are an important contribution, the conversation on the future of the priesthood must address the church's current practice of admitting only males committed to celibacy to the ordained priesthood. TSPG asserts that "effective unity and catholicity in the church require ongoing conversion to deeper holiness as well as creative fidelity to the apostolic tradition; these are all sure signs of the Spirit" (TSPG, 21). Creative fidelity to the apostolic tradition must take into account the reality of the priest shortage and the many scandals caused by clericalism and cover-up that are pervasive in the hierarchy. Discerning the priesthood in our current reality is not based only on a call to serve the church's mission but is limited in its requirements of only admitting celibate males. In its introduction, the document acknowledges that some may be disappointed that the document does not address the possibility for women's ordination and married priests. It gives the reasoning that "the *consensus fidelium*, the 'breathing-together' of the whole church, does not yet exist in relation to those possibilities" (TSPG, 12). Yet how can there be *consensus fidelium* when there have not been adequate channels of dialogue to allow for *sensus fidelium* to even be discerned or heard? This lacuna and oversight surely call us to a time of fresh discernment of an inclusive priesthood, which is crucial to the future of our church and its ministry to the world.

The current qualifications for entry into the priesthood exclude many of the faithful who are willing and able, and who have a call to serve the church's mission in the world. I have worked with faithful young women who, after deep prayer and discernment, have felt an authentic call to the priesthood, and have either repressed it or chosen to go to denominations that welcome women to ordained ministry. I have witnessed priests in good standing leave their vocation from exhaustion and frustration. I have witnessed men who would have made excellent priests leave the seminary feeling drawn to married life. Many of God's faithful are simply denied the chance to even discern a call to the priesthood. The church must listen and be open to the movement of the Spirit with "creative fidelity to the apostolic tradition." As a Catholic theologian, it is personally threatening to put these words in writing, let alone allow them to be published. Theologians and priests who have even suggested an openness to dialoguing about the qualifications for priesthood have been silenced. Many who are sympathetic to the conversation fear that their careers will be compromised. A culture of silencing and condemning does not leave room for the work of the Holy Spirit nor is it congruent with respecting the *sensus fidelium*.

A theology of the priesthood for the twenty-first century needs to revisit limiting qualifications for entry and the theologies that have been used to uphold them. The current most glaring qualification for priesthood is the necessity to be male. The *Catechism of the Catholic Church* states that only men can receive holy orders because Jesus chose men as his apostles. Pope John Paul II in *Ordinatio Sacerdotalis* (1994) confirmed this teaching as definitive and not open to debate, declaring that the church has no authority whatsoever to confer priestly ordination on women. Women's exclusion from the priesthood in the current hierarchical structure of the church also rests on gender stereotypes and a theology that supports gender essentialism. The longer the church hierarchy upholds the requirement of maleness as the authentic calling to the priesthood, the longer it denies the movement of the Holy Spirit working through many capable women who are willing and able to serve our church as priests. The wisdom, pastoral gifts, and leadership of women will only serve to further the mission of the church in our world. Furthermore, it will create an embodied priesthood that better reflects the inclusivity of Jesus's original community, welcoming all to the table and including women in his inner core of disciples. The principal example, of course, is Mary Magdalene as the primary witness of the Resurrection.

TSPG also avoids addressing the problematic stance of obligatory celibacy for diocesan priests. Pope Paul VI, in his encyclical *Sacerdotalis Caelibatus* (1967), reflected that celibacy is an identification with Jesus Christ, who, it is argued, was himself celibate. Yet, in the church's history, there have been married priests, and there are currently pastoral provisions for married priests from other Christian churches to be received into the Catholic Church as presbyters. This takes away from any definitive argument regarding the necessity of celibacy. We then must ask: Is the requirement of celibacy pastorally effective at this point in time and in our culture? Is it a necessary "requirement" for those discerning new vocations to the priesthood? Given that the church has changed its position on celibacy for admitting married clergymen from other Christian communions to Catholic priesthood, why not allow it to continue to change and transform, opening its ranks to those who choose to be married as well as those called to the charism of celibacy?

A person's marital status and gender have no bearing on the five central characteristics essential for priestly ministry, as outlined in TSPG. The most important characteristics that define a well-formed priest are based in personal maturity and Christian discipleship. The current recruitment of only celibate men for the priesthood hinders the flourishing of the church's mission in the world. My greatest hope is that Catholic theologians, seminarians, priests, and all the faithful are able to enter into an open dialogue about creative fidelity to the apostolic tradition without fear of retribution. I believe this is essential for the sake of the mission of our beloved church and its call to be an effective sign of God's reign in the world.

"Shaping the Future"

TSPG offers clear and succinct ways that seminaries can better cultivate learning environments and formation opportunities to support the development and maturation of seminarians into effective priests. I strongly support the document's focus on developing in priests the abilities needed for diverse collaboration and healthy relationships. Priests can be better formed if seminaries are inclusive and diverse both in their student body and within the teaching faculty. Seminaries that do not take seriously this type of agenda of holistic human formation for seminarians will graduate priests who cannot collaborate or lead effectively amid diversity, and instead will perpetuate a culture of clericalism—a detriment to the entire faith community.

Our church needs well-formed priests to be disciples for mission, disciples who preach the Word of God, preside with the faith community at worship, and engage the gifts of the whole community as pastor. A practical question that remains is how priests can best be prepared to enter realistic parish settings. We must ask this while also sharing our hopes for the future. In the context of the United States, we are witnessing more parishes merge into clusters, and while it makes sense logistically, there is a deep need to articulate the theological and pastoral consequences this has on the priests and the communities they are serving. If a priest is busy presiding at all the sacramental events at two or three parishes, there is virtually little time for anything else. A danger in clustering is that priests only become known as sacrament dispensers. We should seriously discern and reflect on the consequences of clustering and how to better support priests and their faith communities.

Priests must be able to empower the people around them to use their gifts for the good of the community. This takes a healthy understanding of power and how best to use their power *with* rather than *over* people. Priests preparing to go out into communities must be aware of explicit and implicit power dynamics that are often associated with the priesthood and the hierarchy. A priesthood emphasized as discipleship for mission would tremendously challenge a hierarchical model that has enabled clericalism to thrive—where clerical leadership equates to unchecked power *over* people's lives. This is especially urgent given the sexual abuse crisis, where a culture of clerical privilege and unchecked power tragically allowed abuse and cover-up to flourish.

This task of grappling with power dynamics and clericalism in parish life should not fall only on the priests. The church as a community of faith must intentionally discern how to disembed from the pervasive culture of clericalism. This is a larger structural challenge that requires the whole faith community to take ownership in addressing—and also a cultural shift in thinking about power and authority in our church. My hope is that not just in seminaries but in all Catholic formation settings—whether they are for children or adults—there is an emphasis on cultivating a culture of participation and active engagement in parish life by all the baptized. While priests can draw on the gifts of the community, it is from within the community that people should discern how they are called to engage actively, not just in showing up for mass but in leadership and participation in their parishes' faith life.

Conclusion

The purpose of this chapter is to present my hopes for the future of the priesthood by reflecting on the document "To Serve the People of God." Priests must first and foremost be disciples for mission, taking seriously Jesus's words, "I have set you an example that you should do as I have done for you" (John 13:15). My hopes for the priesthood are that (1) priests be prepared as disciples of Jesus Christ, to serve from a posture of humility and to prioritize the needs of the most vulnerable; (2) the requirements for priesthood be based on an authentic call and capacity for the essential functions of priestly ministry, not on gender or marital status; and (3) the shift away from a culture of clericalism is the responsibility of all the faithful.

"To Serve the People of God" is an encouraging contribution in discerning the future of the priesthood that can help enrich the life and mission of the church. I am hopeful that the Spirit will continue to work through the Body of Christ in creative, bold, and new ways, so that the priesthood will be one of true and effective service to the mission of the church in our world.

Questions for Reflection

1. As disciples for mission, how can priests be leaders in supporting the church to prioritize the needs of the most vulnerable?
2. How can we engage in and encourage opportunities for dialogue to discern creative fidelity to the apostolic tradition?
3. What are specific actions that members of the church can take to cultivate a culture of participation and active engagement in parish life by all the baptized?

14

ORDAINED DISCIPLESHIP

Stephen Bevans, SVD

"Get rid of it!" a dear friend of mine exclaimed when I asked her what her own best hopes for priesthood might be. "Think outside the box," said another friend, a priest I deeply admire and who has inspired me greatly over the last years. "We know that each author will bring the love and care for priesthood . . . to imagine its future with openness and courage." This is what the editors wrote in the invitation to contribute to this volume on the future of priesthood.

As I pondered what I might write, I realized that these three statements are in no way contradictory. If my goal is to offer my hopes for priesthood "in ways attentive to both the faith of the church and current circumstances" (TSPG, 2),[1] I need to be "Bold and Faithful," as the unofficial motto of my school, Catholic Theological Union in Chicago, proclaims. That motto was given to us by a truly remarkable priest, Monsignor Jack Egan, and it calls for tearing down what impedes the church's mission in the world, and cherishing and preserving what continues to inspire and challenge it.

The Point of the Priesthood

It is important—essential—to understand deeply that the point of the priesthood is *not* the priesthood. We don't get ordained to be ordained. The point of the priesthood, the reason we are ordained, as the TSPG emphasizes, is for *mission*. And mission is about being co-creators of a community that embodies and works for, as African American theologians Willie Jennings and Bryan Massingale stated powerfully, "revolutionary intimacy,"

---

[1] References to TSPG refer to paragraph numbers in the document reproduced at the beginning of this volume.

"God's just future."[2] This is what Jesus called the reign of God. My hope is that we stop focusing on priestly identity and priestly authority, and focus instead on the "radical kinship"[3] that God has in store for all humanity and indeed for all creation. This is not getting rid of priesthood, but getting rid of a preoccupation that really distorts its meaning and purpose. This is, I think, what my friend was really getting at.

We can shift our focus by acknowledging deeply—not just "notionally" but "really," to use Cardinal Newman's words—that we already share the kingdom's radical kinship by virtue of our baptism. My best hope for the future of the priesthood is that we recognize the centrality of our baptism as our fundamental Christian identity, as what makes us connected to each other, and what makes us connected to the world in mission. Pope Francis writes that "our great dignity derives from our baptism, which is accessible to all" (*EG*, 104), and that "great dignity" is that we are each and every one of us *disciples*—or as Francis expresses it, "missionary disciples" (*EG*, 120). My best hope for priesthood is that we begin to understand *any* ministry in the church, but especially *presbyteral* ministry, as a commitment to lead "disciples in the life of discipleship for the sake of God's mission in the world" (TSPG, 26).[4] Real conversion to this conviction will transform the priesthood.

Disciples, Minister Disciples, Ordained Disciples

My best hope for the priesthood of the future is that we recognize our fundamental identity as *disciples*. It is perhaps a foolish hope—and one that perhaps takes me out of the box—but I would like to do away with the distinction between clerics and lay people. Naturally there has to be order in the church, but the idea of a hierarchy is something that, hopefully, we can eliminate. Order does not necessarily imply hierarchy. Hierarchy blurs the clarity of discipleship.

---

[2] Willie James Jennings, *Acts* (Nashville: Abingdon, 2017), 29; and Bryan Massingale, "Merton, Malcolm X, and Catholic Engagement with Black Lives Matter," *Tuesdays with Merton*, March 9, 2021, https://www.youtube.com.

[3] Gregory Boyle, *Barking to the Choir: The Power of Radical Kinship* (New York: Simon & Schuster, 2018).

[4] See also Kathleen Cahalan, *Introducing the Practice of Ministry* (Collegeville, MN: Liturgical Press, 2014), 50.

What I'd like to propose instead is that we simply speak of Christians as *disciples* with different gifts or responsibilities—or as TSPG expresses it, "positions" in the church. We are all "disciples," all of us called to participate in God's mission by participating in the mission of the church. Some disciples would be "minister disciples," and some "minister disciples" would be "ordained disciples." Minister disciples and ordained disciples would serve the entire community—at various levels of responsibility—to inspire, inform, and strengthen all disciples "to enact in their specific circumstances the faith, hope and love that the Spirit empowers" (TSPG, 27). Both would have rites of commissioning or ordination that would highlight the fundamental equality of all Christians because of baptism, and also the particular ministry to which the minister being commissioned or ordained is called *within* the church.

Supervision and Wisdom

The ministry of *ordained* disciples would offer the service of supervision (*episcope*) and wisdom within the community. Since they are ordained *disciples*, their discipleship alone would qualify them for this ministry—not age, gender, cultural identity, marital status, or anything else. They would need to be in deep relationship to Christ—everyday mystics. Their call to ministry would emerge from the community and require rigorous training, but their training would take place amid the community and would be about developing skills of leadership, communication, and theological reflection, rooted in the church's rich theological and spiritual tradition.

Communities of disciples of various ethnic identities would have ordained ministers taken from among them, but ethnic diversity would be important as well. A further skill necessary for minister disciples and ordained disciples would be leading the community of disciples in a life of interculturality whereby everyone is mutually enriched and challenged, especially by cultural diversity. Communities of disciples would be truly *catholic* communities.

Preaching

As wisdom figures in the community, ordained disciples would be the ordinary preachers or homilists at liturgical services, especially at the Eucharist. Their training would steep them in theology, so that their homilies would really open the scriptures to the community in ways that would help all Christian disciples connect them with their lives. In Pope Francis's wonderful phrase, the ordained disciple preaches with "an ear to the people" (*EG*, 154–55). But ordained disciples would know that wisdom is not their own preserve, that it is lavished throughout the community—so preaching would be something that any disciple might be called upon to do, especially minister disciples who share a kind of collegial leadership with their ordained leaders. My best hope for the priesthood is that ordained disciples recognize that *all* God's people, in proportion to their gifts, share fully in the prophetic mission of Christ.

Furthermore, ordained disciples would ensure that scriptural and theological education, personal and social ethics, spiritual formation, and spiritual direction would be regularly available, and thus form missionary disciples for their prophetic task. Sometimes the ordained ministers themselves would offer this instruction; other times, they would engage as teachers experts in the various fields of scripture, theology, and spirituality. Ordained disciples would ensure that members of their ministry team and other disciples could receive further theological training in specialized theological schools.

Leadership

Because ordained ministers recognize the presence of the Holy Spirit working in all disciples, decision-making would usually involve communal discernment and consensus. Ordained disciples would trust deeply in the *sensus fidei*—that infallible instinct for truth and wisdom—that is present within God's people when they make efforts to listen to and respect one another, and are challenged by one another. As Pope Francis has noted, the Spirit works not just by inspiring church leadership but in and through the community that is truly open to the wisdom of the group. No one has *all* the wisdom; everyone has a *piece* of the wisdom; everyone has a *different* piece of the wisdom.[5] Pope Francis calls this process "synodality," and the Synod of Bishops, which hopefully will include more people than bishops as voting members, will be devoted to this theme in 2023. The practice of synodality makes up a large part of my best hopes for the future of priesthood.

---

[5] Pope Francis, with Antonio Spadaro, SJ, *A Big Heart Open to God: A Conversation with Pope Francis* (New York: HarperOne / America Press, 2013), 26; see also Mary Benet McKinney, *Sharing Wisdom: A Process for Group Decision Making* (Valencia, CA: Tabor, 1987), 12–13.

Discernment and consensus are not exercises in Western democracy. The church—the community of disciples—is a *communion*, not a republic. Ordained disciples, especially those who have greater responsibility of *episcope* in the church—those we now call "bishops"—have real authority. Authority, however, is not the exercise of "power over," but "power with." Authority, it is said, is the ability to help people "author"—that is, to claim their own authority. Most of the time the leadership of the ordained disciple leads the community to consensus, but sometimes synodal leadership means articulating a position or making a decision that captures the sense of the group, even though it has not come to a full consensus. Sometimes that decision might even be contrary to the majority of the group and entails a stance of prophecy.

Pope Francis offers a wonderful description of the pastoral ministry of ordained disciples as

> walking with our people, sometimes in front, sometimes behind and sometimes in the middle, and sometimes behind : in front in order to guide the community, in the middle in order to encourage and support; and at the back in order to keep it united and so that no one lags too, too far behind, to keep them united. There is another reason too: because the people have a "nose"! The people scent out, discover, new ways to walk, it has the *"sensus fidei,"* as theologians call it. What could be more beautiful than this?[6]

Pastoral leadership is an art. It demands wisdom. It demands faith in the Spirit's presence in God's people. It is not handed on mechanically, and it does not come automatically with office. My best hope for the priesthood of the future is that our leaders will be ordained disciples of such wisdom and faith, calling forth the prophetic wisdom of the community and its participation in Christ's office of servant leadership.

Leader of Prayer

The ordained disciple is, in the words of the document, "a leader of worship and prayer" (TSPG, 38). The key word is "leader," not celebrant. The ordained disciple *presides* over worship and prayer, drawing the cele-

---

6   Pope Francis, Pastoral Visit to Assisi, 4 October 2013, www.vatican.va.

brating community into prayer, recognizing the various gifts of reading, music, and other ministries in a liturgical celebration or prayer service. This is a recognition that all disciples share in the priesthood of Christ, and that this is the priesthood of which ordained disciples are *sacraments*—that is, effective signs.

Like leadership, leadership at prayer—presiding—is an art. It demands a deep spirituality, a life of regular prayer, gracefulness, and presence. In the best sense of the word, presiding is performance. The way one holds one's hands, the cadence of the voice, the reverence of gestures all invite the community into the liturgical action, all invite the "full, conscious, and active" participation in the liturgy (Constitution on the Liturgy, 14). One of my best hopes for the priesthood is that the liturgies of the future can be rich occasions of beauty and holiness, with full participation of the people, with improved poetic texts and inspiring music with deep, meaningful lyrics that are ecologically and socially sensitive. Of course, the emphasis on the fundamental equality of disciples might make worship spaces more inclusive. Actions like elaborate entrance processions and the kind of clothing presiders wear might also need to be rethought and reimagined.

The ordained disciple, however, is not the only one who leads and presides at the community's prayer. Recognizing the priesthood of all believers, minister disciples and other qualified disciples might be called upon to preside at a variety of prayer services to offer blessings for other parents or to children, or for their own families. Ordained disciples will understand that these tasks are not important because of the current lack of those who are ordained. Presiding and praying publicly is the privilege, indeed the duty, of every disciple.

Mission

Ultimately, "the heart of ministry"—particularly the ministry of ordained disciples—"lies in forms of service that aid the realization of the church's mission" (TSPG, 29). My best hope for the priesthood is that ordained disciples work not just to form supportive and formative Christian communities, but communities of missionary disciples. Christian communities need to be credible witnesses to the world of the possibility of God's reign of radical kinship and justice, and communities that are committed to sharing Jesus's vision and message with their neighborhood, their civic community, their country, and the world. As Pope Francis expresses, "I dream of a 'missionary option,' that is a missionary impulse capable of transforming everything, so that the church's customs, ways of doing things, times and schedules, language and structures can be suitably channeled for the evangelization of today's world rather than for her self-preservation" (*EG*, 27). Our theology of the church and our theology of ministry both need to be rethought in terms of mission, committed to loving, challenging, and transforming the world.

Ordained Disciples in Religious Communities

"To Serve the People of God" focuses particularly on the ministry and formation of diocesan priests. My best hope for the future of the priesthood, however, is that we recognize another kind of ordained disciple, one who is a member of a religious, vowed community. An article written in 2019 with my colleague Robin Ryan and published in *America* tries to delineate an ordained ministry that is rooted in community, is particularly prophetic through the vows, is loyal though challenging to the institutional church, lives out ordained discipleship by embodying a community's particular charism, and offers the church a consistent global vision.[7] This kind of priesthood could be developed in a special edition of the Program of Priestly Formation and even through a rite of ordination that not only highlights the baptismal identity of those being ordained but also recognizes as well the context of community, prophecy, charism, and global vision from which they would exercise their ministry of ordained discipleship.

Conclusion

Many readers might say that the best hopes for future priesthood outlined here are totally unrealistic in today's male-dominated, hierarchical church. In some ways, this is probably true. In other ways, however, the essence of what I have sketched out here is really possible if our leadership and our people begin to understand that the community of God's people, the church, *really is* "missionary by its very nature" (Decree on Missionary Activity, 2) and so *really called* to be a "community of *missionary disciples*" (*EG*, 24). Such an

---

[7] Stephen Bevans and Robin Ryan, "Why the Catholic Church Needs Two Different Kinds of Priesthood," *America*, April 1, 2019, https://www.americamagazine.org.

understanding—a conversion, really—to the fundamental equality of discipleship and the dynamic reality of the church could really change *already
now* the way that our bishops and priests lead, preach, preside at Eucharist,
and understand themselves. Once the reign of God becomes central in the
church's life, everything can and will change.

Such a hope for the future of priesthood is also possible because, in
many ways, it might be a necessity. At least here in the West, the church
is hemorrhaging members—especially women and young people who are
disillusioned by the doublespeak of our leaders about gender equality, their
fixation on a biology that denies sexual orientations and identities, and their
refusal to face honestly the scandal of clergy sexual abuse. The church is
also hemorrhaging leadership in that its ordained ministers are aging and
are not being replaced by younger people—a phenomenon that may well
be the work of the Spirit to force us to think differently and more creatively.
The church—despite what some say—will not thrive by a restoration of "the
way things were" before the renewal of Vatican II. That renewal needs to
continue—always with an eye on the tradition—and might be more radical
than we think if we imagine new ways to be church and serve God's people
and the world in ministry.

Perhaps my best hopes for the future of priesthood are really a dream.
But if this is so, I am in good company. Pope Francis says that God is a
dreamer. God dreams for the transformation of the world.[8] And Francis is
also a dreamer! He dreams of a missionary church (*EG*, 27); he dreams of a
poor church (*EG*, 198); and he dreams of a new future after the COVID-19
pandemic. With God and with Pope Francis, I want to dare to say, "*Come,
let us talk this over. Let us dare to dream.*"[9]

Questions for Reflection

1. Why are baptism and discipleship central to the hope for the future
    of priesthood?
2. Why is mission central to a hope for the future of priesthood?
3. How can parts of the vision presented in this chapter be already
    realized today in a male-dominated, hierarchical church?

---

[8] Pope Francis, General Audience, May 17, 2017, https://www.vatican.va.
[9] Pope Francis, with Austen Ivereigh, *Let Us Dream: The Path to a Better Future*
(New York: Simon & Schuster, 2020), 7.

15

A NEW VISION FOR PRIESTLY FORMATION

Diane Vella

When I asked about fifty people in the parish where I serve what their best hopes for the future of priesthood might be, some of the most common responses were for priests who are compassionate, pastoral, approachable, and enthusiastic; priests who, because of real-life experience, understand the lives of today's families and youth; priests who lead by serving, who are available, and who are present to the wider community; priests who are not rigid but open-minded, and are good preachers; and priests who are holy (undefined).

I reflect and write from the perspective of one who has—by the grace of God and by the encouragement, support, and affirmation of others—been called to serve for forty years as a lay ecclesial minister on the East Coast in a populous and suburban diocese of the Roman Catholic Church. During those years, I have ministered with and encountered many priests. Some of them have become dear friends, others respected colleagues, and all, for better or worse, coworkers in the vineyard. Being in the trenches for so long has afforded me the opportunity to see priests at their best and their worst, and everything in between. Thankfully, the bests far outweigh the worsts. My experience also means that I have had an ear to the ground on what average Catholic parishioners want and need from their priests.

My best hopes for the future of priesthood spring from my conviction that the Catholic Church in the United States is facing challenges that require a radical reimagination and reshaping of its theory and practice of the ministerial priesthood, and especially of the process of initial and ongoing formation of priests. "To Serve the People of God" (TSPG) is a starting point for identifying and addressing those challenges.

Some years ago, I heard Father Michael Himes of Boston College suggest an unorthodox model for priestly formation that, through years of further reflection, has sparked my imagination with its wisdom and practicality. The model, when applied to the current situation of the church, provides what is needed to nurture the kind of priests envisioned by TSPG—and by the people of my parish. In short, Father Himes proposed that forming "mature and well-balanced priests" requires that the traditional seminary formation model be left behind. That former model had its place in its time, but is no longer adequate for our times. Instead, he proposed a healthier, more balanced, and more "open" model in which those preparing for priesthood would reside and work part-time in parishes and diocesan agencies, and attend school part-time with others preparing for church ministry in seminaries or theological schools.

Reimagining the initial formation of priests along these lines has the potential to breathe new life into a ministry gasping for air. This is not a judgment on the dedicated individuals who seek to respond authentically to the calling they hear, but rather on the system that may not be giving them the initial and ongoing formation and support needed to minister effectively in today's church.

What follows are my own further reflections and application of this seed that Father Himes planted. This model also provides a needed boost to two other aspects of the priestly formation process: (1) vocational discernment on the part of potential candidates and those who decide whether to accept them into the initial formation process, and (2) the implementation of a more structured and sustained plan for ongoing formation, support, and accountability.

Five Aspects of Priestly Ministry Reimagined

There would need to be times—perhaps one weekend each month, and a month over summers—when candidates would gather at a seminary or in an environment suitable for spiritual formation to bond with one another over their common calling, and explore more deeply the spirituality and practicalities specific to priestly ministry. Beyond that, I envision a model whereby, over the course of their five-year initial formation, the candidates could live and work in different parishes that represent the cultural, economic, racial, ethnic, and spiritual diversity of the diocese in which they will serve.

By "live," I mean either in the rectory or in a private home, and take part in all the duties necessary to keep a home functioning; by "work," I mean as employees of the parish or agency, with set hours and responsibilities for which they would be held accountable. They would be assigned to work in various settings in each parish, including the reception desk, each of the pastoral offices, and as members of the janitorial staff. This would give the candidates a complete picture of the life of a parish and its people, and the challenges that people who work and minister there face daily.

A model of initial formation that situates those preparing for priesthood in the real world of the people they serve would go a long way toward readying future priests to fulfill their roles as identified in TSPG—preachers, leaders of prayer and worship, collaborative leaders, public representatives of the church, and practitioners of pastoral charity. As the document notes, "The enclosed settings of the seminary, often insulated from the everyday world of families, budgeting, commuting, and even grocery shopping and laundry, can isolate seminarians" (TPSG, 52). Living among people and encountering them in their homes and parishes, and praying in common with them while apprenticing in their parish and church agency jobs would open the eyes, ears, and hearts of candidates for priesthood so that they will be received by the people as shepherds who know, understand, and love them.

Priest as Preacher

I can say for sure from forty years of ministry experience that a common lament is that homilies are often boring, uninspiring, or out of touch. In homilies and in other instances of preaching, what God's people most need are priests who can "speak to the weary a word that will rouse them" (Isa 50:4), not bore, judge, or condemn them. Unfortunately, the latter can easily happen when priests have little knowledge or understanding of the difficulties and challenges that ordinary people face in trying to live out the Christian ideal.

The answer is not more study of theology or church teaching in seminaries. What is needed are rousing words that come from the heart and mind and lips of priests who themselves have encountered the living God in the world. Priests who have shared the life of the people they serve can connect the scriptures and the wisdom of the church to the needs and concerns that real people—not perfect people—are facing. Effective, relevant preaching must be a principal way, perhaps *the* primary way, in which ordained priests inspire, nurture, and pastor the baptized priests, who are sent into the world to love and serve the Lord and one another.

Priest as Leader of Prayer and Worship

The "boring" complaint is not limited to the preaching at mass. Very often even people who attend mass regularly find the experience less than inspiring. The celebration of the Eucharist and any public worship should *move* the participants. Maybe not every time or in a deeply profound way, but most of the time, people should leave the worship experience having been touched spiritually by a sacramental encounter with Christ.

Whether worship comforts the afflicted, afflicts the comfortable, rouses the weary, calms the anxious, or inspires a new way of thinking or acting surely depends not only on the priest but on the full, conscious, and active participation of everyone in the liturgical assembly, and supported by those with special ministry roles. That said, the priest's role as the liturgical presider is key to pulling together the whole act of worship and enabling the fruitful participation of all. This role is one in which priests function much like orchestra conductors—knowing their players, getting them in the right seats, and conducting them so that together they make beautiful, soul-stirring music.

Liturgy can be celebrated well or poorly. Seminarians whose primary experience of liturgy and worship is in the seminary chapel, the diocesan cathedral, or as senior server during an occasional foray in a parish are insulated from the real dynamics of putting together and leading effective worship. Living in various parishes over the course of their period of preparation provides candidates the opportunity to experience the good and the bad, even as they are educated about the liturgy in their graduate school courses.

Until they are ordained, seminarians would sit in the pews on Sundays, shoulder to shoulder with families with squirmy kids, distracted teenagers checking their Instagram accounts, elderly people frightened by the beginning stages of dementia, and those struggling with or recovering from the alcohol or drugs that have claimed them. They would see regularly and in different settings what does and does not move people at worship. Hopefully, they would in all humility pray to God for the understanding, wisdom, and strength to learn to orchestrate worship experiences that lead all those assembled to an encounter with the Living God. Such liturgies give participants whatever hope, strength, and conviction they need to get through the day, and to better live out their Christian mission in their particular life situation.

Priest as Collaborative Leader

In my experience, very few priests are good at collaboration or delegation in ministry. Those who are good at it may have an innate ability to work with others, and some have chosen to develop these skills. Nobody learned it in the seminary. So how do ministers learn to collaborate and delegate?

Learning to delegate does not happen through full-time graduate study and living in the place where they study, all the while having their meals prepared and served and their home and grounds maintained for them. Nor does it happen by being surrounded by a small group of people of the same gender who are all preparing for the same role. Yet, with few exceptions, this is the normal, enclosed Catholic seminary environment in the United States. While some years ago, in the wake of Vatican II, there was a conscious integration of lay people into seminary classes, there has been a movement away from this in more recent decades. Because the course of study in the seminary is specific to the theological, ecclesiological, canonical, and (less often) practical concerns of priesthood, seminarians generally study, pray, and collaborate with each other.

A model in which those preparing for priesthood attend school part-time in seminaries or theological schools along with lay people offers several advantages. First, those preparing for priesthood gain some understanding of and sympathy for the many people whom they will serve—their struggles to balance work, school, and home responsibilities as they pursue their undergraduate or graduate degrees.

Second, this model exposes those preparing for priesthood to a wider and more diverse course of human, spiritual, intellectual, and pastoral formation than seminaries usually offer. A friend of mine who graduated from the seminary and was ordained around the same time I finished my graduate degree in theology had *never heard of* feminist theology or liberation theology, both of which were in the forefront of Catholic theology at that time. Some priests have never been exposed to the broad range of prayer styles that the Christian tradition offers and have never attended a worship service in a synagogue, temple, or mosque, or prayed with or learned from fellow Christians from other churches and ecclesial communities. Those responsible for the formation of candidates for priesthood should welcome such exposure as a way of creating more humanly, spiritually, intellectually, and pastorally grounded priests for today's world.

Flowing from these first two, the third and most important advantage of this model of study is that it enables priests to enter into truly collaborative relationships with fellow professional ministers, employees, and volunteers, particularly women, who are doing the bulk of church ministry in the United States today. This ability comes from observing good examples of collaborative ministry in the parishes and agencies where they work, but it is also possible that they may not experience it in those settings. The sustained exposure to lay people and religious, particularly women, who are professors, mentors, spiritual directors, and fellow students and ministers will be particularly valuable. Theological and ministerial schools tend to have more diverse faculties, students, courses, and spiritual formation opportunities than most Catholic seminaries, and intentionally foster opportunities for collaborative study and projects. By learning and working collaboratively in a diverse environment throughout their formation, candidates for priesthood learn to respect the ideas, experiences, wisdom, and expertise of others, and to value a team approach to ministry that will better serve and support them as they face the many challenges and burdens of servant leadership after ordination.

Priest as Public Representative of the Church and Practitioner of Pastoral Charity

I have combined these last two aspects of priesthood under one heading because they are intimately related. How priests and the Catholic Church, in general, are perceived by the wider community has much to do with how well the whole church, and particularly its priests, serve the community pastorally both inside and outside the walls of the church buildings and offices.

Jesus's ministry focused on the pastoral concerns of teaching, healing, encouraging, forgiving, and responding to people's real needs, Jew and Gentile alike. In short, it was a ministry of service. When priests make service their priority—and this is recognized inside and outside the parish grounds—then they are truly fulfilling their roles as both public representatives of what the church represents, and as recognized practitioners of pastoral charity.

Here again, our proposed model better equips candidates to fulfill these roles because it offers the opportunity throughout their formation experience to establish connections in the wider community, where they can be recognized as effective leaders and representatives of the gospel the church offers to all people. Such broader experience also prepares them for collaboration with other local clergy and pastoral leaders to bring a religious presence to bear when issues arise calling for strong and united stands from faith leaders in the community.

Before, During, and After Initial Formation

Before. Before anyone can be formed for priesthood, those with the requisite calling need to be identified and encouraged to explore it more deeply. If young people in parishes, colleges, and theological schools had regular contact and interaction with those preparing for priesthood through this new model, might that not spark a fire of recognition in some who may be experiencing such a call themselves, but were unable to put a name to it? Might it even *create* a spark in the hearts of some young people searching for a meaningful way of using their faith, their gifts, and their abilities for the good of the church and the world? Instead of hiding their light under the bushel of the seminary walls, those with a vocation to priesthood would be putting their lamps on a stand for all to see!

During. Not everyone who *wants* to be a priest *should* be a priest. Our model of formation may more effectively discern whether a person is suited to the kind of priestly ministry that TSPG envisions and that our world currently needs. It is easier to hide or suppress troubling personality traits, addictions, or signs of psychosexual immaturity behind the walls of a seminary, despite modest attempts to uncover such tendencies. Candidates who are not comfortable with or suited to a collaborative, servant leader priesthood would likely discover this—or others would discover it—in the course of their work and study among a diversity of priests, deacons, lay ministers, parishioners, fellow students, and formators. Better to know earlier than to deal with the fallout later.

After. What if some of the principles of this initial formation model could be carried into postordination for the ongoing formation of priests? Unfortunately, once ordained, priests are largely free from any obligation to seek further human, spiritual, intellectual, and pastoral formation. There are, generally, no mechanisms for accountability other than making sure the sacraments are celebrated and the books are balanced. There is no required evaluation of preaching or pastoral skills, and no requirement for ongoing professional development. While some priests do choose to engage in balanced, ongoing formation, many do not. If requirements for formation and accountability could be put into place for initial formation *before* ordination, why not continue this model *after* ordination?

Reality or Fantasy?

I am well aware of the major shift in paradigm and practice for which such a vision calls. I am aware too of the practical and logistical difficulties and obstacles that some readers might have already identified, and because of them perhaps dismissed my proposal as fantasy. Some may not even agree that this model is good at all. But I hope that many will see in it a glimmer of possibility and hope for the future. I wonder if the real obstacles might be those we place in our own hearts and minds. Transitioning from a venerable system that has served the church for so long and building something new is a slow, difficult, and painful process. Imagining and implementing such a model may be hard for the church. But nothing is impossible for God if we are willing to consider that it is the Holy Spirit who is prompting us and will provide gracious assistance in bringing it to fruition.

Returning to the people in the parish where I serve, the most common response to my question to parishioners about their hopes for the future of priesthood was for priests who are married. The second, tied with "priests who are compassionate," was for women priests. These second-most-common responses are fascinating, considering that in Hebrew the word "compassion" and the word "womb" come from the same root. These responses actually shocked me, because the parish I serve is hardly a hotbed of ecclesial liberalism—in fact, the people are rather conservative in their views on all things church. The question was asked and responded to individually, so this is not a result of groupthink.

Something has been stirring for some time throughout the universal church around the question of mandatory celibacy. While the question of returning to the early church practice of ordaining women as deacons is under discussion at the highest level, the question of ordaining women to priesthood is still considered off limits, partly because it is, admittedly, a "privileged world" concern. Yet we have to ask if those who serve the magisterium of the church are willing to open hearts and minds to the possibility that the Holy Spirit, speaking through a growing *sensus fidelium*, is urging us toward something new. This journey too will be slow, difficult, and painful. If the faithful, ordinary people of my parish are speaking their minds and hearts on these matters, surely the Holy Spirit is trying to break in.

Questions for Reflection

1. Leaving aside the practical and logistical challenges this new model presents, what do you think of its basic idea?
2. What other advantages might this new model have over the current seminary model of formation? What disadvantages can you identify?

16

THE FUTURE OF THE PRIESTHOOD

Archbishop John C. Wester

Priesthood changes the person. In the fall of 1964, I entered St. Joseph Minor Seminary in Mountain View, California. Although I was homesick at first (I was only thirteen years old), my memory of those early years is one of happiness. The seminary was secluded, peaceful, and predictable. For decades, young men had been formed there for a priesthood that was also predictable and well established. However, the serenity of those years belied the tumultuous times of the countercultural sixties, with a war raging in Vietnam, the Haight-Ashbury neighborhood in San Francisco coming into full bloom (pun intended!), and a Vatican Council poised to bring winds of change to the Catholic Church. As I reflect now on those seminary years, what at first seemed like an eternity raced by with lightning speed, and I was ordained into a priesthood that had undergone amazing changes. Father Charles O'Malley in *Going My Way* gave way to Monsignor Eugene Boyle, a San Francisco Bay Area priest who supported the civil rights movement and the United Farm Workers.

My vision of the priesthood has continued to evolve over the past forty-five years, as it should. The Holy Spirit is always at work in the church, breathing new life into the priesthood as it adapts to an ever-developing church in an ever-developing world. In this light, the Second Vatican Council sought to speak to the reality of the Catholic Church as it relates to the world in modern times. In the process, the priesthood received newer and deeper understandings. The "Decree on the Ministry and Life of Priests" (*Presbyterorum Ordinis*), which came late in the council, was a welcome contribution to the understanding of the priest in the modern world. However, the other major documents also had tremendous bearing on the ministry of the priest in the church. The new description of the church found in *Lumen Gentium*, the role of the biblical word in the life of the church outlined in *Dei Verbum*, the new vision of the liturgy described in *Sacrosanctum Concilium*, and the place of the church in the world delineated in *Gaudium et Spes* all combined to form a lens through which priesthood could be seen anew.

Throughout my ministry as a priest and bishop, I have benefited immensely from my interactions with the laity, spiritual directors, seminary professors, theologians, and my brother priests and bishops. All of these encounters, coupled with my ministerial experiences, have helped me to grow in my understanding of priesthood and in my desire for the insights of Vatican II to become more real. In this regard, I was delighted to be invited to a conference hosted by Boston College in January 2020 to discuss an earlier document that came from a seminar at the same college two years earlier titled "To Serve the People of God: Renewing the Conversation on Priesthood and Ministry." The conference helped deepen my reflections on priesthood and led to the invitation to contribute this chapter on my best hopes for the priesthood. I can do this optimally by describing the characteristics that our vocation office team and I look for in a candidate for the priesthood in our Archdiocese of Santa Fe. In particular, four areas refer to the characteristics that I hope for in a priest and that I strive for in my own ministry: the priest as a builder of relationships, as a bearer of mystery, as one who is given to weakness, and as a lifelong learner.

The Priest as a Builder of Relationships

> Every high priest chosen from among mortals is put in charge of things pertaining to God on their behalf. (Heb 5:1)

In the ordination of a priest, the church underscores the paramount importance of preaching and prays that this preaching will bear fruit in the hearts of the faithful. For this to happen, authentic preaching must break open the Word and reveal who God is in the context of the believing community. One of the compelling attributes of God is that God's very being is relational. We cannot speak of God without speaking of a Trinity of Persons who are in relation with each other. Since we human beings are made in the image of God, we too are relational by our very nature, at the core of our being. In this vein, we can say that grace, the life of God, unites us and gathers us in, while sin divides us, breaking down the bonds that unite us. This relational aspect of our lives undergirds the scriptural understanding of faith.

In scripture, faith is more than an acceptance of certain tenets but is better seen as a relationship with God in Christ. Furthermore, being in right relationship with God, each other, and the whole of creation constitutes biblical justice. Karl Rahner used this theme when he defined grace as the human acceptance of God's invitation to be in relationship with the Divine.[1] As mentioned earlier, the Second Vatican Council spent three years reflecting on the relationships within the church, especially at Eucharist, and the relationship of the church to the Word and to the modern world. Little wonder, then, that when I encounter a candidate for the priesthood, I am keenly interested in how he relates to God, to others, and to creation.

Of first importance is his relationship with Jesus Christ, the High Priest of Hebrews. Priesthood is rooted in the relational life of the Trinity and is a lived expression of that dynamic relationship, especially with Christ the Priest. When interviewing a candidate for the seminary, I am attentive to the type of relationship the candidate has with Christ. I am probing whether this early discernment is a response to Christ's call experienced deeply within the candidate's heart or simply a career choice prompted by the candidate's own desires. My hope for the priesthood is that priests have a palpable, tangible, and vibrant relationship with Christ, one that goes beyond rote prayer and rubrics as it sets the heart of the priest on fire with love for Christ and gratitude for the call. Father Thomas Joseph White, OP, notes well,

> The first aim in seeking the priesthood, then, is to stay in the presence of Christ. The vocation makes sense only to the extent that we stay perpetually relative to him, his mystery, his truth, his Church. Christ gives priests a certain interior stability over time. To live in him is to become strong, not unstable. But the stability is dynamic: It only works if the minister remains spiritually poor and docile to Jesus, acting in him and for him.[2]

---

[1] See Karl Rahner, "Nature and Grace," in *Theological Investigations*, vol. 4 (New York: Crossroad, 1982), 165–88.

[2] Thomas Joseph White, "Letter to an Aspiring Priest," *First Things* (March 2019), https://www.firstthings.com.

At the same time, I am looking to see how the applicant relates to the Body of Christ, that is, the church. A dear priest friend of mine likes to say that Jesus Christ is plural. It is his way of saying that we are one in Christ. Before a priest is ordained, he is baptized into a believing community—the Mystical Body of Christ—a concept that has its roots in the letters of the apostle Paul to the Corinthians and the Romans. A priest is called from the community to serve the community. Ordination does not place him above that community but rather equips him to continue as a member of it with a special charism that enables him to accompany people on their path to holiness. Someone once told me that the priest is a chaplain to the laity. I believe that speaks to this reality of the priest's relationship with the people of God.

One of the popular images of the priest when I was first ordained was that of the priest as another Christ (*alter Christus*). That image has evolved since the Second Vatican Council's "Decree on the Ministry and Life of Priests," now seeing the priest as one who represents Christ the Head of the church (*in persona Christi capitis*). In other words, Christ works in the priest as the priest—a member of the community and not above it—ministers to and within the community. As the priest recognizes and remains open to the gifts of the people, his own path of holiness is forged and his ability to serve the church is enhanced. Priesthood changes the person.

The late Archbishop John R. Quinn, a close bishop friend of mine, always noted that a good bishop is formed by his priests and a good priest is formed by his people. This points to the relationship the priest has with his people, grounded in love and service. It contradicts the notion that the priest is set above the community in a position of power and elevated status and reinforces the reality that the community of believers consists of many members with many gifts and different roles, all enlivened by the Holy Spirit. This perspective is in line with the teaching of Pope Francis, who consistently calls for the church to go out to where the people are, encountering them and accompanying them. In a homily the pope gave during an ordination of priests for the Diocese of Rome on Good Shepherd Sunday in 2021, he captured well the relationship a priest has with his people. In speaking of priestly service to the ordinands he said, "It's a service . . . that has a style you must follow. The style of closeness, the style of compassion, and the style of tenderness. This is the style of God—closeness, compassion, tenderness."[3]

---

[3] Pope Francis, Homily for Holy Mass with Presbyteral Ordinations, April 25, 2021, http://www.vatican.va.

What I am hoping for in a future priest, then, is that he is collegial, co-responsible, collaborative, cooperative, and community oriented. I was privileged to be on the subcommittee that authored *Co-Workers in the Vineyard of the Lord*, the document on lay ecclesial ministry that the United States Conference of Catholic Bishops published in 2005. I clearly remember an early consensus of the members that we could not talk about ordained ministry without talking about the laity and vice versa. This interconnection between these two is critical. The priest never stands alone; his relationship with the people is at the core of his ministry, and it defines who he is and what he does, grounding him in love. And this relationship finds its summit at the eucharistic table. The subsequent hopes that I describe briefly now are caught up in this relational aspect of priestly ministry.

The Priest as a Bearer of Mystery

> He is the reflection of God's glory and the exact imprint of God's very being, and he sustains all things by his powerful word. (Heb 1:3)

One of the fruits of a priest's relationship with God and with the people of God is the ability to be a bearer of mystery. At one with Christ, the High Priest, and at one with his people, the priest is uniquely situated, through Holy Orders, to be a nexus of God's mysterious presence in our midst. Karl Rahner explains, "[The priest] is the steward of the mysteries of God. When he speaks this word the personality of the priest sinks farthest into the background and the Christian experiences the directest contact with God. Then, in a sense, only Christ's word rings out through the priest, because there is simply nothing else that he can say but Christ's word."[4] What I hope for in a priest, then, is that he will have this abiding sense of bringing God's presence into every aspect of his life and ministry. Just as Jesus reveals the Father (see John 14:9), so does the priest reveal Christ in every aspect of his being. As the priest and his people interact with each other, Christ's presence will be discerned. Sometimes this happens explicitly, as when a priest is attending a dying parishioner along with that person's loved ones. At other times, it will be more implicit, a subtle recognition that Christ is present in the warmth of a smile or the comfort of a gentle touch.

---

[4] Karl Rahner, *Servants of the Lord* (New York: Herder & Herder, 1968), 76–77.

In other words, the priest is called to bring hope where all else seems lost. He is a constant reminder that to be a Christian means to believe that dead things can come back to life. To use the imagery of George Herbert in his poem "Windows," the priest is a fragile human being, but he can lift his people's spirits to see the possibilities that only the Divine can offer:

> *Lord, how can man preach thy eternall word?*
> *He is a brittle crazie glasse:*
> *Yet in thy temple thou dost him afford*
> *This glorious and transcendent place,*
> *To be a window, through thy grace.*

The priest acts as this beacon of hope through his preaching, as suggested in Herbert's poem, through his sacramental ministry, his teaching, his administration, and his relationships. Since the priest is often allowed into the inner recesses of the human heart, there is always the temptation for him to yield to cynicism, negativism, or skepticism. Thus, I am eager to see if a candidate for the priesthood has an innate ability, grounded in faith, to see new opportunities, new vistas, and new reasons to hope. In the face of so much polarization in the church and in the world, given the huge challenges faced by so many and the countless calamities that beset the human race, we need such priests to bring us good news.

Theologian Trystan Owain Hughes, in an online post, speaks eloquently of the priest as a bearer of mystery:

The overriding call of priesthood is to explore and grasp the mystery and then initiate others into it—opening eyes to God's presence, ears to God's call, hearts to God's love, and ways to God's will. It is in this context that Teilhard de Chardin described the priest as a "border walker," bringing those on earth closer to the kingdom. They stand at the boundaries between the commonplace and the sacred, thus offering the possibility of relationship with the divine. Priests are, therefore, interpreters of Manley Hopkins's "grandeur of God," von Balthasar's "patterns of grace," and Philip Yancey's "rumours of another world." They hold, to use William Blake's phrase, "infinity in the palm of their hand and eternity in an hour" and offer this to those to whom they are ministering.[5]

---

    [5] Trystan Owain Hughes, "What Is a Priest? The Priest as a Bearer of Mystery," Ministry Blog Series 1, April 12, 2021, https://trystanowainhughes.wordpress.com.

The Priest as One Who Knows Weakness

> For we do not have a high priest who is unable to sympathize with our weaknesses, but we have one who in every respect has been tested as we are, yet without sin. (Heb 4:15)

> He is able to deal gently with the ignorant and wayward, since he himself is subject to weakness. (Heb 5:2)

Each year I have the good fortune to participate in the evaluation of our seminarians. I am impressed with the high standards to which they are held in the areas of human, spiritual, intellectual, and pastoral development. Certainly, I hope that a priest will excel in these important aspects of his life and ministry. However, I was recently reminded of an article by Father Michael J. Buckley titled "Because Beset by Weakness." In it, he articulates another hope of mine for the priesthood, namely, that the priest be a man at peace with his weaknesses. Father Buckley writes,

> Is this man weak enough to be a priest? Is this man deficient enough so that he cannot ward off significant suffering from his life, so that he lives with a certain amount of failure, so that he feels what it is to be an average man? Is there any history of confusion, of self-doubt, of interior anguish? Has he had to deal with fear, come to terms with frustrations, or accept deflated expectations? These are critical questions and they probe for weakness. Why? Because, according to Hebrews, it is in this deficiency, in this interior lack, in this weakness, that the efficacy of the ministry and priesthood of Christ lies.[6]

Through a priest's weaknesses he is able to relate to God and others. This openness to one's weaknesses, this humble recognition of limitations, enables God's grace to shine through the priest and enables the people of God to find the priest approachable, real, and believable. It seems to me that this candid acceptance of our human condition is the best antidote to clericalism. An authentically humble priest will not expect favors but rather give them.

When the priest finds it impossible to admit imperfections or faults, then to some extent he loses the ability to relate to God's mercy and

---

[6] Michael J. Buckley, "Because Beset with Weakness . . . ," in *To Be a Priest: Perspectives on Vocation and Ordination*, ed. Robert E. Terwilliger and Urban T. Holmes (New York: Seabury Press, 1975), 125.

compassionate love. Moreover, he renders himself inaccessible to others who will tend to steer away from a priest too filled with his own accomplishments and ego. In his article, Father Buckley points out that it was only when St. Peter began to sink that he called to Jesus for help: "Weakness becomes the vocation of the Lord, our call upon him."[7] It is the priest's "weakness" and vulnerability that make him approachable to his parishioners.

The Priest as a Lifelong Learner

> It was fitting that God, for whom and through whom all things exist, in bringing many children to glory, should make the pioneer of their salvation perfect through sufferings. (Heb 2:10)

In the Gospel of Mark, Jesus performs a very interesting miracle as he cures an unnamed blind man (see 8:22–26). I find it interesting, because it is a gradual miracle. Jesus laid hands on the blind man a second time before he saw clearly. What also makes it interesting is that this miracle introduces the section in Mark's Gospel that deals with discipleship. These two facts lead to the conclusion that discipleship is a gradual, ongoing process in which the Lord Jesus continually lays hands on us, empowering us to reflect his presence clearly in our world. Certainly, this is true of the priest.

As related in the Letter to the Hebrews, Jesus himself, our High Priest, was "perfected through suffering" (Heb 2:10b). This points to a process in Jesus as he "was perfected" through suffering in his carrying out of the Father's will in his life on earth. The priest is called to follow the Master. In this vein, I am looking to see if a candidate for the priesthood is open to growth, learning, and ongoing formation. The Reverend Bernard Bonnot, a retired priest of the Diocese of Youngstown, Ohio, and a founding member of the Association of United States Catholic Priests, recently told me that a priest must be "mature, supple, agile, and flexible. He will be constantly striving to learn and to grow with the church in this era of rapid and endless change, while remaining always deeply grounded in Christ." The church is well served by priests who fit this description.

The Second Vatican Council underscores the importance of ongoing formation by calling the church to read the "signs of the times." Grounded

---

[7] Buckley, "Because Beset with Weakness . . . ," 129.

in scripture (Matt 16:3 and Luke 12:56), this phrase was used by Pope John XXIII when he convoked the council. It captures my hope for the priesthood in that priests are to be good listeners who discern the trajectory of their ministry with the help of the Holy Spirit. This in no way minimizes the priest's role to teach the faith since, as Pope Francis reminds us, in order to teach one must first listen. A priest friend of mine likes to say that the priest must have both a good "receiver" and "transmitter"!

In this light, *Gaudium et Spes* gives insight into the important role that listening and ongoing formation play in the life of the priest. The "joys and hopes, the griefs and the anxieties" (*GS*, 1) of the congregation are those of the priest as he listens to his people with a compassionate heart. It is particularly important that the priest listens attentively to women and lay leaders in the church, as well as to those who represent the diverse cultures that make up the Body of Christ. When a priest listens to his people in this manner, he will find the people relating to him in a way that affirms his ordination and contributes significantly to his ongoing formation. He will glimpse the human face of Christ.

In conclusion, then, my hopes for the priesthood shape my discernment process with those who are answering Christ's call to serve the church in Holy Orders. I pray that candidates for the priesthood will be deeply committed to right relationships in which they are attuned to the mystery of Christ's presence in the midst of the believing community and in the world. My hope is that they will be at peace with their limitations, trusting that Jesus, our High Priest, will shine brightly through their weaknesses. I hope that priests now and into the future will be attentive listeners to the promptings of the Holy Spirit at work in God's holy people. In short, I hope that priests will never cease to give thanks to Jesus Christ, our High Priest, who is constantly at work in them. As priests stand at the altar, praying with and for their people, I hope they will be strengthened to make their lives a continual proclamation of the Word that abides in their hearts.

In the end, it is all about relationships. Cardinal Vanhoye, in his book *Christ Our High Priest*, puts it well: "Union with the heart of Jesus . . . would appear to be the essential thing for the exercise of the ministerial priesthood. We must ask the Lord to give us this intense union with him in filial love for the Father and in fraternal love for all those entrusted to our ministry."[8] Priesthood changes the person.

---

[8] Cardinal Albert Vanhoye, SJ, *Christ Our High Priest*, trans. Joel Wallace (Leominster, UK: Gracewing, 2013), 161.

Questions for Reflection

1. How has your own understanding of priesthood evolved through the years?
2. What gifts would you hope to find in an aspiring priest?
3. Are you surprised by the requirement that the priest be one "who knows weakness"? How might this enhance priestly ministry?

17

THE ONCE AND FUTURE PRIESTHOOD

Phillip J. Brown, PSS

Participation in "To Serve the People of God: Renewing the Conversation on Priesthood and Ministry" at Boston College in January 2020 was an extremely enriching experience. The commitment to the ministry of the church of those who attended and their respect for the priesthood was evident. It is an honor to contribute this chapter to encourage continuing the conversation. Contributors have been asked to reflect on their "best hopes for the future of the priesthood" from their ecclesial context, expertise, and experience. Mine is as a rector of two different seminaries over the past ten years, parish priest, Catholic high school chaplain and board member, head of a clergy personnel board, assistant vocation director, canon law professor, canonical advocate (including many clergy misconduct cases), and past president of the Canon Law Society of America.

I belong to the Society of Saint Sulpice, devoted principally to the formation of parish priests since 1641, and founders of the United States' first seminary, St. Mary's Seminary and University in Baltimore, at the behest of Bishop John Carroll in 1791. My best hopes for the future of the priesthood emerge from thirty-two years as a priest in those various roles, twenty devoted to seminary formation ministry and administration.

Priesthood Today

In its 1965 "Decree on the Ministry and Life of Priests," *Presbyterorum Ordinis (PO)*, the Second Vatican Council noted the vastly changed pastoral and human circumstances affecting priestly ministry at the time. Circumstances have continued to change at an accelerating pace ever since. "To

Serve the People of God" and this volume continue the church's ongoing reflection on the priesthood initiated by the 1965 decree.

Many good things have happened in priestly formation and ministry since 1965. Much of the good has been overshadowed by ecclesial controversies and the clergy sexual abuse scandals during the same period. There is insufficient awareness, I believe, of the many *good* things that have happened—good things that make me hopeful. They provide a solid platform for moving forward and realizing our best hopes for the priesthood.

I see the future of the priesthood every day in our seminarians. They give me great hope. I anticipate a priesthood lived quite differently from what we have been accustomed to in the past. It is an exciting time to be involved in priestly formation and ministry. It is a time when creative, innovative ideas and practices are emerging. I am convinced that these ideas and practices will result in a renewed and more effective priestly ministry, and other kinds of ministry, in the church.

Context: Sacred Scripture and Church Teaching

Presbytorum Ordinis and subsequent reflections on the priesthood and priestly formation, especially the Post-Synodal Apostolic Exhortation *Pastores Dabo Vobis* (1992) of St. John Paul II, provide a context for reflections on the future of the priesthood. *PO* notes that the priesthood is an order established to serve Christ as teacher, priest, and king; it has a share in the ministry of the church for building it up as the people of God, Christ's Body and temple of the Spirit.

Priests receive the sacred power of order, of offering sacrifice and forgiving sins, and of exercising the priestly office publicly in the name of Christ. The ministry of bishops is given to priests in a subordinate degree as coworkers in their order with the episcopal order. The office of priest, because it is joined with the episcopal order, shares in the authority by which Christ himself builds up, sanctifies, and governs his Body. Priesthood is conferred by a particular sacrament through which, by the anointing of the Holy Spirit, priests are signed with a special character and configured to Christ, such that they are able to act in the person of Christ the Head.

The remote origins of Christian priesthood, while rooted in the ministry of Jesus, underwent a complex development over an extended period of time. We know disciples began to follow Jesus and that Jesus chose disciples. He chose others as apostles to follow him and spread the gospel, sending them out two by two (see Luke 6:12–16; Mark 3:13–19, 6:7), later sending seventy-two others out similarly (see Luke 10:1). We know from Acts that the Christian community in Jerusalem adopted a collegial form of governance modeled after the system of elders (presbyters) in the Jewish community (see Acts 11:30, 15:22). In Antioch, there were prophets and teachers: Barnabas, Simeon called Niger, Lucius of Cyrene, Mane'en, and Saul. "While worshiping the Lord and fasting the Holy Spirit said, 'Set apart for me Barnabas and Saul for the work which I have called them.' Then after fasting and praying they laid hands on them and sent them off" (Acts 13:1–3). And we know that Paul and Barnabus appointed presbyters for all the churches (see Acts 14:23). Use of the title "bishop" (*episcopos*) was not always clearly distinct from "presbyter" in the early church (see Acts 20:17; Titus 1:5–7; and 1 Peter 5:1) and is not clearly differentiated until the writings of Ignatius of Antioch (d. 110).

For the Catholic Church, the priesthood has as much to do with its function as its clear establishment—the offering of sacrifice, with the Eucharist understood as representing Christ's sacrifice on the cross and the Last Supper. Protestant scholars deny a clear distinction between priesthood and laity in the early church, tending to see priesthood as a historical development. No one can deny, however, that the Catholic Church has always asserted the ministerial priesthood and the clerical state as a distinct order set apart for particular functions not available to the laity.

Often, the accent has been placed on sacred power, the sacramental nature of the ministerial priesthood, and the authority of priests—that is, on power and authority. But that is not where *PO* begins. It emphasizes that the Lord Jesus makes his whole Mystical Body share in the anointing of the Spirit with which he was anointed. *All the faithful* are made a holy and kingly priesthood, to offer spiritual sacrifices to God through Jesus Christ and proclaim his virtues. There is no such thing as a member of the church who does not share in the mission of the whole Body, the priesthood of all believers. The ministerial priesthood exists to carry out particular ministries for the Body in which all members do not have the same functions:

> For by the grace given to me I tell everyone among you not to think
> of himself more highly than one ought to think, but to think soberly,
> each according to the measure of faith that God has apportioned. For

as in one body we have many parts, and all the parts do not have the same function, so we, though many, are one body in Christ and individually parts of one another. (Rom 12:3–5)

Paul and *PO* conceive of the church as a single integrated Body, made up of many members with different functions, each with its own appropriate and proper role. The ministerial priesthood should never be thought of independently of the Mystical Body of Christ, the priesthood of all believers, the priest serving in the Body, "not thinking of himself more highly than one ought to" but soberly, each member according to the measure of faith God has apportioned.

Self-Understanding and Role

How should ordained priests think of themselves and their role? In two ways, I suggest, one taken from the spiritual tradition of the Society of Saint Sulpice, the other from the teachings of the Second Vatican Council regarding priesthood. My best hope for the future is that renewal will come through careful reflection on the role of the ministerial priesthood as presented in the teaching of the church, especially *PO* and the reflection on it that has followed.

First, from the Sulpician tradition I understand the priest as *animating presence*—not so much one who "governs" or directs the flock, or who dispenses sacraments, as one who animates the Body of Christ in the concrete expression of the Body he serves. Living to serve, not to be served; bringing life to the community of faith, so that, through the community as a whole, the Body of Christ, the ministry of the church will be available to all. More than an organizer or one who "governs," one who calls forth the gifts of others and motivates them to share their gifts generously for the building up of the Body. A recognized leader who encourages, affirms, and empowers the other members of the Body, not reserving all leadership to himself but permitting others to share in leadership. Certainly, one who leads in organizing the efforts of the community, but only as needed. A "captain of the ship," as it were, able to turn the wheel over to other capable hands, intervening only when necessary and according to his proper role. A priest must exercise his sacramental role; the sacraments are at the heart of what animates the community and its members. But it is not the priest's spirit, power, or authority that animates: it is the Holy Spirit, of which he is a conduit through the power of Order and his sacramental role.

Second, from the teaching of the church, priests should think of themselves as *engaged participants*. As much as a priest is an animating presence, his role is not passive. To be effective, he must be engaged and engaging. Following on Paul's observation that the Body has many parts, a priest should serve his function as one of many parts. My best hope for the future of priesthood is that priests will take to heart Jesus's admonition, "You know that the rulers of the Gentiles lord it over them, and the great ones make their authority over them felt. But it shall not be so among you. Rather, whoever wishes to be great among you shall be your servant; whoever wishes to be first among you shall be your slave" (Matt 20:25–28).

You don't have to be a priest long to realize that priests attract attention—both positive and negative—and easily become the center of attention. My hope for the future is that priests will avoid being the center of attention so that they can more effectively be an animating presence and engaged participant. When asked if he was the Messiah, John the Baptist replied, "You yourselves can testify that I said I am not the Messiah, but that I was sent before him. . . . He must increase; I must decrease" (John 3:28–30).

The key to a renewed priesthood is that priests become like John the Baptist, muting the desire for their presence to be felt; to decrease so that Christ may increase; to be not a felt presence but an *animating presence*, an engaged participant; patient and sympathetic; an encouraging and empowering guide to living the gospel life in the fullness of the Catholic faith, and living it themselves; the Christ-self all Christians are called to be, as C. S. Lewis expresses it in *Mere Christianity*; guided by St. Paul: "Do nothing out of selfishness or out of vainglory; rather, humbly regard others as more important than yourselves" (Phil 2:3).

Concrete Recommendations

Here are a few suggestions for shaping a clerical culture of animating presence and engaged participation that if incorporated in priestly formation and life will, I believe, help cultivate humility and competence, even excellence in priestly ministry, to overcome negative images propagated in recent years, and assure that the people of God will have the kind of priests they truly deserve.

Recruitment and Admissions

First, there is a need for deep reflection on and reform of the way seminarians are currently recruited. Many positive things have happened
in this regard in the past sixty years. In particular, the widespread use of
sound psychological assessment has been an important advance, as has the
application of uniform mandatory assessment standards prior to admission required by some seminaries, but which are not mandated by church
authority and are not uniform throughout the seminary system. There are
recommended uniform standards today (Rev. Melvin Blanchette, PSS, has
been a pioneer in developing such standards, admirably followed by Rev.
Steven Rosetti and Rev. David Songy, OFM Cap, at St. Luke's Institute, and
Dr. David Schellenberger at St. John Vianney Center), but no mandated
standards. The quality of preadmission psychological assessments is, therefore, inconsistent. And of course, the most reliable assessment is worthless
if its implications or recommendations are disregarded.

Assessments and decisions should happen at the diocesan level. Sometimes dioceses leave it to the seminary to make decisions about assessments
during or after admission. Doing so sets in motion dynamics that can work
against the best decision. Pressures and incentives external to the seminary
itself to keep a man in formation once he has been admitted are great, for
both seminary and diocese. But it must be recognized that the margins
for remediating significant psychological or emotional deficits are narrow,
and get narrower as the candidate becomes older. Seminaries and vocations offices must work in concert with one another in their willingness to
be realistic about the possibility of remediation in making admissions and
retention decisions. Close collaboration between seminaries and vocations
offices regarding this must begin with the admissions process.

Reform is needed to shift the dynamics of recruitment and admissions
away from quantity toward the quality of candidates. A wide-net strategy
has proven unhelpful, leading to an unacceptable number of priests with
significant issues of maturity and the other elements of sound human
development and formation. I am convinced that paying close attention
to a candidate's maturity, emotional stability, and psychological health,
and being willing to exclude those not demonstrating strong prospects
for successful formation—notwithstanding the current declining number
of ordained clergy and a dearth of seminarians—will, over time, result in
a greater number of well-qualified and suitable candidates for the priest-

hood. It may take an act of faith, but one, I believe, that will be richly rewarded in due course.

Second, there is a need to go beyond the current general psychological assessments in use, while not discarding them, and creating an assessment tool similar to those used in marriage preparation—the FOCCUS instrument, for example. These tools could measure relational skills, compatibility for ministry, and preparedness for entering a highly relational, committed life like marriage or the priesthood. This will require convening experts from the psychological, sociological, and seminary worlds to develop an appropriate instrument. Doing so would be a worthwhile enterprise for the church in support of the future of the priesthood.

Third, all applicants should be required to take the Graduate Record Exam, or a similar examination developed for seminary admissions. This would assure that candidates have the intellectual skills and aptitude to succeed in a seminary academic program and acquire the necessary skills and knowledge to be effective preachers, teachers of the faith, and pastors.

Seminary Formation

St. Mary's Seminary and University, through a generous grant from the Raskob Foundation, has established a full-time position of director of human formation, for monitoring the overall formation program on an ongoing basis to assess the extent to which it supports sound human formation. Formation programs easily get out of balance, emphasizing one of the four dimensions—human, spiritual, intellectual, and pastoral—at the expense of others. The director is responsible for continually monitoring the overall program and advising faculty and administrators on how well it is serving the human formation of candidates. The person is also responsible for developing and administering human formation programs and identifying and administering resources to serve human formation as needed. More is needed than just a "coordinator" of human formation. A dedicated full-time position is required so that holistic human formation can be an integral part of the entire seminary program.

Ongoing Education and Formation

A final recommendation is that ongoing education and formation of priests be made mandatory. Most professions today have mandatory ongoing education requirements. Considering the level of responsibility priests have, and the role they play in people's lives, this absence is a travesty. Virtually all lawyers must complete a prescribed number of hours of continuing ethics education each year. Physicians who do not remain current in their respective fields are not allowed to practice medicine. The same is expected of accountants. Every responsible profession that wishes to be taken seriously requires annual credits of ongoing education. How that would be implemented for priests would have to be worked out, but it should be required and enforced. Priests should be suspended or otherwise restricted in their ability to exercise ministry if they do not regularly renew their knowledge and skills for exercising priestly ministry, remain current with the general culture of what is expected of ordained ministers, and indeed, expand their pastoral skill sets, theological knowledge and formation, pastoral sensitivity, and ethical knowledge and formation regarding appropriate behavior and practices. The time is long past for there to be any more discussion or debate over whether priests should be required to do ongoing education and formation annually. They should.

Conclusion

These reflections are the fruit of thirty-two years of priesthood, pastoral ministry, and seminary formation ministry and administration. The recommendations in this chapter represent my hopes for what will be integrated into the life and ministry of a renewed priesthood. I hope priests will increasingly see and experience themselves as an animating presence and as engaged participants in the life of the church, the Body of Christ. I am hopeful because I know too many good priests and too many outstanding seminarians not to be, and too many Catholics and others who desire that there be priests, who respect them, and who know and appreciate how priestly ministry, when exercised well, adds to their lives, the life of the church, the larger communities in which they live, and the world.

I believe the church and Catholics want a renewed priesthood and the kind of priests they truly deserve. I foresee this as possible, and I hope for it: a priesthood in which priests know their role and do not exceed it; have self-confidence and self-respect; and are spiritual men and competent pastors, who will be engaged participants and an animating presence in the lives of their parishioners and the life of the church.

Questions for Reflection

1. In what ways might seminary formation programs cultivate future priests who wear their authority lightly and serve as an animating presence that gives guidance gently, calling forth and empowering the giftedness of members of the communities they serve?

2. Assuming the development of an assessment instrument for seminary admissions—like the FOCCUS marriage prep instrument—what aptitude qualities should such an instrument reveal for effective pastoral ministry?

3. In what ways should future priests be willing to turn over the wheel of the ship to other capable leaders in the communities they serve, while not relinquishing their proper role as pastors as envisioned by the church in its documents on the priesthood?

4. In what ways can the church establish an effective system of mandatory ongoing education and formation for priests? How can such a system create in priests a positive desire for ongoing education and formation and cause them to value and embrace it willingly and enthusiastically?

18

THE CATECHESIS OF PRIESTHOOD

Thomas H. Groome

A lifetime ago, in an old Irish seminary, I decided to become a catechist, a decision that has endured. This choice was to embrace as my own the particular vocation of "echoing onward" (*kate khein*) the faith handed down. Long ago, however, I recall that my discernment was prompted by the memorable statement in *Gaudium et Spes*, Vatican II's "Pastoral Constitution on the Church in the Modern World" (then hot off the press, 1965): "The split between the faith which many [Christians] profess and their daily lives deserves to be counted among the more serious errors of our age" (*GS*, 43). The paragraph goes on to urge Christians to put their faith to work in daily life, rather than as if it is fulfilled by "acts of worship alone" and separated from "earthly affairs."

This text lent me three convictions that have since shaped the horizon of my ministry: (1) the primary task of catechesis is to teach for a *living* faith; (2) we must ever be alert and consciously guard against teaching "error"; and (3) everything about the life of the church in the world "educates." For good or ill, how we participate in "earthly affairs" is effective (or defective) catechesis.

My concern in this chapter is our present catechesis of the priesthood. In particular, and honoring the alert from *Gaudium et Spes*, how are we to teach the priesthood's enduring truths and avoid teaching error, either intentionally or by implication? As with all education, catechesis in faith always has both an explicit and implicit curriculum—the latter being what we teach by present church practices of priesthood. I focus primarily on the explicit curriculum but will offer a brief word on the implicit as well. We must attend to both if we are to educate for *living* faith.

The church urges that catechesis begin with very young children.[1] The domestic catechesis of the home from infancy is then to be supported by a crafted parish or school curriculum. Typically, by first or second grade, children are prepared for First Holy Communion and sometimes the sacrament of Reconciliation; through both, they encounter and are catechized in the ministry of priests.

Catechesis, then, must represent an understanding of priesthood that will endure as true, perhaps seventy or eighty years from now, throughout the life span of our first-graders. A constant counsel I offer my students is never to teach any aspect of our Catholic faith so that a later catechist or teacher will need to correct or deny what was first taught—for example, don't teach Genesis 1 and the seven days of creation, even in the early grades, as if literally true. Thus, we must not teach what is essential to priesthood now in ways that catechists coming after us might have to correct or have people unlearn; this could hazard their *living* faith.

Let me give an example of misguided catechesis that had very negative consequences for the *living* faith of the church, encouraging what Pope Francis refers to often as "the curse of clericalism." Undoubtedly, clericalism has many causes, but it was particularly encouraged by the exaggerated portrayal of priesthood that emerged from the Council of Trent (1545–1563). Now the historical context makes this somewhat understandable: the Reformers had championed the "priesthood of all believers," and often over against the ordained priesthood; in consequence, Trent, and particularly through its *Catechism*, also known as the *Roman Catechism*, went over the top in heralding ordained priesthood.

Note, parenthetically, that Trent's *Catechism* was the most influential resource in promulgating the council's decrees, which were not even translated into English until 1848. The *Catechism* was first published in Latin and Italian in 1566, and the council had ordered that it be translated immediately into other languages. Thereafter, it was used widely as a basic text in seminaries, then emerging as mandated by Trent. And it was widely used as the primary text for Sunday sermons in many Catholic cultures, being reviewed repeatedly in a three-year cycle.

Within the *Catechism*'s presentation of Holy Orders, and with outlandish proof-texting, we read as follows: "Priests and bishops . . . act in

---

[1] *Directory for Catechesis* (United States Conference of Catholic Bishops, 2020), 124–26.

this world as the very person of God. It is evident that no office greater than theirs can be imagined. Rightly have they been called angels (Mic 2:7), even gods (Exod 22:28), holding as they do among us the very name and power of the living God."[2]

It uses the lower case for "gods" here, and we might even find this humorous today, if such exaggeration had not encouraged a pedestalized clericalism that has had very negative consequences for the church. The memory of such misguided catechesis encourages us, first, to imagine what *not* to teach of priesthood; and second, to craft a catechesis that reflects the best of priesthood's past and present theology for our time.

What Not to Teach

So what should the church *not* teach about priesthood to avoid our catechesis needing correction over the next seventy or eighty years? I choose the two most notable issues to avoid to represent what might later need to be untaught: the current requirement of *celibacy* and that of *maleness* for all three holy orders. Let us begin with the easier case of celibacy.

• *Don't teach celibacy as necessarily required for priesthood.* Clearly, that priests be celibate is a pastoral practice of the church rather than a matter of doctrine; neither scripture nor tradition require it as a precondition. It is a chosen practice of the Western church, and often for poor reasons, including some negativity toward human sexuality and concern for the inheritance of church property by the children of priests. It has been an established requirement for priesthood in the Catholic communion since the Second Lateran Council of 1139, with varied practice before then, but was never required by the Orthodox churches, nor in the Eastern Catholic churches affiliated with Rome. Indeed, the more recent admission into Catholic priesthood of married clergy from churches not in full communion with Rome makes clear that the church allows exceptions to its celibacy requirement.

Surely, the church will always cherish the vowed religious life of poverty, chastity, and obedience as an inspiring vocational choice for those gifted with the needed charism. Likewise, the choice to live a celibate life should always be welcomed and supported for diocesan priests who personally discern such a generous calling. However, as the church moves forward, our

---

[2] *The Roman Catechism*, trans. Robert Bradley and Eugene Kevane (Boston: Daughters of St. Paul, 1985), 308.

catechesis should not present celibacy as a necessary precondition for diocesan priests.

Indeed, Pope Francis's clear encouragement of conversation around the ordination of *viri probati* (mature and credible men) signals that celibacy as a requirement for Catholic priesthood is not beyond discussion. Perhaps the wisest way for the church to proceed in discerning this issue is through what Pope Francis encourages as a synodal path. Among other things, synodality suggests that "each country or region can seek solutions better suited to its culture and sensitive to its traditions and local needs" (*Amoris Laetitia*, 3). It seems that the German and Australian bishops and their churches are actively engaged in such a synodal process. They are responding to Pope Francis's rhetorical question in *Querida Amazonia*: "How can we not consider an inculturation of the ways we structure and carry out ecclesial ministries?" (*QA*, 85).

Following on, that *viri probati* may be admitted to priesthood should at least prompt conversation if the church might make it possible for priests who set out on a celibate path to change their decision as their spiritual journey unfolds. The church has lost countless thousands of good priests by insisting otherwise.

Furthermore, if mandatory celibacy for diocesan priests continues, at least in some cultures, there needs to be a reeducating of public opinion about its witness value. For example, in Western cultures, it would seem to be a deterrent for many from entering priesthood as reflected in the significant drop in numbers; for example, between 1967 and 2017 the number of priests in the United States dropped by some twenty-five thousand—many who left would have stayed if permitted to marry—and predictions for the decline ahead are even more stark. Additionally, rightly or wrongly, celibacy is often perceived as contributing to the clergy sexual abuse scandal, greatly diminishing the "sign" value that it once enjoyed. To conclude, then, our catechesis should never present celibacy as essential to diocesan priesthood, albeit continuing for now as an ecclesial requirement in Western Catholicism.

• *Don't teach maleness as necessarily required for priesthood.* In imagining a catechesis that will still ring true some eighty years from now, likely the most challenging issue concerns the admission of women to priesthood and, indeed, to all three holy orders—deacon, priest, and bishop (traditionally understood as a sacramental threesome). First, we must briefly address whether this is a "closed" issue—beyond dispute or change.

The first post–Vatican II statement in this regard was *Inter Insigniores: A Declaration of the Sacred Congregation for the Doctrine of the Faith on the Question of the Admission of Women to the Ministerial Priesthood* (1976). In brief, it offered a threefold rationale for its stance: (1) there were no women among "the Twelve"; (2) it would be contrary to long tradition; and (3) only men can be "icons" of Jesus Christ. This rationale, however, was roundly refuted immediately by such magisterial scholars as Karl Rahner,[3] Sandra Schneiders,[4] and many mainstream Catholic theologians thereafter. *Inter Insigniores* did not stem the debate.

Then, in 1994, Pope John Paul II issued *Ordinatio Sacerdotalis* (1994), which declared that "the church has no authority whatsoever to confer priestly ordination on women and that this judgment is to be definitively held by all the church's faithful" (*OS*, 4). Given this magisterial statement, the crucial question for a faithful catechist like myself is whether it must be considered an infallible and irreformable teaching of revealed truth.

My systematic theologian friends declare a resounding "no"—that *Ordinatio Sacerdotalis* does not fulfill the necessary conditions to be a universal infallible statement. Even when issued, then-cardinal Ratzinger recognized that it reflected "the ordinary magisterium of the Supreme Pontiff" rather than the ordinary universal magisterium of the world's bishops, and as a result was "not a solemn definition *ex cathedra*." And, as the Code of Canon Law declares, "No doctrine is understood to be infallible unless it is clearly established as such" (Canon 749.3).[5]

In other words, it is at least imaginable, and likely, that women will eventually be admitted to all three holy orders, and it may not take eighty years. For the present, however, and as noted in "To Serve the People of God" (TSPG), "the *consensus fidelium*, the 'breathing together' of the whole church, does not yet exist in relation to these possibilities."

Meanwhile, there seems to be a growing consensus among Catholic theologians, scripture scholars, and the sense of the faithful that welcoming women to holy orders is past due. (This conviction is often kept private for

---

[3] See Karl Rahner, *Concern for the Church* (New York: Crossroad, 1981), ch. 3.

[4] Sandra M. Schneiders, "Did Jesus Exclude Women from Priesthood?," in *Women Priests: A Catholic Commentary on the Vatican Declaration*, ed. L. and A. Swidler (New York: Paulist Press, 1977).

[5] See also Richard Gaillardetz, "Infallibility and the Ordination of Women," *Louvain Studies* 21 (1996): 3–24.

fear of reprisal; there are certainly many bishops who hold it and as much as 95 percent of the members of the Catholic Theological Society of America.) Might the recent appointment by Pope Francis of another commission to study ordaining women to the diaconate imply such openness? While the diaconate is an ordained ministry in its own right—as evident in the restoration in 1967 of the Permanent Diaconate for men—if women are admitted to one holy order, why not the other two? Meanwhile, in this between-time, what are we to catechize regarding this practice of the Catholic Church, keeping the question open and yet not pretending that women can now be ordained?

Here I sound a personal note. I have been the primary author of two widely used grade-school catechetical curricula, kindergarten to eighth grade: the *God with Us* series, completed in 1984, and the *Coming to Faith* series, completed in 1995 (W. H. Sadlier); and an eleven-book high-school theology curriculum: the *Credo* series, completed in 2018 (Veritas / RCL Benziger). All these catechetical texts (a total of thirty), affirmed by *nihil obstat* and *imprimatur*, present an orthodox Catholic understanding of priesthood, as appropriate to grade level, and yet without specifying that it is necessarily limited to men.

The key to such catechesis is threefold. First, we need to catechize a robust and faithful theology of priesthood without posing maleness as essential to the "sign" of the sacrament. Second, we must be rigorously careful of the language pattern used when referring to priesthood's participants and candidates. Most obviously, never use male-only language regarding priesthood; instead, speak of "person," "people," and "they," instead of "man," "men," or "he." (Note that this careful language pattern appears in TSPG.)

Third, say what needs to be said to represent faithfully a Catholic understanding of the sacrament but without saying what does not need to be said. Having cited the *Catechism of Trent* for saying far too much, let me now surprise, perhaps, by citing the *Baltimore Catechism* of 1885 as it named the requirements for Holy Orders. There we read the question, "What is necessary to receive Holy Orders?" The dated-to-its-time but wonderfully sparse answer was, "To receive Holy Orders worthily it is necessary to be in the state of grace, to have the necessary knowledge, and a divine call to this sacred office."[6] Let such brevity inspire us not to teach what does not need to be taught for a faithful catechesis of priesthood.

---

[6] *A Catechism of Christian Doctrine, Enjoined by the Third Council of Baltimore* (New York: Sadlier and Co., 1885), 48.

Of course, should the issue be raised, perhaps in the upper grades, we must be clear about the church's present requirements. However, to be true for the next eighty years or so, it would surely be wise to add that limiting priesthood to men may change in the years ahead.

A brief word now on what the church teaches by excluding women from priesthood—its implicit curriculum. This very public sign from the church can become a legitimating symbol for the sexism and gender discrimination practiced in the world at large. Regardless of how the church explains its practice, it yet implies that women are not equal to men, even, or especially, in the eyes of God. Such exclusion can be "an effective symbol that causes what it symbolizes," but surely this is not the sacramentality we want to mediate to the world. No matter how loudly the church teaches about the dignity and equality of men and women, the latter's exclusion from priestly ministry makes its teaching ring hollow.

In the meantime, while many wait and work for better days, the church must be aggressive to advance the public leadership roles of women in the church. Pope Francis has made significant efforts in this regard.

What to Teach

So what are we to catechize *now* of priesthood, regardless of what may unfold in the future? Here I echo much of its theology as proposed in TSPG; to so catechize would mark a new day for priesthood, even within its present form.

Whether intended or not, it was Vatican II's reclaiming of a radical theology of baptism (as in *radix*, going to the root) that turned upside down the hierarchical ordering of ministry, moving to situate all within the common priesthood of the baptized. Note that the council did not address ministry in general. In the index of Abbott's edition of *The Documents of Vatican II*, there is no entry for "ministry," and under "minister" it says, "See clergy or priest." Yet by the council's reclaiming of the understanding of baptism reflected in the early Christian communities, it released what theologian Thomas O'Meara well named "an explosion of ministries."[7]

In brief and by Paul's imagery, all the baptized are to function together as the *Body of Christ* in the world; "now you are the body of Christ" (1 Cor

---

[7] Thomas O'Meara, *Theology of Ministry,* 2nd ed. (New York: Paulist Press, 1999), 6.

12:27). Within this "body," there are "different kinds of spiritual gifts," with all given "for some benefit" to the life and mission of the whole community (1 Cor 12:4–7). As the Spirit gives varied gifts "for building up the body of Christ," all have responsibilities to fulfill as gifted so that they "may no longer be infants in their faith" (Eph 4:12, 14). We hear a similar theology in the First Letter of Peter, who assures the baptized, "You are a chosen race, a royal priesthood, a holy nation, God's own people" (2:9).

Among this general ministry of all the baptized, particular functions were to be fulfilled. Scripture scholars count as many as twelve in the early Christian communities: apostle, prophet, evangelist, teacher, pastor/shepherd, miracle worker, healer, administrator, helper, deacon, elder, and overseer. Insofar as these functions were structured, they seem to have worked together more as a collaborative circle than a top-down pyramid. In particular, a consistent pattern of how one came to be a community leader who presided at Eucharist does not emerge until well into the third century.[8] Even up to the end of the fourth century, Cyril of Jerusalem was still addressing the newly baptized as "other Christs"; in time, however, this designation of *alter Christus* became limited to priests.

That early church theology of baptism was taken up by Vatican II, which stated that "the baptized, by regeneration and the anointing of the Holy Spirit, are consecrated into a spiritual house and a holy priesthood" (*LG*, 10). Though claiming a difference "in essence" by way of function, all are to exercise rights and fulfill responsibilities within "the common priesthood of the faithful" (*LG*, 10). Indeed, all the baptized are "made sharers in the priestly, prophetic, and kingly functions of Christ" (*LG*, 31). Within this Body of Christ, "All share a true equality with regard to the dignity and to the activity common to all the faithful for building up the body of Christ" (*LG*, 32).

This inclusive portrayal of ministry has been echoed repeatedly since Vatican II; for example, "By baptism, all share in the priesthood of Christ, in his prophetic and royal mission. . . . Baptism gives a share in the common priesthood of all believers" (*Catechism of the Catholic Church* §1268).

Therefore, priesthood is to be realized in the midst of a priestly people. Like a concentric circle rather than a top-down pyramid, the ordained are "ordered" to the circle's center only for their ministry to ripple out to collaborate with full-time, part-time, and volunteer ecclesial ministers,

---

[8] See Raymond Brown, *Priest and Bishop* (Paramus, NJ: Paulist Press, 1970), 40–41.

and this in service to all the baptized for their *living* faith in the midst of the world.

We must catechize now that the *essential* functions of ordered priesthood, again echoing TSPG, are to be an effective *preacher* of the Word to people's lives, to *preside* prayerfully at liturgy, and to *pastor* in ways that empower the whole faith community, especially in works of compassion and justice for all. Moreover, going forward, we should not catechize *essentialism* regarding maleness or celibacy for priesthood.

Preparation for such ministry must tend to the *human, spiritual, academic,* and *pastoral* development of candidates. It is preferable that this be done in educational contexts that reflect the whole people of God, with both female and male faculty and students.

In discerning a person's call to ordained ministry, again our catechesis should reflect the criteria listed at the end of TSPG:

- The capacity and preparation to preach the Word of God in life-giving ways for all
- The ability to lead parish communities in spiritually enriching prayer and worship
- To be collaborative leaders within the community, encouraging all the gifts to work together in holy order
- To commit to a life of exemplary Christian discipleship
- To lead pastoral outreach in works of compassion and justice

In choosing candidates for priesthood, there should be a real rather than a token consultation of the laity. This requires the laity being catechized in an understanding of priesthood and its requirements as reflected in "To Serve the People of God."

Questions for Reflection

1. What is your own position on the current requirements of celibacy and maleness for priesthood? Why do you hold your opinion?
2. Imagine yourself presenting a catechesis on priesthood. What would you be sure to highlight? To leave out? Why?

19

The Prophetic Ministry to the Word

Susan K. Wood, SCL

The restoration of the Word of God to its rightful place in the lives of Catholics ranks among the most important contributions of the Second Vatican Council. *Dei Verbum*, the Dogmatic Constitution on Divine Revelation, takes its place alongside *Lumen Gentium,* the Dogmatic Constitution on the Church, as one of the two dogmatic constitutions of the council. Its explicit encouragement to all Catholics to be familiar with the Bible sharply departed from the pre–Vatican II fear that Catholics would misinterpret the biblical text if they read it on their own. In contrast, *Dei Verbum* describes the Bible as "food of the soul" and "source of everlasting life" (*DV*, 21) and quotes St. Jerome's statement, "Ignorance of the Scriptures is ignorance of Christ" (*DV*, 25).

For too long, the Liturgy of the Word took a back seat to the Liturgy of the Eucharist for Roman Catholics. For evidence of this inequality, one only has to remember that before Vatican II, one could arrive by the offertory to validly attend mass. The pre–Vatican II liturgy focused on the consecration of the bread and wine into the body and blood of Christ. Vatican II tried to redress this by speaking of the two tables: the table of the Word and the table of the Eucharist, by providing for a revision of the lectionary and emphasizing the importance of preaching on the scriptural texts or the liturgical season. The council taught that all preaching should be ruled and nourished by sacred scripture (*DV*, 21) and that the homily forms part of the liturgy itself (*SC*, 52).

It is no surprise, then, that this renewed emphasis on the Word of God is also embedded in the council's enactment of ministerial identity within the rites of ordination, beginning with the bishop. The person being ordained a bishop not only promises to preach the gospel with constancy and fidelity, but just prior to the prayer of consecration, the principal ordaining bishop places the open book of the Gospels upon the head of the bishop-elect. Two assisting deacons hold the book of the Gospels above his head until the prayer of consecration is completed. While there has historically been a number of interpretations of this gesture, one interpretation coming from John Chrysostom (ca. 349–407) or possibly a Pseudo-Chrysostom, suggests that the gesture is a symbol of the submission of the bishop to the law of God. Another interpretation, from Pseudo-Dionysius, is that the book of the Gospels represents the word of the gospel and the work of proclaiming it that is given to the bishop.[1] Whatever its origins, this gesture mirrors the teaching of *Lumen Gentium* that "among the more important duties of bishops, that of preaching the Gospel has pride of place" (*LG*, 25). This is not a new responsibility but repeats the teaching of the Council of Trent that the preaching of the gospel is the chief duty of the bishops and that they are bound to do so unless lawfully hindered, in which case they are to appoint competent persons to do so.[2]

Priests, as coworkers of bishops, share in this responsibility to preach the gospel. The prayer of consecration reflects this relationship, stating, "May he be faithful in working with the order of bishops, so that the words of the Gospel may reach the ends of the earth." The ordinand promises to exercise the ministry of the word worthily and wisely, preaching the gospel and teaching the Catholic faith. The homily for the ordination of a priest exhorts the ordinand to apply his energies to the duty of teaching in the name of Christ, the chief Teacher, and to share with all humanity the Word of God he has received with joy. It summarizes, "Meditate on the law of God, believe what you read, teach what you believe, and put into practice what you teach" (Homily, paragraphs 5 and 6). Vatican II's Decree on the Ministry and Life of Priests (*Presbyterorum Ordinis*) states that "priests, as co-workers with their bishops, have the primary duty of proclaiming the Gospel of God to all" (*PO*, 4).

Yet the identity of the priest traditionally was centered on his ability to transform bread and wine into the body and blood of Christ and to offer sacrifice. Vatican II expanded and developed both the theology of priest-

---

[1] Paul Bradshaw, *Ordination Rites of the Ancient Churches of East and West* (Collegeville, MN: Liturgical Press, 1990), 40.

[2] Council of Trent, "Decree Concerning Reform," session 5, ch. 2, n. 9; and session 24, canon 4.

hood of the baptized and the ministerial priesthood in terms of the priestly, prophetic, and kingly roles of Christ. The priestly role was associated with worship and liturgical leadership, the prophetic with lives of witness and ministry to the word in preaching and teaching, and the kingly or shepherding function with work for the reign of God and pastoral leadership.

Priestly and Prophetic

Too often, the priestly and prophetic roles of the priest remain unrelated to one another. However, a study of the structure of the Liturgy of the Word and the Liturgy of the Eucharist, and the role that the ordained minister fulfills in both, reveals a profound parallelism in these two hinges of the eucharistic liturgy and show how all three roles of the priest are interrelated.

This becomes clear when we refer to Louis Marie-Chauvet's analysis of the Liturgy of the Word.[3] The texts proclaimed in the liturgy belong to a canon accepted by the community, thereby indicating an authority of the texts acknowledged by the community. The scriptures have been officially received in the church. The ongoing reception of this canon occurs as the assembly recognizes the scriptural text as an exemplar of its identity. In other words, the proclaimed texts become the autobiography of the faith community. The reading of the texts gives the community its identity since the texts proclaim a past experience of the people of God as the living Word of God for the community today. The ordained minister guarantees both the apostolicity of what is read and assures that these texts function as an exemplar of the community's identity.[4] In addition to proclaiming the text in his role as leader of the community, he is also himself a member of the assembly, who stands within the assembly and testifies that this text reflects the present life and faith of the community. The ordained minister is both the believing one who preaches and the proclaiming one who believes.

The official proclamation of the gospel in liturgical prayer belongs to an ordained minister, because it is not just a matter of reading a text from a book, a function that any literate person can perform, but an act of official witnessing on behalf of the community and in the name of the apostolic tradition. Thus, even though a lector who reads from the Old Testament,

---

[3] Louis-Marie Chauvet, *Symbol and Sacrament* (Collegeville, MN: Liturgical Press, 1995), 190–227.

[4] Chauvet, *Symbol and Sacrament*, 210.

the Letters, or the Acts of the Apostles may be an installed minister or lay person, the Gospel is always read by an ordained minister—a bishop, presbyter, or deacon.

To summarize, there are four constitutive elements of the Liturgy of the Word: (1) texts of past events accepted as authoritative, (2) texts proclaimed as living today, (3) their reception by a community recognizing its own identity in them, and (4) ordained ministry that guarantees their apostolicity and exemplarity.[5]

The biblical narrative is no longer a story of past events but becomes the interpretive lens through which the community interprets its present life. As a proclamatory speech-act, the word itself assumes a sacramental dimension insofar as it makes present under word-symbol the event it proclaims in the life of the community. The narrative is no longer literature, but the very life of the community. The salvation event proclaimed in the scriptures is accomplished in the life of the assembly. Yet the assembly is a pilgrim people still on the way to their final goal, not having arrived at the end of their journey. The prophetic role of the presbyter calls the community into its future in addition to linking it to its apostolic roots. This is facilitated by an over-against nature of the ordained to the community he serves. He is not simply a representative of the community who can only repeat back to the community its own prejudices and biases but challenges it, bringing something new.

A similar pattern occurs in the Eucharistic Prayer. The link between the Liturgy of the Word and the Liturgy of the Eucharist is that both proclaim and sacramentally represent God's plan of salvation as it was enacted in the past, becomes a living event in the present, and looks forward to completion in the future. The Preface to the Eucharistic Prayer commemorates the events of salvation history. The Eucharistic Prayer itself recalls the actions of Jesus on the night before he died. In a first epiclesis invoking the Holy Spirit over the gifts, the priest prays that these gifts be transformed into the body and blood of the risen Christ present now within the assembly. In a second epiclesis invoking the Holy Spirit over the assembly, he prays that they, too, be transformed into the body of Christ. The Eucharistic Prayer anticipates a future when all will be gathered in Christ. In the memorial acclamation, it

---

[5] Susan K. Wood, "Participatory Knowledge of God in the Liturgy," in *Knowing the Triune God*, ed. James J. Buckley and David S. Yeago (Grand Rapids: Wm. B. Eerdmans, 2001), 103.

recalls Christ who has died, who is presently risen, and who in the future will come again. The past that is celebrated in the present under the modality of real symbolism will one day be realized in fullness as the veil of sacramentality is removed to reveal the completion of all in Christ.

The parallelism between the Liturgy of the Word and the Liturgy of the Eucharist is found in the congruence between (1) the eucharistic symbol of meal that commemorates a past meal and anticipates a future eschatological banquet, and (2) a liturgical reading of the scriptures that proclaims a past event that becomes the autobiography of the present community, and yet also draws it forward into a hope-filled future. Both the Liturgy of the Word and the Liturgy of the Eucharist participate in the dynamic interplay of past-present-future, of anamnesis-epiclesis-eschatological anticipation as the community commemorates past saving events, celebrates them as present in the life of the community, and anticipates their final future completion and realization.

A second parallelism occurs in the role of the ordained ministry in both the Liturgy of the Word and the Liturgy of the Eucharist. In the Liturgy of the Word, the ordained ministry, as charged with preserving the apostolicity of the community, proclaims the canonical scriptural text to the community as normative of its faith. In doing so, the ordained minister confronts the community with the Word of God. Yet, at the same time, the ordained minister is a member of the community and brings to the scriptural text the living faith of that present community. In doing so, the minister witnesses to the exemplarity of the biblical text as reflective of the present faith of the community. Thus, there is a movement of presentation, of over-againstness of both the text confronting the community and eliciting its faith, and the over-againstness of the ordained minister empowered to preach a prophetic word calling the community to transformation in Christ. In a second movement of recognition the community acknowledges its faith in the text proclaimed, and the ordained minister functions as representative and recapitulative of the community.

In the Liturgy of the Eucharist, the priest speaks the words of institution in the first-person singular of "I," in the person of Christ: "This is *my* body; this is the cup of *my* blood." He prays the rest of the Eucharistic Prayer as a member of the community in the first-person plural of "we" as in "We offer. . . ." These are the two representative functions of the action of the ordained minister that theologians have identified as acting *in persona*

Christi in a posture of being over-against the community and *in persona ecclesiae* in a posture of representation and recapitulation of the community. These two representative functions enable us to say that the ordained minister acts *in persona Christi capitis*, in the person of Christ insofar as Christ is the head of his mystical body, the church.

Thus, just as in the Eucharist the priest functions both *in persona Christi* and *in persona ecclesiae*, representing Christ to the community and the community to Christ, so in the liturgical proclamation of the word, the ordained minister connects the community to the faith proclaimed in the text and represents the canonicity and apostolicity of the text to the community. Perhaps we can say that the function of liturgical proclamation by an ordained minister is to stand *in persona Verbi*. The Word is the ultimate and definitive Word of God, the incarnate self-utterance of God. In standing *in persona Verbi*, the priest stands *in persona Christi*. The parallelism between the Liturgy of the Word and the Liturgy of the Eucharist reveals the proclaimed word to be sacramental and the symbolic action to be enacted proclamation. Together they form a diptych mutually interpreting and enacting the Christ event as living within and formative of the Christian community today.[6]

Karl Rahner had a similar understanding of priestly identity with respect to the word. His definition of priestly ministry is, "The priest is the proclaimer of the word of God, officially commissioned and appointed as such by the Church as a whole in such a way that this word is entrusted to him in the supreme degree of sacramental intensity inherent in it. His work as proclaimer of the word in this sense is essentially directed towards the community (which is at least potentially in existence)."[7] For Rahner, far from being two unrelated entities, a theology of the word becomes the basis for a theology of the sacraments. More precisely, the sacrament is understood as one quite specific word-event within a necessarily broader and more general theology of the word.[8] Both word and sacrament are expressive of

---

[6] Susan K. Wood, "Presbyteral Identity within Parish Identity," in *Ordering the Baptismal Priesthood*, ed. Susan K. Wood (Collegeville, MN: Liturgical Press, 2003), 175–94.

[7] Karl Rahner, "The Point of Departure in Theology for Determining the Nature of the Priestly Office," in *Theological Investigations*, vol. 12 (New York: Seabury, 1974), 36.

[8] Karl Rahner, "What Is a Sacrament?," in *Theological Investigations*, vol. 14 (New York: Seabury, 1976), 137–38.

grace, are moments of human intercommunication, and express a reality that is brought about through them. The event of really hearing and imbibing the word is parallel to the event of receiving a sacrament in faith. Both constitute a *kairos* moment of accepting the salvation offered in word and sacrament. Both are events of grace and thereby saving events.

Embodied Word

Proclamation of the word is not limited to a liturgical context. For the text to become the autobiography of the community presupposes that in some way the faith embodied in the community precedes its liturgical proclamation. It may be an inchoate faith that underlies relationships, commitments, and values in the life of the community. The scriptural word proclaimed is recognized by the *sensus fidei* of the people, and what was inchoate is brought to sacramental visibility and explicit articulation. That same faith is then recognized, strengthened, and affirmed in the liturgy. This illustrates the conviction that sacraments presuppose faith and lead to faith. Here we have a perfect hermeneutical circle. The entry point is proclamation of the word—one not necessarily within a liturgical context and one that may be a proclamation through witness even without words. One is reminded of Paul's words, "But how are they to call on one in whom they have not believed? And how are they to believe in one of whom they have never heard? And how are they to proclaim him unless they are sent?" (Rom 10:14–15).

This extraliturgical proclamation of the word as an inherent component of priestly ministry provides a theological foundation for the priestly ministry of those priests not working primarily in parochial settings. For these priests, the prophetic function of ordained priesthood may be the primary identity for those who serve as educators, as scholars, as poets, as social workers among immigrant communities, as traveling missionaries, as spiritual directors, or any of the activities that characterize the ministry of members of apostolic orders. While they may all at times engage in liturgical proclamation of the word, celebration of the sacraments, and parochial pastoral leadership, these activities do not exclusively define their priestly ministry, which may more accurately be identified with the prophetic function of ordained ministry in their service to the word either in the cloister or in the world. This prophetic proclamation of the word also has a sacramental dimension in bringing to explicit consciousness, articulation, and visibility God's word and faithful response to that word.

The proclamation of the word is not exclusively directed to the church or to other Christians but to the whole world. As such, it inherently carries out the mission of the church to transform the world in service to the reign of God. "The Pastoral Constitution on the Church in the Modern World" (*Gaudium et Spes*) is a word of the church addressed to all people, not just members of the church. Its opening line announces that "the joys and the hopes, the griefs and the anxieties of the men of this age, especially those who are poor or in any way afflicted, these are the joys and hopes, the griefs and anxieties of the followers of Christ. Indeed, nothing genuinely human fails to raise an echo in their hearts" (*GS*, 1). It speaks of the mission of the church—and by extension the proclamation of its ministers—to heal and elevate the dignity of the human person, to strengthen human society, and to help humanity discover the deeper meaning of their daily lives (see *GS*, 40). This mission, in addition to a robust theology of the word, breaks down any dichotomy between the sacred and the secular, between an ecclesial mission *ad intra* and another one to the world *ad extra,* between any division between word and sacrament, or between the prophetic and priestly identity of ordained ministry, all the while expanding the scope and venue of the ministry of proclamation—literally to the ends of the earth.

Questions for Reflection

1. What kind of content in a homily best elicits and articulates faith within the hearer?
2. What are the conditions in which the gospel message becomes the autobiography of the assembly?
3. How do the "nonchurchy" activities of apostolic religious priests represent proclamation of the gospel?

20

The Dawn of "Crisis"

Richard Lennan

Ultimis Temporibus (*UT*) is an obscure document. Compared to the great constitutions of the Second Vatican Council or numerous writings of post-conciliar popes, the text attracts little attention. Fifty years on from its publication by the Synod of Bishops in 1971, *Ultimis Temporibus* is probably the object of very few Google searches, and rarely receives a mention in literature on the church's ministry. Regardless, the document's acknowledgment fifty years ago that all was not well in the life of the Catholic Church remains striking. The text is sober in its tone, but it would scarcely be an exaggeration to describe the opening articles of *Ultimis Temporibus* as cataloguing an existential crisis in the church's ordained priesthood.

In the decades since the *Boston Globe* published its revelations of clerical sexual abuse, that crime has defined "crisis" in relationship to the priesthood. In *Ultimis Temporibus*, "crisis" applies to the widespread lack of confidence among priests about the future of their ministry—a fear that had increased exponentially *ultimis temporibus* ("in the most recent times"). Those "times" are the handful of years between the end of the Second Vatican Council in 1965 and the release of the synod's document in 1971. The content of the text, however, especially its first section, supports translating *ultimis temporibus* as "in the end times," a phrase consistent with what is evident in the text: the anxiety that the last days of the priesthood were at hand.

The document identifies two catalysts for the crisis: the whirlwind of contemporary social change, which rendered uncertain the church's place in the world and prompted priests to question whether they were capable of responding to the then-current world; and the reception of Vatican II's teaching on the common priesthood of the faithful, which challenged the long-prevailing centrality of the ordained priesthood. Both developments prompted a series of questions indicative of anxiety about the future. Those questions, and how to address them, are the focus of this chapter that considers the questions in light of the fifty years of the church's life since the appearance of *Ultimis Temporibus*.

Anxiety and Questions

The social upheavals of the late 1960s led priests to wonder whether "in their pastoral and missionary care" they were using "methods which are now perhaps obsolete to meet the modern mentality" (*UT*, 1). *Ultimis Temporibus* records that the specter of a church irrelevant to the world was especially troubling for priests, who feared that their ministry and way of life were under threat.

A specific concern of priests was that the gulf between the church and the world had echoes in the life of the church itself, noticeably in the distance between priests and the laity. This perception launched troubled musings: "Is it possible to exhort the laity as if from the outside? Is the church sufficiently present to certain groups without the active presence of the priest? If the situation characteristic of a priest consists in segregation from secular life, is not the situation of the layman better?" (*UT*, 1). Allied to these questions was a fear that celibacy separated priests from the wider community of the baptized and increased the gap between the priest and the surrounding culture.

Exacerbating the burgeoning unease among priests was their experience of tensions within the church, especially in the relations among priests and between priests and bishops. Here, "The very fact that the exercise of ministry is becoming more diversified" resulted in "problems concerning brotherhood, union and consistency in the priestly ministry" (*UT*, 4). Priests, in short, felt isolated and increasingly peripheral to the church and society.

In relation to the reception of the council's teachings on the common priesthood, the second source of priestly angst, *Ultimis Temporibus* lists the new circumstances and new difficulties that confronted and troubled priests:

> Many activities which in the past were reserved to priests—for instance, catechetical work, administrative activity in the communities, and even liturgical activities—are today quite frequently

carried out by lay people. . . . Hence a number of questions are being asked: Does the priestly ministry have any specific nature? Is this ministry necessary? Is the priesthood incapable of being lost? What does being a priest mean today? Would it not be enough to have for the service of the Christian communities presidents designated for the preservation of the common good, without sacramental ordination, and exercising their office for a fixed period? (*UT*, 4)

The authors of the synodal text expressed some sympathy for the plight of priests. They acknowledged that the apprehension driving the questions reflected "real difficulties" rather than—"although this is sometimes the case"—being solely the expression of "an exasperated spirit of protest" or "selfish personal concerns" (*UT*, 1). The bishops also understood that some of the circumstances burdening priests were inseparable from modernity's suspicion toward institutions, a suspicion that assumed such institutions lacked integrity: "Is the present-day church too far removed from its origins to be able to proclaim the ancient gospel credibly to modern [people]?" (*UT*, 5).

As already mentioned, the candor of *Ultimis Temporibus* about problems in the priesthood remains noteworthy, far exceeding the standard episcopal commentary on today's clerical sexual abuse crisis. What, then, of the bishops' response to the questions in the text? Sadly, the answers are less memorable than the questions. Largely a compilation of points drawn from Vatican II, the answers do not engage directly with the questions priests were asking, but reflect a context-free, nonspecific presentation of the priesthood.

Extraneous Answers

The bulk of *Ultimis Temporibus* is a recitation of the church's doctrine about Jesus's intention in establishing the church and its ordained ministry. When the document does address the practice of priesthood, in a section titled "Guidelines for the Priestly Life and Ministry," its primary contention is that a healthier priesthood requires the intensification among priests of "pastoral charity," as well as the renewal of their spiritual life. Significantly, the text's reaffirmation of celibacy as an element of that spiritual life receives, in general, double the space dedicated to priestly spirituality.

There is, of course, nothing doctrinally dubious about the document's approach to the ordained priesthood or its presentation of the priest's place in the life of the church, and in the church's mission in the world. Nor would it be productive to dispute the importance of pastoral charity and spiritual renewal. Still, in light of the honest, and somewhat anguished, questions at the beginning of the text, *Ultimis Temporibus* seems like a missed opportunity.

The lack of congruence between the questions and answers is not difficult to understand. When added to the upheaval that had followed in the wake of *Humanae Vitae* (1968), it is likely that the breadth and depth of the gloom among priests exceeded any tools accessible to the synodal bishops for their response. Since priestly ministry had been such a settled aspect of the ecclesial community—and that for more than a millennium—the church at large, including the bishops, was ill-prepared for an environment of crisis.

In the wake of all that has transpired in the history of the priesthood since Vatican II, it is important to recall that a major assessment of the priesthood was not part of the council's agenda. Indeed, the bishops at Vatican II, confident in the typical theology of the time, did not focus on the ordained priesthood until very late in the council's proceedings. Even then, what drove their reflections was not the conviction that the priesthood was ripe for scrutiny, but the recognition that insights from other aspects of Vatican II's texts—the church as a communion, the ministry of bishops, the liturgy, and the church's relationship to the world—all had implications for the ministry and life of priests. When the council focused on the priesthood, the looming end of Vatican II's final session left insufficient opportunity to develop a comprehensive document on the ordained ministry. Accordingly, *Presbyterorum Ordinis* (1965), the council's decree on priestly ministry, is far less groundbreaking than other conciliar texts.

It is unlikely that even a more creative conciliar text would have anticipated all that began to convulse the experience of priests after 1965. Nor is it conceivable that words or actions from the Synod of Bishops would have reversed the large-scale exodus from the ordained ministry that was already evident in 1971, and was accelerated by the controversy over *Humanae Vitae*. The fact that *Ultimis Temporibus* refers to this exodus only obliquely suggests that openness on that subject was a step too far for the bishops. Nonetheless, had the bishops at the synod confronted the anxiety of priests more explicitly, less predictably, and even with a measure of personal and pastoral vulnerability, they might have laid a foundation for something other than the prolongation and proliferation of "crisis."

The remainder of this chapter considers possibilities for alternative responses to the questions that *Ultimis Temporibus* raised. I write with an awareness of the last half-century in the landscape of the priesthood, and with an eye to the future of the ordained ministry.

The Priesthood in a Changing World and Church

What makes revisiting *Ultimis Temporibus* other than an exercise in antiquarianism or quirky nostalgia is that its questions are still relevant for the church and the priesthood. True, the temptation to "revolutionary activity" (*UT*, 2) as an alternative to the church's ministry might not be as attractive today as it seemed to some in the late 1960s, but priests today must still evaluate their ministry in light of the church's relationship with the world. If they are not to sink inexorably into irrelevance, contemporary priests must remain self-critically attentive to the goals and methods of their ministry. Today's priests must ask themselves, for example, what role they might play in the racial reckoning that confronts all citizens and members of the church in the United States. The failure to do so can only widen the gulf between priestly ministry and the mission of the church to be sacrament of the reconciliation and justice integral to God's reign.

Priests share with all the baptized faithful the graced imagination and creativity necessary for gospel-informed responses to social challenges. It is difficult to see how priests "in segregation from secular life" could live out the implications of the discipleship proper to every Christian. For a priest living such segregation—a condition more descriptive of a mind-set than a monastery—the proclamation of the gospel and presiding at communal worship, including the Eucharist, would be unlikely to nurture the community of faith or resonate with the church's mission in the world.

Since priestly ministry is more than—indeed, other than—a form of private piety, the priest's ministry must attest to the church's continuing foundation in the incarnate Word of God and the Holy Spirit, whose grace is active in the world. To fulfill this mission, priests must identify themselves as part of a church whose "shoes get soiled by the mud of the street" (*EG*, 45). Preaching, in particular, must embody the gospel's grounding in everyday life. Doing so requires homilies that avoid addressing "questions that nobody asks," a form of futility against which Pope Francis explicitly cautions ordained ministers (*EG*, 155).

Even without trespassing against Vatican II's description of the "essential" difference between ordained priests and other members of the baptized community of faith, it is critical that ordained priests understand themselves as part of the one pilgrim people of God. Priesthood finds its rationale within the communion of this people, every member of whom the Holy Spirit summons to the holiness integral to faithful discipleship. Outside of this framing, the "essential" difference of the priests can foster a corrosive clericalism.

The guiding premise common to many of the questions in *Ultimis Temporibus* is that the priesthood would be meaningless without a clear understanding of all that made the priest "different." Long before the council, "difference" was a dominant motif of the priesthood: "One of his duties consists in a mission of dissimilarity and an apologetic of severance. . . . Ordination gives priests a grace which is at once a capacity for and a call to sanctity higher than that of those who have simply been baptized."[1] Depicting the priesthood in this way can foster the isolation of the priest or reduce the ordained ministry to what "only a priest can do," a designation that leaves the priest marooned on a narrow strip of land, surrounded by an ocean of the laity.

A more constructive envisioning locates the specificity of priests in terms of the priest's particular, Spirit-formed relationship to Jesus Christ and the community of the church. Specificity, then, is not distinct from the ministry of the priest, from the priest's relationship to the ecclesial community. The communal emphasis reflects the relational dynamics of the Trinity, within which difference builds unity, just as unity enables difference. Such an outlook underscores the irreducibly ecclesial aspect of the ordained ministry, an emphasis not always evident when the accent was on the priest's "difference" from "those who have been simply baptized."

Similarly, creative answers to the question about the "necessity" of priestly ministry require more than a catalogue of priestly prerogatives. A fruitful discussion of necessity in the context of the priesthood must have a grounding in the lived history of the church, not simply in ontology or

---

[1] Cardinal Emmanuel Suhard, *Priests among Men* (South Bend, IN: Fides, 1951), 88.

function. Historical studies can bring into relief the sacramental relationship between the ordained priest and the wider community of the faithful, a relationship that embraces the proclamation of the word, the building up of a community, direct pastoral care that includes all that serves justice and compassion, and the leadership of communal worship.

Historical studies can also demonstrate the effect of an exclusive concentration on the role of the ordained priest in the eucharistic liturgy. This emphasis contributed not only to the eclipsing of other forms of ministry in the community of faith, but also, and most dramatically, to the "sacralizing" of the priesthood. This phenomenon, which elevated priests above all other members of the church, laid the groundwork for the segregation of priests from the secular world. Seminaries—often physically remote and abstracted from many everyday realities—became emblematic of this segregation—from the world, certainly, but even from the community of the baptized. Developing more fruitful models of priestly ministry requires conscientious reviews of current practices, including those that limit the participation of women in activities such as the spiritual direction of seminarians.

The defensiveness evident in many of the questions in *Ultimis Temporibus*—perhaps especially, "Is the priesthood incapable of being lost?"—is indicative of a perspective that associates continuity in the church's life with the absence of change. In other words, the presumption seems to be that priesthood can have only one form, such that any change becomes tantamount to the priesthood "being lost." The fact that the ordained ministry, like all elements of the church's life, has a history—that it did not begin with the form it had in 1965—indicates the need for the ecclesial community, and especially for priests, to recover a sense of the church's eschatological orientation, and therefore, the imperative to remain open to the movement that the Holy Spirit inspires and sustains.

Discerning Change

As a body moving toward the fullness of life in Christ, the church participates in a graced pilgrimage in history. The faithfulness that is to be a hallmark of this pilgrimage, the journey that the Holy Spirit sustains, requires more than the endless repetition of a single model. The form that faithful expressions of the ordained priesthood might take going forward needs the ongoing discernment of the entire ecclesial community.

This discernment is not in competition with the tradition of faith, nor is it in opposition to the role of ecclesial authority. Discernment, a key dimension of the church's synodal reality, involves faithful—as distinct from "unchanging"—reception of the tradition, attentiveness to the contours of the church's mission in the present context, and instruments of decision-making that channel the presence of the Spirit in the whole community of faith. The outcomes of such a process in relation to the ordained priesthood will be far from the "loss" of that ministry, but they will showcase its participation in the church's pilgrimage. This participation implies the potential, and need, for change.

If the content of *Ultimis Temporibus* stamps it as a missed opportunity, it is not alone in that regard. The response of bishops around the world to the clerical sexual abuse crisis, to take the most high-profile instance, follows a similar trajectory. It is understandable, and necessary, that the bishops would insist on zero-tolerance policies in the hope of ensuring an end to abuse. Yet the dearth of official and public efforts to identify and investigate the "why" of the crisis is desperately disappointing. There remains the need to unearth all that the crisis discloses about myriad facets of the church's life—including programs of formation, decisions on suitability for ordination, the well-being and ongoing formation of ordained priests, and the relational capacity of priests, especially with those they are to serve. If *Ultimis Temporibus* represents a failure to answer directly important, albeit disturbing questions, much of the response to the sexual abuse crisis represents answers given without clearly identifying the questions and opening them to the wisdom of the church and the wider world. In both instances, the desire to "get back to normal," to "business as usual," seems to be dominant. The reality, however, is that the normal and usual no longer exist.

Questions about the priesthood did not cease in 1971. In fact, the questions broadened and deepened, ensuring the health and longevity of "crisis." Even the magnitude and persistence of those questions, however, is not a sure harbinger that the extinction of priesthood is nigh. A hopeful future for the ordained priesthood requires from bishops, priests, and the whole church the "real daring" that *Ultimis Temporibus* endorsed in its conclusion. The document did not deliver that boldness, but the Holy Spirit is surely still urging the church to "allow the Lord to rouse us from our torpor, to free us from our inertia" (*Gaudete et Exsultate*, 137).

Questions for Reflection

1. How might creative responses to present-day crises enhance the church's ordained ministry?
2. In what creative ways might priests express the relational dimension of their ministry?
3. What would constitute "real daring" in shaping the future of the ordained priesthood?

Bibliography

Church Documents

A Catechism of Christian Doctrine, Enjoined by the Third Council of Baltimore. New York: Sadlier and Co., 1885.

———. "The Pastoral Conversion of the Parish Community in the Service of the Evangelizing Mission of the Church," July 20, 2020, http://www.clerus.va.

———. "*Ratio Fundamentalis Institutionis Sacerdotalis*" (The Gift of the Priestly Vocation), 2016, http://www.clerus.va.

"Instruction on Certain Questions Regarding the Collaboration of the Nonordained Faithful in the Sacred Ministry of Priests," August 15, 1997, http://www.vatican.va.

International Theological Commission. "Synodality in the Life and Mission of the Church," March 2, 2018, http://www.vatican.va.

Pope Francis. "Address to Clergy, Consecrated People, and Members of Diocesan Pastoral Councils," October 4, 2013, http://www.vatican.va.

———. "Address of His Holiness Commemorating the 50th Anniversary of the Institution of the Synod of Bishops," October 17, 2015, http://www.vatican.va.

———. "Address to the Leadership of the Episcopal Conference of Latin America," July 28, 2013, http://www.vatican.va.

———. "Letter to the Popular Movements," April 12, 2020, http://www.vatican.va.

———. Post-Synodal Apostolic Exhortation *Evangelii Gaudium*, "The Joy of the Gospel: On the Proclamation of the Gospel in Today's World," 2013, http://www.vatican.va.

———. Apostolic Exhortation *Gaudete et Exsultate*, "Rejoice and Be Glad: On the Call to Holiness in Today's World," 2018, http://www.vatican.va.

Pope John Paul II. Apostolic Letter *Ordinatio Sacerdotalis*, 1994, https://www.vatican.va.

Pope Paul VI. Encyclical *Sacerdotalis Caelibatus*, "The Celibacy of the Priest," 1967, https://www.vatican.va.

The Roman Catechism. Translated by Robert Bradley and Eugene Kevane. Boston: Daughters of St. Paul, 1985.

Synod of Bishops. *Ultimis Temporibus* (1971). In *Vatican Council II—More Postconciliar Documents*, edited by Austin Flannery, 672–94. Northport, NY: Costello Publishing Company, 1982.

United States Catholic Conference of Bishops. "The Program of Priestly Formation," 5th ed., 2006.

Vatican Council II: The Conciliar and Postconciliar Documents. Edited by Austin Flannery, OP. Collegeville, MN: Liturgical Press, 1996.

Other Resources

Augustine. *Confessions*. Trans. Peter Brown. Indianapolis: Hackett, 1993.

Beinert, Wolfgang. "Priestly People of God." *Irish Theological Quarterly* 85 (2020): 3–15.

Bevans, Stephen, and Robin Ryan. "Why the Catholic Church Needs Two Different Kinds of Priesthood." *America*, April 1, 2019, https://www.americamagazine.org.

Boyle, Gregory. *Barking to the Choir: The Power of Radical Kinship*. New York: Simon & Schuster, 2018.

Bradshaw, Paul. *Ordination Rites of the Ancient Churches of East and West*. Collegeville, MN: Liturgical Press, 1990.

Brown, Raymond. *Priest and Bishop*. Paramus, NJ: Paulist Press, 1970.

Cahalan, Kathleen. *Introducing the Practice of Ministry*. Collegeville, MN: Liturgical Press, 2014.

Chauvet, Louis-Marie. *Symbol and Sacrament*. Collegeville, MN: Liturgical Press, 1995.

Gaillardetz, Richard. "Infallibility and the Ordination of Women." *Louvain Studies* 21 (1996): 3–24.

Jennings, Willie James. *Acts*. Nashville: Abingdon, 2017.

Kenny, Nuala. *Still Unhealed: Treating the Pathology in the Clergy Sexual Abuse Crisis*. New London, CT: Twenty-Third, 2019.

Lennan, Richard. "Ministry in the Church." In *The Cambridge Companion to Vatican II*. Edited by Richard Gaillardetz, 248–65. Cambridge: Cambridge University Press, 2020.

Massingale, Bryan. "Merton, Malcolm X, and Catholic Engagement with Black Lives Matter." *Tuesdays with Merton*, March 9, 2021, https://www.youtube.com.

McKinney, Mary Benet. *Sharing Wisdom: A Process for Group Decision Making*. Valencia, CA: Tabor, 1987.

O'Collins, Gerald, and Michael Keenan-Jones. *Jesus Our Priest: A Christian Approach to Priesthood*. Oxford: Oxford University Press, 2012.

O'Meara, Thomas. *Theology of Ministry*. New York: Paulist Press, 1999.

Philibert, Paul. *The Priesthood of the Faithful: Keys to a Living Church*. Collegeville, MN: Liturgical Press, 2005.

———. *Stewards of God's Mysteries: Priestly Spirituality in a Changing Church*. Collegeville, MN: Liturgical Press, 2004.

Pope Francis, with Antonio Spadaro, SJ. *A Big Heart Open to God: A Conversation with Pope Francis*. New York: HarperOne / America Press, 2013.

Pope Francis, with Austin Ivereigh. *Let Us Dream: The Path to a Better Future*. New York: Simon & Schuster, 2020.

Puglisi, James F. "Presider as Alter Christus, Head of the Body?" *Liturgical Ministry* 10 (2001): 153–58.

Rahner, Karl. "Christian Pessimism." *Theological Investigations*, vol. 22, trans. Joseph Donceel, 155–62. New York: Crossroad, 1991.

———. *Concern for the Church*, vol. 20. *Theological Investigations*. New York: Crossroad, 1981.

———. "The Point of Departure in Theology for Determining the Nature of the Priestly Office." In *Theological Investigations*, vol. 12, 31–38. New York: Seabury, 1974.

———. "What Is a Sacrament?" In *Theological Investigations*, vol. 14, 135–48. New York: Seabury, 1976.

Rush, Ormond. *The Eyes of Faith: The Sense of the Faithful and the Church's Reception of Revelation*. Washington, DC: Catholic University of America Press, 2009.

Schneiders, Sandra M. "Did Jesus Exclude Women from Priesthood?" In *Women Priests: A Catholic Commentary on the Vatican Declaration*, ed. L. and A. Swidler, 227–33. New York: Paulist Press, 1977.

Schuth, Katarina. "Assessing the Education of Priests and Lay Ministers." In *The Crisis of Authority in Catholic Modernity*, ed. Michael J. Lacey and Francis Oakley, 317–48. New York: Oxford University Press, 2011.

Williams, Rowan. *Wound of Knowledge: Christian Spirituality from the New Testament to St. John of the Cross.* Boston: Cowley, 2003.

Wilson, George B. *Clericalism: The Death of the Priesthood.* Collegeville, MN: Liturgical Press, 2008.

Wood, Susan K. "Participatory Knowledge of God in the Liturgy." In *Knowing the Triune God*, ed. James J. Buckley and David S. Yeago, 95–118. Grand Rapids: Wm. B. Eerdmans, 2001.

———. "Presbyteral Identity within Parish Identity." In *Ordering the Baptismal Priesthood*, ed. Susan K. Wood, 256–267. Collegeville, MN: Liturgical Press, 2003.

LIST OF CONTRIBUTORS

John F. Baldovin, SJ, is a Professor of Historical and Liturgical Theology at Boston College School of Theology and Ministry.

Liam Bergin is a priest of the Diocese of Ossory (Ireland) and a Professor of the Practice in the Theology Department of Boston College.

Stephen Bevans, SVD, is the Louis J. Luzbetak Professor of Mission and Culture Emeritus at the Catholic Theological Union in Chicago.

Phillip J. Brown, PSS, is the President-Rector of St. Mary's Seminary and University in Baltimore.

Catherine E. Clifford is Professor of Systematic and Historical Theology in the Faculty of Theology, St. Paul University (Canada).

Boyd Taylor Coolman is a Professor of Theology in the Theology Department of Boston College.

Richard R. Gaillardetz is the Joseph Professor of Catholic Systematic Theology in the Theology Department of Boston College.

Raúl Gomez-Ruiz, SDS, is the President-Rector of Sacred Heart Seminary and School of Theology in Hales Corners, Wisconsin.

Thomas H. Groome is a Professor of Theology and Religious Education at the Boston College School of Theology and Ministry.

Bradford E. Hinze is the Karl Rahner Professor of Theology in the Theology Department of Fordham University in New York.

Emily Jendzejec is a doctoral candidate in Theology and Education at the Boston College School of Theology and Ministry.

John Kartje is a priest of the Archdiocese of Chicago and Rector/President of the Mundelein Seminary / University of St. Mary of the Lake in Chicago.

Richard Lennan is a priest of the Diocese of Maitland-Newcastle (Australia) and a Professor of Systematic Theology at the Boston College School of Theology and Ministry.

Reinhard Cardinal Marx is the Archbishop of the Archdiocese of Munich and Freising (Germany).

Jacqueline M. Regan is Associate Dean of Student Affairs and Career Services at the Boston College School of Theology and Ministry.

John Stowe, OFM Conv., is the Bishop of the Diocese of Lexington, Kentucky.

Diane Vella is a Pastoral Associate at St. Bernard's Parish, Levittown, New York.

John C. Wester is the Archbishop of the Archdiocese of Santa Fe, New Mexico.

Susan K. Wood, SCL, is the Academic Dean and Professor, Regis College, Toronto School of Theology (Canada).